PICTURE P VALUES

GW00634570

formerly IPM Catalogue of Picture Postcards and Year Book

Compiled by Phil & Dave Smith

Consultant C.R.Smith

"PPV, his legacy, is dedicated in perpetuity to the memory of J.H.D., and to the postcards and people he loved so well". The Family.

Published by:

IPM
Promotions
130 Brent Street
Hendon London,
NW4 2DR

Tel: 020 8203 1500
enqs@ppv.uk.com
www.memoriespostcards.co.uk

Printed by:

Adlard Print
The Old School
The Green
Ruddington
Nottingham
NG11 6HH

Tel: 0115 921 4863
calvin@adlardprint.com
www.adlardprint.com

Visit our website at:
www.memoriespostcards.co.uk

FOREWORD

Welcome to the 31st edition of this catalogue which was first published in 1975. We have replaced most of the illustrations in the hope that it will make identification of subjects easier to identify, which should help newcomers to the hobby to understand this vast and complicated collecting field.

Once again we have priced more than 300 illustrations of postcards,

If Golf is your game then take a look at page 164 to see a comprehensive list and some illustrations of the fantastic Wrench series of golfing postcards, very kindly supplied by Philip Truett, a golf collector and historian.

Our thanks again to our regular experts, Tom Stanley, our Shipping expert, Tony Davies for his expert advice with the Naval and overseas sections and Tony Merrill. Also to Clive Smith who has contributed his wealth of knowledge across many areas.

We can only re-iterate the message that this catalogue is a guide to pricing with many variations the prices given will help the uninitiated, but it is only with specialist knowledge that one can truly price a postcard. The vast majority of cards are not worth more than a pound, it is only a select few which command the larger prices. The social history cards, which include topographical, have many collectors including local and family historians.

Subject cards have a more international appeal and consequently can generate high prices, the bigger the demand the better the price will be. The condition of the card is more important for a subject card. A topographical collector is more likely to buy a damaged card, the reason for this is it may be the only one in existence.

Happy hunting for 2006,
Phil & David Smith

This is a very poignant edition of the Picture Postcard Values, because this year we have to mark the passing of J.H.D.Smith the man who first produced this publication way back in 1975 as the IPM catalogue. John helped us with this edition, as he had done over the last few years and we are very sad that he isn't around to see it finished. John had a real passion for the hobby and was without doubt, the champion of the postcard world. He was still working with them until quite close to his death in July of this year.

We hope to keep this catalogue improving as a tribute to John, who always worked hard to ensure it was of the highest standard.

He is sadly missed by us all.

JOHN SMITH 1937-2005

AN INTRODUCTION TO POSTCARD COLLECTING

It has long been felt that the PPV catalogue and indeed the whole hobby of postcard collecting, is 'inaccessible' to the general reader. Therefore with this edition we are presenting a brief introduction to the subject, sketching in the historical background, and taking a look at the present state of the art.

The Early Beginnings

The first plain postcards appeared in Austria in 1869. One year later Britain followed, and shortly afterwards in the mid-1870s, the first picture postcards began to appear. The Paris Exhibition of 1889 gave a tremendous boost to this still novel form of sending a message, and from then on picture postcards were produced in ever increasing numbers by almost every country in the world. Britain joined the game in earnest in 1894 when the first picture cards were permitted and in 1902 was the first country to divide the back, thus allowing the message and address on one side and a complete picture on the other, a move which saw an explosion in picture postcard production as other countries quickly followed. This period is dealt with in more detail in the Catalogue under 'Early Cards'.

The Golden Age

The period from 1902-1914 has been termed the 'Golden Age' of picture postcards, for it was in these years that the hobby reached a height of popularity that it has never exceeded. It was a time when nearly everybody sent postcards, because in a pre-telephone era they represented the cheapest and most reliable form of communication. And what cards they were ! Almost every conceivable subject could be found on picture postcards, as publishers competed with each other to produce the most attractive designs. As a result, postcard collecting became a national pastime where almost everybody young or old had their own albums into which went cards showing Father Christmas and Fire Engines, cards showing Pigs, Pretty Ladies and Political Figures, and cards of just about any other subject you care to name! And the hobby was not confined to Britain, for by now every country in the world was producing postcards, resulting in uncountable millions being issued world-wide throughout this period.

World War I

For reasons of quality and price, the majority of British postcards had been printed in Germany, and the guns of 1914 brought this quickly to an end. But although the Great War did see many Patriotic and Military cards issued, in the words of Brian Lund, Editor of Picture Postcard Monthly, It 'destroyed a national mood '.

Between the Wars

From 1918 a number of things combined to bring about a virtual end to the hobby. A nation trying to come to terms with the tragedies of the Somme and of Flanders, was in no mood for the fripperies of the picture postcard. In addition, the doubling of the inland postage rate for postcards, the wider acceptance of the phone as a means of communication, not to mention the difficulties which many firms found themselves in after the war - all these factors combined to bring about the end. Perhaps quite simply, nobody, neither the postcard houses, nor the collectors, wanted to 'start again'. Of course, postcards were still being produced, but in much smaller quantities. The seaside comic market was still there, and some firms were producing local views, while others reflected the current Art Deco craze with some fine issues, but effectively the 'Golden Age' had passed.

World War II

The Second World War saw a minor revival in postcard production, with a number of Military and Aviation series being produced, as well as other cards dealing with issues of the time, but the hobby lay relatively dormant until the late 1950s.

The Postcard Revival

Throughout the post war years, a small band of enthusiasts had kept things going, until in 1959 two collectors, James Butland and Edward Westwood established a regular magazine. 'The Postcard Collectors' Guide & News, full of articles about the hobby, and closing with a short sales list. 1961 saw the foundation by Drene Brennan of the 'Postcard Club of Great Britain', and at this time in the early 1960s, several collectors' shops could be found stocking old postcards. The hobby gathered momentum until in 1968 the compiler of this catalogue established the monthly 'IPM' sales magazine. This was the first real attempt to establish classifications for postcards and to put the hobby on to a commercial basis, and this issue also carried the first auction of picture postcards. From then on things further progressed. Postcard Fairs were already being held under the aegis of the PCGB and these were complemented by the first big specialist events held by John Carter, and in the early 1970s by RF Postcards. The hobby received a massive boost with the Victoria & Albert Museum Centenary Exhibition of 1970, later to travel round the country, and supported by an ever increasing number of books, magazines and sales lists, culminated in 1975 with the appearance of the first IPM Catalogue. The following year, 1976, saw the formation of the Postcard Traders Association, the first sale held by "Specialised Postal Auctions', now our leading auction house, and the foundation of the annual British International Postcard Exhibition, while in 1977 came the first Postcard Fair at Bloomsbury Crest Hotel, now an institution among collectors. Our regular monthly journal 'Picture Postcard Monthly' first saw the light of day in 1978, and set the seal on what has become known as the postcard revival. For now we had the dealers, the collectors, the fairs and auctions, and the magazines, books and literature. Everything was there, ready to move postcard collecting into the national hobby it has now become, taking its place alongside Stamps and Coins as one of the top three collecting hobbies in the country.

The Present Day

The hobby today supports some 500 Dealers and many more smaller collector/dealers. There are an estimated 20,000 serious collectors, many of whom belong to one of nearly 70 Postcard Clubs. We have over 20 Auction Houses specialising in picture postcards, and a national network of Postcard Fairs. There is the PPV Postcard Catalogue, a national magazines, and a substantial number of books on the subject. We can now look briefly at the operation of the hobby today.

The Collectors

Why do people collect picture postcards? Why do people collect anything! For pleasure, interest, and perhaps profit, are some of the reasons which may be advanced. Yet in this hobby, the collecting of postcards is now divided into two worlds. That of Art & Subject Cards, and that of Topographical, or Local History. The former are perhaps the 'real' postcard collectors, while the latter group are essentially more interested in representations of their own locality as it used to be, than in picture postcards as an art form.

The Dealers

The Postcard Trade operates in much the same way as the Stamp or Coin Trade, in that we have a national network of dealers whose task it is to find and supply postcards to collectors. Many of them carry substantial stocks of up to 100,000 cards, all priced, and filed in boxes or albums under their respective Subject or Location headings, although others carry smaller stocks, perhaps specialising in several chosen themes or areas. Many dealers will conduct business through the post, sending approval selections of your choice, while many more can be found at Postcard Fairs throughout the country. A comprehensive list of dealers will be found in 'Picture Postcard Annual', while dates of current Fairs are listed in 'Picture Postcard Monthly.'

Auctions

There are now 20 Auction Houses holding regular specialised sales of picture postcards. All produce catalogues obtainable on subscription, and all will accept postal bids for the Lots on offer. While the more common cards tend to be lotted in some quantity, there is now an increasing trend for the better cards to be offered as individual items in single lots, a reflection of the current strong demand for these cards. A word of advice, when buying at auction do try to ensure that cards are in the best possible condition, particularly if buying through a postal bid. This is made easy by certain leading Auction firms, whose descriptions always include a very clear statement of condition, but is less visible in the catalogues of some firms, where at times you will find nothing at all regarding condition.

Fairs

Led by the gigantic IPM Promotions Fair which has been held every month since December 1977 at Bloomsbury, London WC1, there are now over 50 organisations holding regular Postcard Fairs throughout the country, dates of which may be checked with the Diary published in 'Picture Postcard Monthly'. The largest of these by far is Bloomsbury, which every month has up to 130 stands packed with picture postcards, displayed by over 80 stand holders. Other large provincial events include the 2-day Fairs held at York, Twickenham, Guildford and Yeovil, with major one day events at Cheltenham, Birmingham, Nottingham, Folkestone, Wickham and Haywards Heath. The prestige event, and most important show of the year, is the annual 4-day Picture Postcard Show (formerly BIPEX), held in late August at the Royal Horticultural Hall, SW1, while every weekend many smaller events are held regularly up and down the country. Here you will find the Postcard Trade at work, and will be able to meet the Dealers in person. Ask them for what you want, and you will find them all very helpful, particularly in guiding the new collector.

What to Collect

This depends entirely upon the individual. Visit the Fairs and look around at the enormous selection of cards you will find there. Perhaps after a few visits you may find yourself attracted to one particular Artist or Subject, or possibly you may wish to specialise in old views of your town or village. Whatever you choose, remember to look for cards in the finest possible condition. This is not perhaps so important in the Topographical field where only a few copies of a particular card may remain, but it is important in Art & Subjects. Generally you will want to ensure that the higher the price asked, the better the condition of the card.

How to Collect

At the Fairs. and in Dealers' advertisements, you will find a good range of accessories offered. Many collectors store their cards in albums, while others prefer loose storage in cardboard boxes. You may also consider it advisable to protect your loose cards by keeping them in protective envelopes now available. Some collectors prefer the old-fashioned Edwardian paper albums. rather than the modern PVC types. It is entirely up to you.

Postcard Clubs

As your interest grows, you may wish to join one of the many Postcard Clubs, a list of which may be found in Picture Postcard Annual. Here you will meet other local collectors who share your interest in the subject and who will be able to broaden your horizons by showing you some of their own collecting themes.

Investment

This is not something to be attempted by the new collector, for while it is always pleasant to see your collection grow in value, as indeed it will do, to set out to buy postcards with the sole aim of making money is an exercise fraught with difficulties. Wait until you know a lot more about the hobby. Then it may be possible to put some spare cash into an area you feel is under-valued, but a study of past Catalogues and past prices will clearly reveal that while some cards have risen dramatically in price, others have remained on the same mark for years, while some cards have even fallen in value.

Selling your Cards

All collectors wish to sell at different times. Perhaps they are giving up, or maybe turning to another subject. Whatever the reason, you have four basic methods of disposing of unwanted cards. You can take a table at one of the Postcard Fairs, and with your stock properly marked up and laid out, you can become a 'Dealer' yourself! If you know of other collectors in your field, you could offer your cards to them for sale by private treaty. Alternatively you can offer your stock to a dealer, but his response will depend very largely upon what sort of cards they are, their condition, and at the end of the day, whether he wants them! All cards must have a Catalogue value, but it does not necessarily follow that anyone wants to buy them! Most dealers will only willingly buy those cards in the collectable categories which they have some chance of re-selling at a profit. Finally you can offer your cards for sale by Auction, but remember that here you take a chance on the final price. You may of course put a reserve on your cards, and if they fail to meet this figure they will be returned to you. You may be pleasantly surprised at the price you obtain at Auction, or in some cases you could be disappointed.

Certainly you may do better with particularly good single items if offered for sale by this method, but you have to meet the Auctioneer's commission, which may be up to 20% of the price realised. If you have a valuable collection, you may wish to discuss various methods of sale with an established Auctioneer or Dealer.

Modern Cards
The past 10 years has seen a phenomenal growth in the production of Modern postcards, and this can be seen as almost a separate industry, with cards on every conceivable subject now being issued by many leading companies. After some initial hesitation by the traditional postcard collecting world, Modern cards are now making considerable inroads into the hobby. Perhaps the great advantage of Modern Cards lies in their price, where for a nominal 50p, or so,one may buy superbly designed and printed cards on almost any subject you care to name.

Conclusions
In this brief survey we have tried to show how the hobby originated, and how it operates today. It is still growing, and I sincerely hope that all of you, particularly if you are a new collector finding out about postcards for the first time, will gain through this, and through the pages of this Catalogue, something of the nostalgia we collectors all feel for those long hot summer days at the turn of the century. It was for many a golden age, a time of faded sepia, and croquet on the lawns. Of knickerbocker suits, Sunday School and Mr. Polly, when the event of the year was annual trip to the seaside, with its toffee apples, winkles and busy, sad-eyed donkeys. A time of endless summer, when small boys looked for tiddlers under the bridge, oblivious to the voices calling them home across the fields, peacefully unaware of the later call of destiny which they would face in 1916 in the green fields of France.

A time without television, video, or computer games, when young girls and boys spent their evenings carefully putting all their new cards into their postcard albums. It is these cards which are so highly prized today, and which form the subject of this Catalogue.

ACCESSORY SUPPLIERS

Vera Trinder Ltd.
38 Bedford Street, London WC2 9EU   020-7836-2365

G. Barrington Smith*
Cross Street, Oadby, Leicester LE2 4DD   0116-271-9181

Sherford Stamp Co.
66 Bridge Street, Taunton, Somerset   01823-283327

Murray Cards International Ltd.
51 Watford Way, Hendon Central, London NW4 3JH   020-8202-5688

Rob Roy Cards
Crosshall, Chelsfield Village, Orpington, Kent   01689-828052

The firms listed above are trade wholesalers and between them carry an extensive range of Accessories including: Postcard Catalogues - Books - Albums - Leaves - Plastic Envelopes - Film Front Bags - Postcard Wallets etc.

Vera Trinder, G. Barrington Smith, and **Sherford Stamp Co.** also specialise in Philatelic and Numismatic albums and accessories, while **Murray Cards International** and **Rob Roy Cards** carry large stocks of Cigarette Card albums and leaves.

Most of the firms above will deal with individual customers, but a telephone call will confirm this, and determine whether the firm have the item you require currently in stock.

In addition many postcard dealers carry smaller stocks of Books, Albums and Accessories.

*Trade only supplied.

GLOSSARY OF POSTCARD TERMS

Applique
A term used to describe a postcard which has some form of cloth, metal, or other embellishment attached to it.

Art Deco
Artistic style of the 1920's recognisable by its symmetrical designs and straight lines.

Art Nouveau
Artistic style of the turn of the century, characterised by flowing lines and flowery symbols, yet often depicting impressionist more than representational art.

Bas Relief
Postcards with a heavily raised surface giving a papier-mache appearance.

Catch-phrases
Many pre-1914 Comic postcards are captioned by phrases such as "When Father says turn", often alluding to other spheres of contemporary life.

Chromo-Litho
The finest of all colour-printing methods, the colour being applied in solids as opposed to modern screen printing. There are no 'dots' in chromo-lithographic printing. Cards produced by this method have a rich and deep colour, where often the original shiny surface remains. Usually found in 'Gruss Aus' and other early undivided back cards.

Composites
A number of cards which together form a large picture.

Court Cards
The official size for British picture postcards between 1894-1899, measuring 115mm x 89mm.

Divided Back
Postcards with the back divided into two sections, one for the message, the other for the address. Great Britain first divided the back in 1902.

Early
A term loosely used to describe any undivided back card.

Embossed
Postcards with a raised surface. Often found among Greetings and Heraldic types.

Fab Cards
Produced by W.N. Sharpe of Bradford. These cards contain a small printed silk square which could be removed and used for other purposes.

Full out
Usually found in the Heraldic classification, meaning a design which fills the whole of the card.

Giant Postcards
Novelty cards, some of which were as large as 305mm x 165mm.

Glitter
Postcards sprinkled with tinsel.

Gruss Aus
German for "Greetings From". A term used to describe these highly pictorial continental Greetings Cards.

Hold to Light
Referred to as "HTL". Postcards with small cut out windows, through which appear different colours when held to a strong light.

Intermediate Size
The link between Court Cards and Standard Size, these were cards of 130mm x 80mm.

Kaleidoscopes
Postcards where a rotating wheel reveals a myriad of colours when turned.

Midget Postcards
Novelty cards of size 90mm x 70mm.

Montage
A term usually employed to describe a picture formed by cutting up postage stamps.

Novelty
A postcard which deviates in any way from the norm. Cards which do something or have articles attached to them, or are printed in an unusual size or on strange materials.

Official
Postcard printed by a Government or other established body to advertise their services. The Railway companies printed many 'Official' cards.

Oilette
A trade name used by the publishers Raphael Tuck to describe postcards reproduced from original paintings.

Panel Cards
These are postcards printed on heavy board.

Poster Advert
A reproduction of an advertising poster, or a postcard done specifically in that style.

Pullouts
Postcards containing a strip view insert.

Real Photographic
Abbreviated to 'RP'. Used to describe a card which has been produced by a photographic rather than a printing process.

Reward Cards
Given away to reward school-children for good work.

Standard Size
Introduced in GB in November 1899, this size of 140mm x 89mm corresponds to 5.5 x 3.5 in.

Topographical
A term used to describe postcards showing street scenes and general views, where the view is more prominent than any other feature, e.g. if a Post Office or Public House were to form the dominant feature of a card, then it would be classified and priced under that heading.

Transparencies
Postcards which change colour or reveal a hidden object when held to a strong light.

Undivided Back
Postcards with a plain back where the whole of this space would be used for the address. A term often used loosely to describe Early Cards, although undivided backs were in common use until 1907.

Vignette
Usually found on undivided back postcards, and consisting of a design which does not occupy the whole of the picture side. Vignettes may be anything from a small sketch in one corner of the card, to a design covering three-quarters of the card. The essential idea was that some space should be left for the message, as the reverse of the card could only be used for the address.

Write-Away
A term used to describe a postcard bearing the opening line of a sentence, which the sender would then continue. Usually found on early Comic postcards.

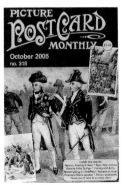
9

SRP COLLECTORS FAIRS

POSTCARDS ~ CIGARETTE CARDS
FOOTBALL MEMORABILIA ~ COINS
PHONECARDS ~ BOOKS ~ PAPER
EPHEMERA ~ STAMPS ~
MEDALS MAPS

ORPINGTON

THURSDAY EVENING FAIR
Crofton Halls
Nr. Orpington BR Station, Kent
50+ Stalls
4pm - 8pm Free entry
January 12th,
February 9th, March 9th,
April 13th, May 11th,
June 8th, July 13th,
August 10th, September 14th,
October 12th,November 9th,
December 14th.

Orpington Halls,
High Street, Kent.

70+ Tables
6ft.Table £20,
12ft. Table £35

Parking & Refreshments
FREE ENTRY
Postcards, Cigarette
Cards, Football
Memorabilia,
Books,China,
Jewellery, Ephemera,
Silverware, Wade,
C.D's, L.P's, Coins,
Militaria, Antiques.

**Curios,
Collectables &
Antiques Fair**

2006

February 5th,
March 5th,
April 2nd,
May 7th,
June 4th,
July 2nd,
August 6th,
September 3rd,
October 1st,
November 5th,
December 3rd.

Toy and Train Collectors Fairs
Orpington Halls
Leigh City Tech. Dartford
Sweyne Park School, Rayleigh
Bexhill High School, Bexhill On Sea
Swallowfield Parish Hall, Reading
Saturday Market - Orpington Halls

DARTFORD SUNDAY TOY SOLDIER, WAR GAMING & MILITARY MODEL FAIR
*Leigh City Tech College, Green St. Green
Road, Dartford, Kent.*
80 + Stalls
10.00 - 2.30pm
9th April & 10th September

 Information: 01689 854924 Mobile: 0776 6021633
Email: srptoys@hotmail.com www.srptoyfairs.com

12

Postcard Traders Association

▓▓▓▓ PROMOTING POSTCARDS THROUGH FAIR TRADING ▓▓▓▓

Established in 1975. The Postcard Traders Association represents the UK's foremost dealers (and also many from overseas) auctioneers, fair organisers, publishers and accessory distributors amongst its members.

The principal aim of the 'PTA' is to promote postcards and the collecting hobby. Much of this work is carried out by the elected members and officers of the PTA committee, on a purely unpaid/voluntary basis, who are dedicated to ensuring a prosperous future for postcards and collecting. We also acknowledge other individuals, businesses and societies that assist us with our promotional work.

Membership of the PTA is open to anyone (over 18) who is in business trading in picture postcards or associated accessories. Members are vetted to ensure high standards in helping to protect the public against unfair or dubious trading practices.

For further information please contact our hon. secretary..
Peter James, 9 Paray Drive, Wells, Somerset. BA5 3HW
tel/fax 01749-679662 email: ptasec@postcard.co.uk

PLEASE VISIT OUR POSTCARD INFORMATION PAGES at www.postcard.co.uk

19

Top Left: Postmen of the
Empire early chromo-litho £20.
Top right: Chromo-litho Pig
theme £15.
Left : Nippon Yusen Kaisha
Line chromo-litho advert £20.
Bottom Left: Gruss Aus £12.
Below: Sufragette cartoon,
'My Valentine' £30

24

BLOOMSBURY

POSTCARD & COLLECTORS FAIR

n the Galleon Suite at The Royal National Hotel

Bedford Way, London WCI

POSTCARDS, EPHEMERA, AUTOGRAPHS, MOVIE JUMBLE,
SPORTING MEMORABILIA, PRINTS, SCRAPS, PROGRAMMES,
PHOTOGRAPHS, CIGARETTE CARDS, TRADE CARDS,
CARTE DE VISITES, STEREOCARDS,
POSTAL HISTORY, MAGAZINES,
BOOKS, POSTERS, ACCESSORIES Etc;

COLLECTORS
FESTIVAL
Bank Holiday Monday
January 2nd

A Right Royal Drink

HORNIMAN'S PURE TEA

2006 Sundays:

January 22nd
February 19th
March 26th
April 23rd
May 28th
June 25th
July 23rd
August 27th
September 24th
October 22nd
November 26th
December 17th

Open 10 a.m. to 4.30p.m. Admission £1
(Incl. FREE postcard)
Early entry available at 8.00 a.m.

MEMORIES Collectors shop
130 Brent St, Hendon, London NW4.

Tel, 020 8202 9080 020 8203 1500 Fax 020 8203 7031
e-mail dave@memoriespostcards.co.uk
web page www.memoriespostcards.co.uk

Edgar Longstaffe (1884-1906) *specialised in landscapes and travelled extensively in Scotland and the North-East of England for various postcard companies.*
Most of his work was published by S.Hildersheimer & Co Ltd. Six of his pictures were exhibited at the Royal Academy.
Cards are currently valued at £1.50

Alexander Young *was born in Scotland and flourished as a painter between 1885 & 1920, his water colours were published in the main by Faulkner in their early series.*
Young also painted a large number of inland beauty spots of Scotland.
Cards are currently valued at £1.50

Walter Hayward Young (1868-1920) *was born in Sheffield although he started out as a clerk to a lawyer he was soon lured by his talent to paint.He called himself 'Jotter' and in 1899 he was commissioned to paint famous beauty spots by Raphael Tuck and these were published in the "Oilette" series.*
He produced over 800 paintings for the postcard industry.
'Jotter' died at the height of his creative talents in1920 at the age of 52.
Cards are currently valued at £3

George Parsons-Norman (1840-1914) *Born in London he achieved considerable success as a painter. In 1880 he settled in Lowestoft. There he painted pictures of the Broads and many views which featured poppies. Many of his paintings have been published as postcards, some by Jarrold & Co of Norwich.*
Cards are currently valued at £1.50

ARTISTS ON POSTCARDS

Here are a few examples of the many famous artists who painted large numbers of superb scenes from all around the British Isles. Many of these are available from dealers for just a few pounds.

Henry B. Winbush was one of Raphael Tuck's stable of hard working and highly productive water colourists who was a Royal Academian, exhibiting between 1888 and 1904.
Wimbush was kept busy covering London as well as places of interest around the British Isles, Channel Isles and the Isle of Wight.
Cards currently valued at £2

Charles E. Flowers was born in 1871 and studied at the Royal College of Art in London.He exhibited at the Royal Academy in 1902. Flowers training in draughtmanship is evident in the minute detail of architectural features. Castles, churches and Inns are found in many of his pictures. He died in 1957.
Cards are currently valued at £2

Robert Gallon (1845-1925) was a succesful landscapist who achieved the distinction of exhibiting at the Royal Academy between 1868 and 1903. Publisher S.Hildersheimer & Co commissioned him to paint a number of views from around the British Isles. He lived most of his life in London and died at his home in St.John's Wood.
Cards are currently valued at £1

Postcards by J Lévy Sons & Co - LL

The letters LL on a lively seaside view or a busy street scene make the postcards of Lévy Sons & Co. instantly recognisable. The skill of their photographers in capturing animated scenes contrasts with the views of buildings and empty streets favoured by many others. However the origin of the LL imprint is still the source of debate and some confusion. The latest understanding is that it was the trademark of an old established photographic firm based in Paris, rather than the initials of any one individual.

The LL Collectors' Circle has some sixty members exchanging information and compiling listings of the cards published by the firm. Twelve illustrated newsletters have been distributed. Volunteers are collating checklists for each location covered in the UK and beyond. Information on earliest posting dates and highest numbers known is developing rapidly. Cards of England, France and other countries are being actively studied, as part of compiling a more detailed history of the firm and their output.

Two meetings a year are held to share and exchange information. Contact between individual members is also actively encouraged. A website is under development. The subscription for four newsletters is £8 to addresses in the UK and Europe or £12 elsewhere. **Contact: Geoff Ashton, Wahroonga, Clarefield Drive, Maidenhead, Berks SL6 5DP (01628 637868) or e-mail: geoff @backhome.globalnet.co.uk**

Below and Right are some examples of LL postcards with a guide price to give some idea of the of value and variety of subject matter and location.

74 London Bridge £2

210 London – Marble Arch £4

524 Hampton Court– Arrival of 'Queen Elizabeth '£5

928 – The Zoo (London) – The Llama Ride £6

A guide to the values of J Lévy Sons & Co - LL

35 Canterbury – Old House £8

6 Oxford – Balliol College £3

34 Swanage – Victoria Terrace £12

1 Stratford-on-Avon,Shakespeare's Birthplace £1.50

29 Eastbourne – On the Beach £4

27 Dover – Arrival of the Ostend Boat £6

5 Seaview (Isle of Wight) – The Pier £5

25 Ryde (Isle of Wight) – Yachting at Ryde £7

WHAT THE PRICES MEAN

With a few exceptions, all cards in this Catalogue have been given a single price, representing a broad average figure for the majority of cards in their respective classification. For example:

ART and SUBJECT CARDS

The stated price may be taken as a broad average figure for all Art and Subject cards. You will find C.E. Flower listed at £2. There are many common cards by this artist which are worth no more than £1, while his rare cards would certainly be worth £3. The great bulk of his output therefore would be expected to sell at the broad average figure of £2.

TOPOGRAPHICAL and SOCIAL HISTORY

With any relevant entry, e.g. Motor Bus . Tram . Street Market . Windmill etc. the stated price, or broad average figure, is for a card, *either RP or Printed, fully identified and showing a 'Close-up at a named location',* with real photographic cards being the most desirable. (Logically it will be appreciated that to qualify for listing at all, a Bus or Tram etc. has to be a *"Close-up"* in the first place and as such would represent the *majority of cards in that classification*). Generally speaking, anything less would be classified as a street scene at a lower price. If you think of a Bus or Tram in the middle distance, that is a street scene, while a Windmill in the middle-distance would similarly be priced at a lower figure.

With this in mind, it is then necessary to apply certain other criteria before formulating a final price, as with all Topographical and Social History cards, it is neither realistic nor practical to subdivide each entry into considerations of: Real Photographic . Printed . Close-up . Far Distance . Located . Unlocated . Identified . Unidentified . Common . Scarce . Publisher . Condition etc., not to mention whether the card is in a saleable area or even if it forms part of a remaindered stock! (You will begin to appreciate the problems in pricing these cards!). Put simply, the card has to be a Close-up to qualify for the price given. Consideration of all these other factors will then enable you to arrive at a final valuation.

A real photographic Motor Bus is catalogued at £35. A distant view of a Bus trundling along a country road may fetch £5, while a common, mass produced card of Buses in Trafalgar Square would only be worth 50p. On the other hand, a spectacular real photograph of a bus in a provincial town, taken by a local photographer, where the image fills the whole of the card, may fetch £50. Real Photographic cards are generally worth more than Printed cards, but a middle distance RP would be worth less than a superb Printed close-up. Admittedly, this is not easy for collectors new to the hobby, but as you gain more knowledge you will quickly see how it all works! Pricing is not an exact science, nor would we ever wish it to be!

It is further pointed out that in all relevant classifications, 'Accidents' would carry a price toward the higher end of the scale.

FURTHER INFORMATION

It must always be borne in mind that an exceptional card or complete set in any classification may fetch a price well in excess of Catalogue valuation. There are many reasons for this. In the dealer's stock any particularly rare or desirable item may be felt to be worth a premium, given the number of potential buyers, while at auction the same card, or complete set, would be offered to a totally different world-wide clientele, with a resulting number of high bids being received. It does not therefore follow that any auction realisation can be taken as representing current market value as perceived by the majority of dealers throughout the country.

In many Subject classifications, for example, Animals, Children, Greetings etc. one finds many cards printed by the early chromo-litho method. The superior quality of these cards would put them at the higher end of the price range.

It is not possible to be more specific given the huge numbers and types of postcards produced, neither is it realistic to have an entry for 'Chromo-Litho' under hundreds of Subject listings!

A single figure has been for all classifications where the majority of cards are of similar content, e.g. Bamforth Song Cards. One would expect to find such cards in any dealer's stock, priced at around the stated price.

The Price Range has been retained for classifications where one finds a wide divergence of content in available cards, e.g. 'Advert Cards/Poster Type'. Here only knowledge and experience can be your guide, though it is quite practical to take a middle average price for any particular card. This will enable you to form a realistic assessment of the value of your collection.

Unless otherwise stated, all cards in this catalogue are priced as being commercially published. Private and family photographs have no value other than what they may be worth to a particular collector. There are certain exceptions e.g. 'Contemporary Fashion, Weddings' and similar collectable cards.

Unless clearly stated in the text, all prices are for singe cards.

In all cases, prices are for cards in fine condition, with no marks or bent corners etc. This is particularly so with Art and Subject cards, whereas in the Topographical and Social History fields, the image may be felt to outweigh considerations of condition.

The cards listed in this Catalogue are with very few exceptions pre-1939 and all standard size 5.5 x 3.5 in. This date may be extended to 1945 for the issues of World War 2, and as far as 1970 for GB Topographical Views, Civil Aviation, Cinema and one or two other subjects as indicated in the listings.

Certain issues in the larger 6 x 4 size did occur during this period, and are listed as appropriate, but with the odd exception, this Catalogue does not concern itself with anything later than 1970 in either size.

All prices in this Catalogue, many of them covering thousands of cards with one figure, must be taken as a broad average of that particular classification. Please do not say "PPV gives £3 for this". PPV does not give £3 for this. PPV suggests £3 as a mean average figure for the majority of cards of that type. Some cards may be worth £1, while others may be worth £5. Please bear this in mind when buying or selling.

N.B. It must be pointed out to non-collectors wishing to sell cards, that perhaps 75% of all postcards are virtually worthless! Postcards are like Stamps or Coins, in that huge quantities of common, or low-denomination material exists in today's market. I refer to Greetings cards - Landscapes - Seasides - Tourist Areas - Churches - Cathedrals - common Foreign views etc. All these cards are catalogued, and all must have a price, but it does not follow that anyone wants to buy them! Such cards may be picked up from auctions or trade sources in bulk at nominal cost. Effectively, what dealers want to buy are the better cards catalogued at £1.50 and upwards, which they can sell again. Please bear this in mind when offering cards for sale.

MODERN CARDS

As a brief guide it can be assumed that while certain subject themes may have a value of up to several pounds each, the vast majority of subject cards can be purchased new for 50p or less and secondhand or used for a few pence each.

As for topographical views, the same price structure applies, although it is pointed out to prospective vendors that views of foreign holiday areas are worth very little.

ADVERTISING

One of the most popular and widely collected postcard themes. Many different types of Advertising cards were produced during the early years of this century, both by the companies whose products they advertised, and by the independent publishers. They range from the very attractive 'Poster Types', designed in the form of an advertising poster, or sometimes reproducing an established poster such as Fry's classic 'Five Boys' design, to the many plainer types known as 'Giveaways'. These were published by the company for promotional purposes, and were often given away with the product, although many more do show themes such as the gathering, processing, or manufacture of the product. Companies across the whole spectrum of industry produced Advertising cards of one sort or another, and we have cards from the Food and Drink industry, Animal Feed Manufacturers, Newspapers and Magazines, the Tobacco Industry, and many more. In addition, many of the Railway and Shipping companies, as well as other more specialised issues are listed under those respective sections. We also include 'Reward Cards' under the main entry, as these were given away to school-children for good attendance.

Market Report
The better Poster Types and certain themes do sell steadily, as do the more interesting Giveaways, but no significant increases have been seen this year.

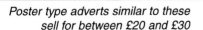

Poster type adverts similar to these sell for between £20 and £30

POSTER TYPE

Beecham's Pills
Tom Browne designs   £25

Beer & Baccy
Victoria State 1896   £30

Berry's Boot Polish   £20

Bird's Custard   £20

British Army
Recruiting Poster   £30

Bryant & May   £35

Cadbury's   £40

Camp Coffee
Harry Payne designs   £60
Other designs   £30

Campbell's Soups
G. Weidersheim designs   £25

Capern's Bird Foods   £15

Cerebos Salt   £25

Champion Vinegar   £12

Claymore Whiskey
Defenders of the Empire   £10

Continental Tyres   £25

C.W.S
Pelaw Metal Polish   £18
Other Products   £18

Epps Milk Chocolate   £25

Fletcher's Sauce   £25
GP Government Tea   £15

Gossage's Soap   £25

Heinz H.J. & Co.   £18

H.P. Sauce   £30

Horniman's Tea   £25

Hudson's Soap   £25

James Keiller   £15

John Knight Soap   £25

Mustad Horse Nails   £25

Nestle's Milk   £30

North British Rubber Co.   £30

Ovaltine   £15

Palmer Tyres   £25

Peek Frean
Tom Browne designs   £25

Raleigh Cycles   £30

Schweppes   £12

Wm Younger Poster Advert £30

Skipper Sardines   £10

Wood Milne Rubber Heels   £15

Miscellaneous Products   £10/£30

Suchard Chocolate/Cocoa
One of the earliest companies to employ the medium of the picture postcard for advertising purposes, Suchard were producing cards from c.1890 onwards.

Early Vignette/Gruss Aus type   £20

SETS & SERIES

C.W.S. Packet Teas

Dickens sketches/Trade back	£8
Time Around the World/Trade back	£10

Epps Cocoa

Nature series	£8

Famous Posters in Miniature

H.M.& Co.	£30

GP Government Tea
Set 6/KEVII at Windsor

Price per set	£130

Lemco

Coronation series	£15
Types of Lemco Cattle	£10

Quaker Oats

Smiles/Set 10	£12

Shell Oil

Original series	£35
Reproductions	.50

Walker, Harrison & Garthwaite

Phoenix Poultry Foods	£10
Viscan Pet Foods	£10
VC Winners	£12

For other Advertising cards on Aviation, Motoring, Railway, Shipping and Theatrical, please see those headings.

CHROMO-LITHO

Standard-size cards, mainly of French origin, and printed Chromo-Litho, usually in early vignette style. They carry the brand name of a product on an often quite unrelated design.

Arlatte Chicory
Tuck R. & Sons/Flowers £10

Belle Jardiniere

Art sketches	£20

Chocolat Lindt

Children/Art sketches	£20

Chocolat Lombart

Children/Art sketches	£20

Lipton

Language of Flowers	£18

Scott's Emulsion

French Departments/Set 92	£8

COURT SIZE

These are among the earliest examples of Advertising cards. Smaller than standard postcard size, and usually printed chromo-litho in vignette style.

Hutchinson Novels

Literary adverts	£25

Johnston's Corn Flour

Some Methods of Travelling/Set 24	£35

Nestle's Swiss Milk

Military vignettes	£40

St. Ivel Cheese | £20 |

FRIENDLY SOCIETIES

Not exactly Poster Type, although some very attractive designs may be found on these cards.

Grand United Order of Oddfellows	£6
Hearts of Oak Benefit Society	£6
Independent Order of Rechabites	£6
Order of the Sons of Temperance	
Heraldic Designs	£6
Bridges/Castles/Churches	£10
Twentieth Century Equitable Friendly Society	£6

Rechabites Society £6

POSTER TYPE/SERIES

FRY J.S. & SONS

Prices

As with Tuck Celebrated Posters, a wide divergence exists in the current market value of these cards. Some are very common, others remarkably scarce.

Tom Browne designs	£15/£30
With Capt Scott at the South Pole	£50
Other designs	£20/£40

Caption	Artist
Showcard Replica Series	
What's good for the bee	
His heart's desire	
A perfect dream	
The tired traveller	
On the top	
A perfect food	
Sweeter than honey	

Vivian Mansell &Co.
Unapproachable
This is my brother Billy
A source of delight
Is the best
Keeps out the cold

Various Publishers	
John Bull says support home industries	R.C. Carter
Cow being milked	R.C. Carter
The prize winner	Chas. Pears
If you feel cold	Chas. Pears
My eye! Ain't Fry's Chocolate nice	Chas. Pears
Far too good to share	Chas. Pears
The diver's lucky find	
Cocoa Sah!	Edgar Filby
Good old mater	
Fry's Milk Chocolate (White Cow)	

It's worth the risk	
Unrivalled ... etc.	
A double first	
The bloom of health	
No better food	
Design as above/C.W. Faulkner	
The little connoisseur	
Over the top and the best of luck	
Fry's for good	
So near and yet so far	Tom Browne
Highway robbery	Tom Browne
See their eyes as she buys	
Fry's	Tom Browne
One touch of nature	Tom Browne
Right up to date	Tom Browne
Fry's Cocoa (rich girl)	Tom Browne
Hello Daddy	
Whom God preserve	
Compliments of J.S. Fry & Sons Ltd.	
Fry's Coca (Boy with train)	
Fry's Chocolate for endurance	
Well, if you know of a better cocoa!	
Going by leaps and bounds	
Jolly good for the money	
Sustaining and invigorating	
Fry's, it's good	
The best is good enough for me	
Fry's Pure Cocoa/	
Design as above/J.S. Fry & Sons Ltd.	
Tuck CP 1500	Gordon Browne
Fry's Milk Chocolate/Tuck CP 1502	

TUCK R. & SONS
Celebrated Posters

Prices

There exists a considerable variance in price for these cards, even for the same card, if sold at auction or by a dealer. Basically the lower numbered series are the more common, and would range from about £15-£30 depending upon the artist, design, product, condition etc. But even here we find particular cards occurring more frequently than the others. Indeed some are positively commonplace!

The higher series from 1504 onwards are less often found, with the contrary position that certain cards seem almost non-existent! Here the price range would be from £30-£75, although prices as high as £150 for particular cards have been noted in the stocks of certain dealers!

For a more comprehensive study of this subject J.H.D.Smith has published 'The Picture Postcards of Raphael Tuck & sons'. Price £30. See page 36 for more details.

TOBACCO

A special classification for these cards reflects a shared interest with the cigarette card world.

Havelock Tobacco advert £20

Adkins Tobacco
Tom Browne posters £150+

Cavander's Army Mixture
Poster type £25

Dimitrino Cigarettes
Chromo-Litho £15

Gallaher's Park Drive Cigarettes
Poster type £12

Gitanes Cigarettes
Poster type/Art Deco £30

Godfrey Phillips
Set 30/Beauty Spots of the Homeland £8
Set 24/Coronation Series £8
Set 26/Famous Paintings £8
Set 24/Film Stars £60
Set 48/Film Stars £60
Set 30/Garden Studies £6
Set 12/Jubilee Series £6
Set 30/Our Dogs £90
Set 30/Our Glorious Empire £12
Set 30/Our Puppies £40

Grapevine Cigarettes
Southend Lifeboat 1906 £15

Gray's Cigarettes
Views £3

Job Cigarette Papers
Vercasson/Poster type:
Chromo-Litho £50
Early vignettes £25

Lea R. & J./Chairman Cigarettes
O.E. Pottery and Porcelain/Set 24 £6
With supplier's imprint £8

Mitchell's Prize Crop
Glasgow Exhibition 1901 £75

Murad Turkish Cigarettes £30

Nicholas Sarony
Film Stars £3

Ogden's
Poster type £90

Players
Poster type £75
Other types £30

Sandorides Lucana Cigarettes
Poster type £20

U.K. Tobacco Co./The Greys
Beautiful Britain £2

Wills W.D. & H.O.
Poster type: Capstan/Gold Flake/
Three Castles/Westward Ho! £100

Miscellaneous Companies
Poster type £15/£40
Views etc. £2+

Tuck's celebrated poster No 1501 £90

GIVE AWAY/INSERT CARDS

This section covers those cards given away or distributed by commercial firms, newspapers and magazines, etc., for promotional purposes. Subjects depicted are varied, and often have no relation to the product advertised. Here again the total number of firms who produced these cards is incalculable. We list below the more common and collectable cards.

Amami Shampoo
Prichard & Constance — £2

Answers — £4

Bazaar, Exchange & Mart
Comic sketches — £8

Beecham's Pills
GB views — £1

Bees Ltd. — £1

Bensdorp Cocoa
Pierrots — £12
Dutch Scenes — £3
London views — £1.50
Isle of Marken — £1

Books/Magazines/Newspapers
Military/Mail/Front Page — £3
French Newspapers/Front Page — £3
Other publications — £3

Boon's Cocoa
European views — .75

Bovril
Art Reproductions — £1

Brett's Publications
GB views — £1.50

British Dominions Insurance
Art studies/Set 24 — £1.50

Bromo Cocoa
Plantation sketches — £2

Brooke Bond
Silhouettes of Manchester — £12

Butywave Shampoo
Film Stars — £3

Cadbury Bros.
Bournville village — £1.50

Canadian Dept. of Emigration
Canadian views — £1.50

Canary and Cage Bird Life
Cage Bird Studies/32 cards
  /pc back — £5
  /trade back — £3

Capern's Bird Foods
Cage bird studies/pc back — £3
  /trade back — £1.50

Captain Magazine
Tom Browne sketches — £8

Carter Paterson
Art sketches — £2

Carter's Seeds — £1.50

Chelsea Flower Show — £3

Chick's Own — £5

Chivers & Sons
Studies of English Fruits — £2
Aerial views of Histon — £2

Christian Novels
GB views — £1.50

Colman's Starch
Postmen of the Empire — £12
GB sketches — £3

Connoisseur
Art Reproductions — .50

Cook E./Lightning Series
Aviation studies — £8

Crawford's Cream Crackers
Russo-Japanese war map 1905 — £8

CWS Soaps — £5

Daily Chronicle
Fashion adverts — £5

Daily Express — £2

Daily Mirror
Fair of Fashions Competition — £2
Beauty Contest — £2

Daily News/Wallet Guide
GB views — £1.50

Daily Sketch
The Daily Sketch Girl — £3

Dainty Novels
Greetings/Coloured — £2
Other subjects — £1.50

De Beukelaer's Cocoa
Topographical sketches — .75

Dewar's Whisky
Gems of Art series — £1.50

Eagle Insurance Co.
Head Office building — £4

Elliman's Linament
Tuck R. & Sons — £5

Family Reader
Various subjects — £1.50

Feathered World
Poultry studies £5

Field J.C./Toilet Soaps
Childhood sketches £4

Field The
Military sketches £4

Fine Arts Publishing Co.
Burlington Proofs .75

F-M-N Complete Novels
Theatrical portraits £1.50

Formosa Oolong Tea
Sketches on Rice Paper £10
Japanese prints £3

Fry J.S. & Sons
Non-poster types £8
Views of Somerdale Works £2

Garden City Association
Letchworth Garden City/
   Set 12/Frank Dean £4
   Set 6/W.W. Ratcliffe £4

Gentlewoman
Royal Artist Post Card Series £4

Girl's Own Paper
Art sketches/4 designs £10

Glaxo
Various subjects £3

Goss W.H.
Oates S. & Co. £8

Guinness A.
Cartoons/6x4 size/
Three sets of 6 cards (per card) £8
Brewery scenes £8
Brewery scenes/6x4 size £4

Harland & Wolf
Valentine & Sons £6

Hartley W.P.
Jam production scenes £2

Haydock Coals
Art Reproduction/GB views £1

Health and Strength
Physical Culture studies £8
Hoffman's Starch £1.50

Home Words
Various subjects £1.50

Horner's Penny Stories
Various subjects £3

Horniman's Tea
Invisible Picture £8
GB views £2

Hotels/Restaurants
GB/Artist sketches £3
GB Photographic/Printed £5
Foreign/Gruss Aus type £3
Foreign/Later issues £1

Ideas Weekly
The Imps £8

Idle Moments
Various subjects £1.50

Imperial Fine Art Corporation
Art Reproductions .75

International Horse Show £8

Jacob W. & R.
Biscuit production scenes £3

King Insurance Co.
GB Royalty sketches £6

Lever Bros.
Port Sunlight village £1.50

Liberty's £8

Liebig Fray-Bentos
Oxo Shackleton Expedition £25
Meat processing scenes £4

Lipton
Tea Estate sketches £1.50

Liverpool, China & India Tea Co. Ltd.
Atlantic Liners £15

Lord Mayor Treloar Home
Institution scenes £1.50

Maggi
European views .75

Manchester Dock & Harbour Board
Topographical sketches £6

Mazawattee Tea & Chocolate
Louis Wain Cats/Postcard £85
  /Trade Back £50

Mellin's Food
Costume & Flags/Set 12 £6
Various subjects £6

Melox
Animal Foods £6

Menier Chocolate
Paris sketches £1

Miniature Novels
Various subjects £1.50

Mirror Novels
Theatrical/Bookmark type £3

Molassin Meal/Dog Cakes
Various subjects £8

My Pocket Novel
Various subjects £1.50

My Queen & Romance
Various subjects   £1.50

Nestle's
Animals & Birds/Set 12   £6

New Zealand Govt. Department
Topographical sketches   £1.50

New Zealand Lamb
Dairy Farming scenes   .75

North British Rubber Co.
Golfing sketches   £45

Norwich Union
Motor Fire Engine   £12

Ocean Accident & Guarantee Corp.
Insurance Post Card Series   £4

Odol Dentifrice
Actresses   £4

Oetzmann's Cottages
Exhibition cards   £1.50

Old Calabar
Animal Foods   £10

Oliver Typewriters
Writing through the Ages   £6

Overprints
Advertising copy overprinted on to otherwise standard commercial postcard. Value as latter plus nominal premium.

Oxo
Oxo Cattle Studies   £15

Peark's Butter/Tea
Various subjects   £2

Pears A. & F.
Various subjects   £2
Bubbles   £1

Peek Frean
Invisible Picture   £10
GB views   £2

Pickfords
Transport sketches   £8
Reproductions   .50

Pitman Health Food Co.
Ideal food series   £5

Postcard Connoisseur
Dore's London/1904 Facsimile £50

Price's Candles
Military sketches   £8
Nursery Riddles   £8

Princess Novels
Various subjects   £1.50

Red Letter/Red Star Weekly
Greetings/Coloured   £3

Eastmans Poster Advert £20

Jacob & Co £25

40

White rose Advert £12

Waldorf Hotel £15

Remington Typewriters
Poster type £20

Ridgway's
Tea Estate scenes £3

Rowntree
Louis Wain Cats £75
Rowntree's Postcard Series £2

St. Bartholomew's Hospital
Reconstuction Appeal £1

St.Ivel
GB views/Set 12 £1.50

St. Paul's Hospital/Set 12
£1,000 Competition £1

Sainsbury's Margarine
Crelos/Early Days of Sport £15
/Fairy Tales £15

Selfridge Co. £3

Shippam's
Food production scenes £5

Shops/Stores
Artist sketches £5
Photographic/Printed £15

Shurey's Publications
Twopenny Tube/Set 12 £6
Various subjects £1.50

Singer Sewing Machines
Sewing Machines Worldwide £10
Aviation studies £6
Battleships £3

Sketchy Bits
Various subjects £1.50

Smart Novels
Dance Band Leaders/Set 10 £6
Greetings/Coloured £1.50
Various subjects £1.50

Spillers £12

Sportex Cloth
Dog studies £8

Spratt's Dog Foods
Dog studies £8

Sutton & Sons
Flowers/Vegetables £1.50

Swan Fountain Pens
Comic sketches £6

Symond's London Stores
Comic sketches £8

T.A.T.
The `Months' Series £4
Other subjects £1.50
Thomson D.C.
Various subjects £1.50

Thorley
Cattle photographs   £6

Time Magazine
Subscription cards   .75

Tiny Tots
Greetings/Coloured   £8

Tit-Bits
Poster type   £6

Tower Tea
Proverb Series   £10

Trent Pottery
Trent Bridge Publishing Co.   £6

Tussauds Madame
Tableaux/Set 12/Tuck R. & Sons   £3

Two Steeples Hosiery
Hunting sketches   £3

Typhoo Tea
Various subjects/Oilette   £3

Underwood Typewriters
Poster type   £20

Van Houten's Cocoa
MGM Film Stars   £5
Colouring Cards of Birds/
Set of 6 in Folder/Price per card   £4
Dutch scenes   £2
Art Sketches/Uncaptioned   £1.50

Virol
Children of all Nations   £6

Vitality
Physical Culture studies   £6

Ward Lock
Naval photographs   £3

Weekly Tale-Teller
Various subjects   £1.50

Weekly Telegraph
Tom Browne sketches   £8

Weldon's Bazaar
KE VII Coronation Souvenir   £10

White Horse Whisky
Maggs Coaching studies   £2

Wood-Milne Rubber Heel
Glamour studies/Sager   £15
GB views   £1.50

Wrench
Insurance cards   £8

Yes or No
Various subjects   £1.50

Nectar tea Company £4

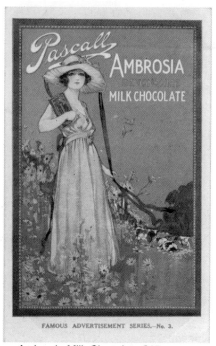

Ambrosia Milk Chocolate £15

National Telephone Company £10

Thermos advertising £10

REWARD CARDS

Given away for good school work and attendance etc.

COMPANIES

Cadbury Bros.

Birds/Set 25	£6
Birds and their Eggs/Set 12	£6
Butterflies/Set 32	£8
Map Cards	£8

Ficolax

Fruit sketches	£4

Milkmaid Condensed Milk

Royalty sketches	£8

Nectar Tea

Bird sketches	£6
Tea Estate sketches	£4

Reckitt

Naval History	£6

Scott's Emulsion | £5 |

EDUCATION AUTHORITIES

Barking Education Committee

Homeland Series/Court Size	£6

County Borough of West Ham

Court Size	£6

Erith Education Committee

Tuck R. & Sons/Castles etc.	£3

Hampshire County Council

GB views	£1.50

Huddersfield Education Committee

GB views	£3

Isle of Ely Education Committee

Nature Notes	£3

Leyton School Board/Pre-1902

Various sizes and series	£4

London County Council

Battleships/6 x 4 size/ S. Cribb	£5
Various Subjects	£1.50

Oxfordshire Education Committee

British Wild Flowers	£3

Reading EducationCommittee

Animals/Historical	£3

School Board for London

Various subjects/Pre-1895	£5
Various subjects/1895-1902	£3

Surrey Education Committee

GB views	£1.50

Walthamstow Education Committee

Paintings/Views	£3

Wanstead School Board

Flowers	£4

ANIMALS

If postcard collecting was originally the province of the young girls of the Edwardian age, then it is to them, and their interest in this subject, that we owe the great legacy of Animal cards bequeathed us. Always an attractive collecting area, then as now. Animal cards were produced in considerable quantity, with almost every type of bird or beast depicted somewhere. Today's collectors tend to prefer Artist-drawn cards, rather than the photographic studies.

Market Report
Still a very popular area, although the higher prices are reached by the quality art cards by popular artists, for example Louis Wain or Arthur Thiele.

ANTHROPORMORPHIC
(Animals in human dress)

Chromo-Litho	£10
Photographic/Printed	£3

BIRDS

NVP Sluis Birdfood	£1.50
Racing Pigeons	£5
Scilly Isles/C.J. King	£1
Art Studies	£2
Photographic Studies	£1

Tuck R. & Sons

British Birds & their Eggs/ Aquarette Series 9218/9399/9519	£6

BUTTERFLIES

Art Studies	£3
Photographic Studies	£1

Tuck R. & Sons

Butterflies	£6
British Butterflies and Moths	£6
Butterflies on the Wing	£6
Educational Series No. 8/Set 6	£8

CATTLE

Miscellaneous Studies	£1.50

CATS

Chromo-Litho	£12
Mainzer, Alfred/Post-war	£2
Art Studies	£3
Photographic Studies	£1.50

DOGS

Military Dogs/WW1	£6
Spratt's Dog Foods	£8
Art Studies	£3+
Photographic Studies	£2

Dog Carts

Belgian	£3
French Milk Carts	£25+
French other Carts	£25+
Swiss	£5
Other European types	£5

Within these prices, named breeds would be worth more than un-named.

DONKEYS

Donkey Carts/RP	£6
Seaside	£2
Domestic	£2

FISH

Art Studies	£3
Photographic Studies	£1.50

Photographic cats £1.50

Photographic Dog £2

Horse, Photographic study £2

ZOO ANIMALS

Art Studies	£3
Photographic Studies	£2

Official Issues

London Zoo/Whipsnade	£2

Series

Zoological Society of London/	
H.A.J. Schultz & Co.	£5

London Zoo   £2

HORSES

Horses and Carts	£6
Ponies and Traps	£4
Working Horses	£3
Art Studies	£4
Photographic Studies	£2

Coaching

Vanderbilt Coach	£12
Holiday types	£3
State/Ceremonial Coaches	£1.50
Old Coaching Inns of England/	
Set 16/J.C. Maggs	£2

PIGS

Early/Chromo-Litho	£15
Farmyard scenes	£2
Art Studies	£5
Photographic Studies	£3

POULTRY

Easter Chicks	£1.50
Art Studies	£4
Photographic Studies	£1.50

Tuck R. & Sons

Prize Poultry/Oilette	£6

TAXIDERMY

Booth Museum/Brighton	£2
Bramber Museum	£1.50
Stuffed Animals/Fish	£3

WILD ANIMALS

Frogs	£3
Rabbits	£3
Art studies	£3
Photographic Studies	£1

Tuck R. & Sons

Wild Animals/Oilette	£3

Leopards and their keeper Tuck's £5

SERIES

Tuck R. & Sons

Educational Series	£9

WELFARE SOCIETIES

Abattoir scenes/U.S.A.	£8
Anti-Bloodsports	£12
Anti-Vivisection	£12
Cat Protection Organisations	£10
National Canine Defence League	£10
Our Dumb Friends League	£10
R.S.P.C.A./R.S.P.B.	£10
Vegetarian Society	£10
Veterinary Services	£12

ART DECO

Art Deco remains an important postcard classification, reflecting as it does the work of many leading artists of the twentieth century. Art Deco began in the early years after 1900, as a reaction to the swirling and complex designs of Art Nouveau. The style was characterised by a more severe and economical line, and was later to be inspired by cubism. It reached its height in 1925 with the Paris Exposition des Arts Decoratifs et Modernes, but died out in the 1930s. At its peak, the Art Deco style reached into many other branches of the arts, and its influence was particularly notable in the design of contemporary architecture, furniture and fashion. The `Odeon' cinemas of the period are a typical example. Artist signed postcards are difficult to price accurately while unsigned work can only sell for what the buyer is prepared to pay.

Much current business is conducted through the auction rooms where this subject always sells well, with the better artists much in demand.

Art Deco cards similar to these sell for around £15 to £20 each

ART NOUVEAU

This is a highly specialised field which, like Art Deco, reaches into the Fine Art World, with the consequent high price structure of many of its Artists.Typified by a swirling, flowing style, Art Nouveau reached its apogee at the turn of the century in the work of Mucha, Kirchner and Basch, among others, but died out about ten years later. Like Art Deco, the postcards are

difficult to price, for although the style is quite popular with British collectors, most business today is conducted through the auction houses selling single cards, often at widely differing figures. It is fair to say however, that considerable opportunities remain for the informed collector, whose specialised knowledge may be used to advantage at postcard fairs or retail outlets.

The work of top artists is keenly sought by an exclusive clientele, with much interest coming from the USA and the Continent. Both Art Nouveau and Art Deco, however, remain a rather heady mix for the average British collector.

Left; Raphael Kirchner £60
Below Left: Raphael tuck's Christmas series £20
Below; Tuck's Art series no. 843 £20

ARTISTS

This is a select index of better known artists who designed for the picture postcard in both Subject and Topographical fields. It is not comprehensive, as many thousands of artists world-wide have contributed to the medium during the past century. The price stated may be taken as a guide to the most typical and representative work of the artist concerned, although in the Subject field, this price may be qualified by the theme depicted. With all artists so much depends upon the individual card, the design, the period, the publisher and of course the condition. I have done nothing more than indicate the general price area into which the artist falls,but certain rare cards by particular artists may dramatically exceed this figure. The great majority of artists listed below are either British, or have produced cards which are collected in this country. There are some excellent catalogues available which list the artists of France, Italy, Russia, USA etc. but I do not consider it practical to copy out several thousand names which would have little relevance to the British market.

Market Report
Still a good area for investment. If you can find a little known artist and build a collection, it should be well worth your while.

M.A.	Comic	£1	Aris, Ernest	Comic	£3
S.A.	Comic	£1.50		General	£1.50
T.A.	Comic	£1.50	Armitage, A.F.	General	£1.50
Abeille, Jack	Art Nouveau	£60	Asti, Angelo	Glamour	£8
	Glamour	£50	Attwell, Mabel Lucie	Children/	
Acker, Flori Von	General	£1		Pre-1918	£12
Ackroyd, W.M.	Animals	£3		1918-1939	£10
Adams, C.J.	General	£1		1940 on	£6
Adams, Frank	General	£3		Modern Repros	.50
Adams, J.T.	General	£1.50	Austen, Alex	General	£1
Adams, M	General	£1	Austerlitz, E	Comic	£3
Adams, Will	Comic	£1.50	Austin E.H.S. Barnes	Animals	£12
Addison, W.G.	General	£1.50	Austin, Winifred	Animals	£4
Ainsley, Anne	Animals	£3	Aveling, S.	General	£1.50
Albertini	Glamour	£6	Azzoni, N.	Children	£4
Aldin, Cecil	Animals	£6	H.S.B.	Comic	£1.50
Allan, A	General	£1	J.O.B.	Comic	£2
Allen, S.J.	General	£1	Baertson	Military	£4
Allen, W.	General	£1.50	Bailey G.O.	Glamour	£4
Alys, M	Children	£1.50	Bairnsfather, Bruce	Comic	£3
Ambler, C	Animals	£3		Theatre	£30
Anders, O	Animals	£6	Baker, G.	Military	£4
	Comic	£3	Baker, H Granville	Military	£6
Anderson, Anne	Children	£6	Bakst, Leon	Art Deco	£50
Anderson, V.C.	Children	£4	Balestrieri, L	Glamour	£8
				General	£4
Andrews, E	General	£1.50	Ball, Wilfred	General	£2
Anichini, Ezio	Art Deco	£15	Bamber, George A	Comic	£2
Aranda, Pilar	Art Deco	£8	Baness	General	£1

48

Bannister, A.F.D.	Aviation	£4
	Shipping	£4
Bantock	Art Deco	£8
Barbara, S	Art Nouveau	£25
Barber, Court	Glamour	£4
Barber, C.W.	Children	£3
	Glamour	£3
Barde	Flowers	£1.50
Barham, S	Children	£8
Barker, Cecily M	Children	£12
Barnes, A.E.	Animals	£20
Barnes, G.L.	Animals	£15
	Comic	£8
Barraud, A	General	£1.50
Barraud, N	Animals	£5
Barribal, W	Children	£12
	Glamour	£12
	Theatre	£25
Barthel, Paul	General	£1.50
Bartoli, Guiseppi	General	£5
Basch, Arpad	Art Nouveau	£110
Bask, W	General	£1
Bateman, H.M.	Comic	£7.50
Bates, Marjorie C.	Literary	£5
	General	£3
Bayer, R.W.	Flowers	£1.50
Beards, Harold	Comic	£1.50
Bebb, Rosa	Animals	£6
	General	£1.50
Becker, C.	Military	£8
	Sport	£8
Bee	Comic	£1
Beecroft, Herbert	General	£4
Beer, Andrew	General	£1.50
Beerts, Albert	Military	£5
Belcher, George	Comic	£4
Beraud, N	Animals	£4
	Military	£5
Berkeley, Edith	General	£1
Berkeley, Stanley	Animals	£3
Berthon, Paul	Art Nouveau	£80
Bertiglia, A	Children	£8
Bianchi	Glamour	£4
Biggar, J.L.	Comic	£2

Billing, M	General	£1.50
Billinge, Ophelia	Animals	£5
Birch, Nora-Annie	Children	£4
Bird, H	Sport	£5
Birger	Art Deco	£20
Birtles, H.	General	£1.50
Black, Algernon	Shipping	£8
Black, Montague B.	Shipping	£8
Black, W. Milne	Comic	£3
Blair, Andrew	General	£1.50
Blair, John	General	£1.50
Bob	Comic	£2
	General	£1.50
Boccasile, Gino	Art Deco	£45
Boecker, A.G.	Flowers	£1.50
Boileau, Philip	Glamour	£10
Bolton, F.N.	General	£1
Bompard, S	Glamour	£6
Boriss, Margret	Children	£6
Borrow, W.H.	General	£2
Bothams, W	General	£1
Bottaro, E	Glamour	£10
Bottomley, Edwin	Animals	£3
Bottomley, George	Glamour	£3
Boulanger, Maurice	Animals	£10
	Comic	£10
Bourillon	Military	£5
Boutet, Henri	Art Nouveau	£35
Bowden, Doris	Children	£6
Bowers, Albert	General	£2
Bowers, Stephen	General	£2
Bowley, A.L.	Children	£12
Bowley M.	Animals	£6
Boyne, T	General	£1
Bradshaw, Percy V	Comic	£6
	Political	£8
Braun, W	Glamour	£6
Breanski, Arthur de	General	£2
Brett, Molly	Children	£3
Bridgeman, Arthur W	General	£2
Brisley, Nina	Children	£5
Broadrick, Jack	Comic	£2
Brown, Maynard	Glamour	£4

Name	Category	Price
Browne, Stewart	Theatre	£15
Browne, Tom	Adv/Inserts	£10
	Adv/Literary	£10
	Posters	£15/£75
	Cathedrals	£6
	Comic	£4
	Theatre	£20
Brundage, Frances	Children/Chromo-Litho	£15
	Others	£6
	General	£4
Brunelleschi, U	Art Deco	£100
Buchanan, Fred	Comic	£3
Buchel, Charles	Theatre	£18
Budge	Comic	£1
Bull, Rene	Comic	£4
Burger, R	General	£1
Burgess, Arthur	Shipping	£8
Burnard, Victor W.	General	£1.50
Burton, F.W.	General	£1.50
Bushby, Thomas	General	£3
Busi, Adolfo	Art Deco	£12
	Glamour	£6
Bussiere, G	Art Nouveau	£30
Butchur, Arthur	Children	£4
	Glamour	£4
Butler, G.	Animals	£2
Buxton, Dudley	Comic	£2
A.S.C.	Comic	£1.50
C.C.	Comic	£1.50
Caldecott, Randolph	Children	£1.50
Calderara, C	Art Deco	£6
Calland, H.J.	Animals	£5
Cameron, Archie	Comic	£1.50
Cane, Ella Du	Flowers	£1.50
Capiello Leonetto	Art Nouveau	£75
Caport	Comic	£1
Carey, John	Comic	£2
Carline, George	General	£1
Carnell, Albert	Comic	£3
Carr, Paddy	Children	£2
Carrere, F.O.	Glamour	£8
Carruthers, W	General	£1.50
Carson, T.	Art Nouveau	£20
Carter, R.C.	Comic	£1.50
Carter, Reg	Comic	£1.50
	Southwold Rly.	£4
Carter, Sydney	Comic	£2
	General	£2
Cascella Basilio	General	£10
Cassiers, H	General	£6
	Royalty	£10
	Shipping	£18
Cattley, P.R.	Comic	£2
Cauvy, Leon	Art Nouveau	£50
Chalker	Comic	£1.50
Chandler, E	Comic	£2
Chaperon, Eugene	Military	£8
Charlet, J.A.	Glamour	£10
Chatterton, F.J.S.	Animals	£6
Cheret, Jules	Art Nouveau	£75
Cherubini, M	Glamour	£6
Chidley, Arthur	Military	£12
Chilton, G.	Art Deco	£20
Chiostri	Art Deco	£25
Christiansen, Hans	Art Nouveau	£100
Christie, G. Fyffe	Comic	£4
Christy, F. Earl	Glamour	£6
Church, Bernard, W	Shipping	£6
Clapsaddle, Ellen H.	Children	£6
	General	£4
Clarkson, R	General	£1
Cloke, Rene	Children	£8
Coates, A	General	£1
Cobbe, B	Animals	£4
Cock, Stanley	Comic	£3
Coffin, Ernest	Exhibitions	£2
Colbourn, Lawrence	Comic	£2
Cole, Edwin	General	£1
Coleman, W.S.	Children	£8
	General	£6
Coley, Hilda M.	Flowers	£1
Colls, H.	General	£1.50
Colombo, E.	Children	£6
	Glamour	£8
Combaz, Gisbert	Art Nouveau	£100
Comicus	Comic	£1.50
Cook, C.K.	Comic	£4
Cooper, A. Heaton	General	£1
Cooper, Phyllis	Children	£10
	Later Issues	£2

Bilibin	Art Nouveau	£55
Copping, Harold	Glamour	£4
	Literary	£4
	Military	£4
Coppola, A	General	£2
Corbella, Tito	Art Deco	£18
	Glamour	£8
	Political	£8
Cordingley, G.R.	General	£1.50
Corke, C. Essenhigh	General	£2
Cottom, C.M.	Children	£5
Cowderoy, K.E.	Children	£8
	Art Deco	£18
Cowham, Hilda	Children	£8
	Comic	£6
Crackerjack	Comic	£4
Craftanara	General	£2
Craig, Janie	Flowers	£2
Cramer, Rie	Art Deco	£20
	Children	£15
Crane, Walter	Political	£18
Cremieux, Suzanne	Glamour	£8
	Military	£8
Croft, Anne	General	£1
Crombie, C.M.	Comic	£4
	Golf	£25
Crow	General	£3
Croxford, W.E.	General	£1.50
Cubley, H. Hadfield	General	£1.50
Cumming, Neville	Shipping	£8
Cuneo, Cyrus	Military	£8
Cynicus	Comic/	
	Court Size	£12
	Und. back	£5
	Later Issues	£2.00
J.C.D.	Comic	£1.50
J.W.D.	Comic	£1.50
Daniell, Eva	Art Nouveau	£110
Dauber	Comic	£2
Davey, George	Comic	£2
Davidson, Nora	Children	£3
Davo	Comic	£1
Daws, F.T.	Animals	£6
Dawson, Muriel	Children	£8
Dean, Frank	Sport	£4
	General	£4

Dexter, Marjorie M.	Children	£5
Diefenbach, K.W.	Art Deco	£8
Diemer, Michael		
Zeno	General	£4
Dinah	Children	£4
Dink	Sport	£8
Dirks, Gus	Comic	£4
Dixon, Charles	Shipping	£10
Dobson, H.J.	General	£1.50
Docker, E. Jnr.	Art Nouveau	£60
	Animals	£5
Dodd, Francis	Military	£3
Donaldini, Jnr.	Animals	£6
Douglas, J	General	£1.50
Downey, Thos. P.	Comic	£2
Doy, H.	Comic	£1
Drallek, Yaran	Comic	£1
Drayton, Grace	See under Wiederseim	
Driscoll	Comic	£1
Drummond, Eileen	Animals	£5
Drummond, Norah	Animals	£6
Ducane, E & F	General	£1
Duddle, Josephine	Children	£8
Dudley, Tom	General	£1
Dufresne, Paul	Glamour	£5
Duncan, Hamish	Comic	£2
Duncan, J. Ellen	Children	£2
Dupre, G	Art Deco	£6
Dupuis, Emile	Military	£4
Dwig	Comic	£6
Dyer, Ellen	Flowers	£1
Dyer, W.H.	General	£1
Dymond, R.J.	General	£1
E	Comic	£2
A.E.	Comic	£2
Earbalestier, C.	General	£1.50
Earnshaw, Harold	Comic	£3
Ebner, Pauli	Children	£8
Eckenbrecker, T von	Shipping	£10
Edgerton, Linda	Children	£8
Edler, Edouard	Shipping	£12
Edmunds, Kay	Military	£1.50
Edwards, Edwin	General	£1

Edwards, Lionel	Comic	£4
Eliott, Harry	Comic	£8
Elks	Comic	£1
Ellam, W.R.		
Breakfast in Bed	Comic	£10
Other Series	Comic	£10
Elliot, K.E.	Flowers	£1
Emanuel, Frank, L.	General	£2
Endacott, S.	General	£3
Esmond,	Comic	£5
Ettwell, Elliot	General	£2
Evans, Percy	Comic	£2
A.E.F.	Children	£1
Fabiano, F.	Glamour	£15
Feiertag, K	Children	£3
Felix, P.E.	Art Deco	£8
Fernoel	Art Nouveau	£8
Feure de	Art Nouveau	£160
Fidler, Alice Luella	Glamour	£8
Fidler, Elsie Catherine	Glamour	£8
Fidus, H.A. von	Art Nouveau	£60
Finnemore, J	General	£1.50
Fisher, Harrison	Glamour	£10
Fitzpatrick	Comic	£1.50
Fleury, H.	Comic	£2
	Railway	£2
Flower, Charles E.	General	£2
Folkard, Charles	Children	£15
	Literary	£15
Fontan, Leo	Glamour	£12
Forres, Kit	Children	£2
Forrest, A.S.	Shipping	£3
Forsberg, J.	General	£1.50
Foster, Gilbert	General	£1.50
Foster, R.A.	General	£1.50
Fowell, G.M.	General	£1
Fradkin, E.	Children	£1.50
Francis,	General	£1
Frank, Raoul	Shipping	£18
Fraser	Comic	£1.50
Fredillo	Art Nouveau	£20
Freer, H.B.	Shipping	£8
French, Annie	Art Nouveau	£100
Fry, John H.	Shipping	£10
Fuller, Edmund	Comic	£6
	Postal	£6
Fulleylove, Joan	General	£1.50
Fullwood, A.H.	General	£5
Furniss, Harry	Political	£5
Gabb	Comic	£1.50
Gabriel, E	Shipping	£12
Gallon, R.	General	£1
Ganz	Comic	£3
Gardener, E.C.	General	£1.50
Garland, A.	General	£1.50
Gassaway, Katherine	Children	£6
Gay, Cherry	Children	£1.50
Gayac	Glamour	£15
Gear, M.	Animals	£5
Gerald, Brian	General	£1.50
Gerbault, H	Glamour	£6
Gervese, H.	Comic	£3
Gibbs, May	Comic	£25
Gibson Charles Dana	Glamour	£2
Giglio	Glamour	£5
Gilbert, Allan	Glamour	£4
Gill, Arthur	Comic	£3
Gilmour	Comic	£1.50
Gilson, T.	Comic	£2
	Military	£2
Gioja, G	General	£5
Gladwin, May	Comic	£5
Glanville	Comic	£1.50
Gobbi. D	Art Deco	£20
Goethen E. van	Children	£10
Golay, Mary	General	£3
Goodman, Maud		
/Tuck Early	Children	£18
/TuckEarly	General	£18
/Hildesheimer	Children	£4
Gotch, Phyllis, M	Comic	£2
Gould	Comic	£1.50
Govey, Lilian	Children	£8
Gozzard, J.W.	General	£1.50
Graeff	Comic	£2
Graf, Marte	Art Deco	£10
Grant, Carleton	General	£1
Grasset, Eugene	Art Nouveau	£75

Green, Alec E.	Children	£3
Green, Roland	Animals	£3
Greenall, Jack	Comic	£2
Greenaway, Kate	Children/	
	1903 printing	£65
	later printing	£15
Greenbank, A.	Glamour	£8
Greiner, M	Children	£10
Gresley, A.	Flowers	£1.50
Gretty, G	General	£1.50
Grey, Mollie	Children	£2
Gribble, Bernard F.	General	£2
Grimes	Comic	£3
Grin, C.U.	Comic	£1.50
Grosze, Manni	Art Deco	£10
Grunewald	Art Deco	£10
Guerzoni, C	Glamour	£8
Guggenberger, T	General	£1.50
Guillaume A.	Art Nouveau	£75
	Comic	£5
Gunn, A.	Glamour	£5
Gunn Gwennet	Comic	£2
Gurnsey, C.	Comic	£1.50
Guy, T.	General	£1
E.A.H.	Comic	£1.50
F.W.H.	Comic	£3
S.H.	Comic	£1
Hager, Nini	Art Nouveau	£80
Hailey, Edward	General	£1
Haller, A.	Flowers	£2
Halliday	Comic	£3
Hamilton, E	Shipping	£8
Hamish	Comic	£2
Hammick, J.W.	Glamour	£3
Hammond, J.	Flowers	£1.50
Hampel, Walter	Art Nouveau	£85
Hanbury, F. Schmidt	General	£1.50
Hannaford	General	£1.50
Hansi	Children	£15
	Political	£15
Harbour, Jennie	Art Deco	£15
Hardy, Dudley	Comic	£6
	Glamour	£9
	Political	£12

	Shipping	£12
	Theatre	£20
Hardy, Florence	Children	£6
Hardy, F.	Art Deco	£10
Hardy, F.C.	Military	£4
Harriet	Comic	£1
Hart, Josef	Art Nouveau	£35
Hartridge, Norman	Children	£10
Harvey, F.	Comic	£1.50
Haslehust, E.W.	General	£1.50
Hassall, John	Comic	£5
	Court Size	£15
	Theatre	£30
	General	£4
Hauby, S.	Art Nouveau	£12
Haviland, Frank	Glamour	£5
Hayes, F.W.	General	£1.50
Hayes, Sydney	Animals	£1.50
Hebblethwaite, S.H.	Comic	£3
Heinirch	General	£6
Henckel, Carl	Military	£6
Henley	Comic	£1.50
Henley, W.E.	General	£1.50
Henry, Thomas	Children	£6
	Comic	£6
Herouard	Glamour	£15
Hey, Paul	General	£4
Heyermanns,S.	General	£1.50
Heyermans, John A	General	£1.50
Hickling, P.B.	General	£1.50
Hier, Prof. van	General	£1.50
Higham, Sydney	General	£1.50
Hill, L. Raven	Political	£5
Hilton, Alf	Comic	£2
Hines, B.	General	£1..50
Hodgson, W. Scott	General	£1
Hoffman, H.W.	General	£1
Hoffman, J.	Art Nouveau	£90
Hoffmann, Anton	Military	£8
Hohenstein, A	Art Nouveau	£35
Holloway, Edgar A.	Military	£12
Hollyer, Eva	Children	£8
Home, Gordon	General	£1.50
Hood, Eileen	Animals	£4

Hopcroft, G.E.	General	£1.50
Horder, Margaret	Children	£2
Horrell, Charles	Glamour	£4
Horsfall, Mary	Children	£6
	Glamour	£4
Horwitz, Helena	Glamour	£4
Howard, C.T.	General	£1.50
Howard, Jim	Comic	£1.50
Howell, E.	Comic	£1.50
Hudson, Gerald	Military	£4
Hughes, Alun	Comic	£1.50
Hughes, Lloyd	Comic	£1.50
Hughes, R.	General	£1
Hunt, Edgar	Animals	£2
Hunt, Muriel	Animals	£4
Hunter, Mildred C	Animals	£4
Hurst, Hal	Comic	£3
Hutchinson, F.	General	£1
Hyde, Graham	Comic	£6
Ibbetson, Ernest	Comic	£6
	Military	£12
Icart, Louis	Glamour	£12
Innes, John	General	£2
Inskip, J. Henry	General	£1.50
Ironico	Comic	£1.50
Irwin	Comic	£1
J.R.J.	Comic	£1.50
Jackson, Helen	Children	£18
Jackson, Ian	Glamour	£5
Jacobs, Helen	Children	£8
Jafuri, R.	General	£3
James, Frank	Animals	£1.50
James, Ivy Millicent	Children	£10
Jank, Angelo	Art Nouveau	£35
Jarach, A	Glamour	£12
Jay, Cecil	Glamour	£5
Jenkins, G.H.	General	£1.50
Jester	Comic	£1.50
Jo	Comic	£1
Johnson, M.	General	£1.50
Johnson, S.	General	£1.50
Jossot	Art Nouveau	£160
Josza, Carl	Art Nouveau	£60

Jotter	Hotels	£3
	Railways	£3
	Unusual types	£3
	General	£1.50
Jung, Maurice	Art Nouveau	£500
A.H.K.	General	£1
C.K.	Comic	£1.50
E.M.T.K.	Comic	£1.50
Kaby	Glamour	£4
Kainradl, L	Art Nouveau	£100
Kammerer, Rob	General	£1.50
Karaktus	Comic	£1.50
Kaskeline, Fred	Children	£6
Katinka	Art Deco	£12
Kaufmann, J.C.	Animals	£2
Keene, Elmer	General	£1.50
Keene, Frank	Comic	£1.50
Keene, Minnie	Animals	£2
Keesey, Walter M.	General	£1
Kempe	Children	£6
Kennedy, A.E.	Animals	£6
	Comic	£6
	Theatre	£12
Kerr, Tom	Children	£1
Kid	Comic	£1.50
Kidd, Will	Children	£6
Kimball, Alonzo	Glamour	£5
King A. Price	General	£1.50
King, Edward	General	£3
King, Gunning	General	£3
King, Jessie M.	Art Nouveau	£85
King, W.B.	Comic	£1.50
King, Yeend	General	£1.50
Kinnear, J.	General	£1
Kinsella, E.P.	Children	£6
	Comic	£6
	Theatre	£20
Kircher, A.	Naval	£4
Kirchner, Raphael		
/Early	Art Nouveau	£80
/WW1 period	Glamour	£30
/Bruton Galleries	Glamour	£25
Kirk, A.H.	General	£1.50
Kirkbach	Children	£3
Kirkpatrick	General	£1
Kirmse, Persis	Animals	£5

Klein, Christina	General/Chromo-Litho	£6
	Later Issues	£3
Kley, Paul	Chromo-Litho	£5
	Other printings	£2
Koch, Ludwig	Sport	£6
Koehler, Mela	Art Deco	£70
	Art Nouveau	£120
Koehler Mela Broman	Art Deco	£25
Kokoschka	Art Nouveau	£600
Konopa	Art Nouveau	£35
Kosa	Art Nouveau	£100
Koy	Comic	£1.50
Kulas, J.V.	Art Nouveau	£35
Kupka	Art Nouveau	£75
Kyd	Comic	£8
	Literary	£12
	London Life	£10
Lacy, Chas J.de	Shipping	£12
Lajoux, Edmond	Military	£5
Lamb, Eric	General	£1
Lambert, H.G.C. Marsh	Children	£5
Lang, W.	Art Nouveau	£35
Larcombe, Ethel	Art Nouveau	£35
Lasalle, Jean	Glamour	£2
	General	£2
Laskoff F	Art Nouveau	£50
Lauder, C.J.	General	£1.50
Lautrec, H. de Toulouse	Art Nouveau	£600
Lawes, H.	General	£1
Laz	Comic	£1.50
Leete, Alfred	Comic	£4
Leggatt, C.P.	Comic	£2
Lehmann, Felix	Sport	£6
Lehmann, Phil	Comic	£2
Leigh, Conrad	Military	£4
Lelee Leopold	Art Nouveau	£60
LeMunyon, Pearl Fidler	Glamour	£6
Leng, Max	Art Nouveau	£30
Leodud Di	Art Deco	£6
Leonnec, G.	Glamour	£15
Leroux Pierre Albert	Military	£5
Leroy	Military	£5
Lesker, H.	Art Deco	£8
Lessieux, E. Louis	Art Nouveau	£40
	Shipping	£25
Lester, Adrienne	Animals	£3
Lester, Ralph	Glamour	£3
Lewin, F.G.	Children	£6
	Comic	£4
Lilien, E.M.	Art Nouveau	£35
	General	£8
Lime, H.	Comic	£1
Lindsay, J.	General	£1
Lindsell, L.	Glamour	£3
Livemont, Privat	Art Nouveau	£100
Lloyd, T. Ivester	Glamour	£4
	Military	£5
Loffler Berthold	Art Nouveau	£100
Loffler, Lovat	Art Nouveau	£30
Loir Luigi	General	£6
Long, L.M.	General	£1.50
Longley, Chilton	Art Deco	£35
Longmire, R.O.	Political	£10
Longstaffe, Ernest	General	£1.50
Loreley	Art Deco	£15
Love, H. Montagu	Military	£6
	General	£2
Lovering, I.	General	£1.50
Lowe, Meta	Children	£2
Luckcott G.Y.	Comic	£1.50
Ludgate	Comic	£2
Ludlow, Hal	Comic	£2
Ludovici, A.	Children	£5
	Comic	£3
	Political	£3
Luke W.	Comic	£2
Lumley, Savile	Military	£4
Lynen, Amedee	General	£4
C.M.	Comic	£1
M.S.M.	Glamour	£15
P.C.M.	Comic	£1.50
Mac/National Series	Comic	£2
Mac	Animals	£5
	Comic	£3
MacBean L.C.	Comic	£2

Name	Category	Price
McGill, Donald	Comic/Early Dated	£8
	Pre-1914	£5
	1914-1939	£3
	`New'	£1
McIntyre, J.	General	£1.50
McIntyre, R.F.	General	£1.50
McNeill, J.	Military	£12
Macdonald, A.K.	Art Nouveau	£35
Mackain, F.	Comic	£3
Macleod, F.	Comic	£2
Macpherson, John	General	£1
MacWhirter, J.	General	£1.50
Maggs, J.C.	Coaching	£2
Maguire, Bertha	General	£1.50
Maguire, Helena	Animals	£8
	General	£3
Mailick, A.	Glamour	£4
	General	£3
Mainzer, Alfred	Animals	£3
Mair, H. Willebeek le	Children	£8
Mallet, Beatrice	Children	£5
Mallet, Dennis	Comic	£1.50
Manavian, V.	Comic	£2
Mann, James S	Shipping	£12
Marchant, Leslie P.	Comic	£1.50
Marco, M.	Glamour	£3
Marechaux, C.	Glamour	£4
Margetson, Hester	Children	£8
Marisch, G.	Art Nouveau	£75
Maroc	Comic	£1
Marshall, Alice	Children	£12
Mart	Comic	£1.50
Martin, L.B.	Comic	£3
	Children	£5
Martin, Phil	Comic	£2
Martineau, Alice	Glamour	£8
	General	£3
	Children	£8
Martini, A.	Adverts	£35
	Political	£25
Martino R. de	General	£1
Marty, Andre	Art Deco	£15
Mason, Finch	Comic/Sport	£4
Mason, Frank H.	Shipping	£5
Mason, George W	Comic	£4
Mastroianni, D.	General	£2
Mataloni, G.	Art Nouveau	£30
Matthison, W.	General	£1.50
Maurice, Reg	Comic	£2
Mauzan, A.	Children	£6
	Glamour	£10
	Political	£6
	Art Deco	£20
	General	£3
May, F.S.	Comic	£2
May, J.A.	Comic	£2
May, Phil	Comic/Write-away	£8
	Oilette	£4
Maybank, Thomas	Children	£12
Mayer, Lou	Glamour	£5
Meadows, Chas	Comic	£2
Menpes, Mortimer	Children	£3
Mercer, Joyce	Art Deco	£25
	Children	£25
Meredith, Jack	Comic	£2
Merte, O.	Animals	£5
Meschini, G.	Art Deco	£35
Metlicovitz, L.	Art Nouveau	£35
Meunier, Henri	Art Nouveau	£90
Meunier, Suzanne	Glamour	£20
Mich	Comic	£1.50
Mignot, Victor	Art Nouveau	£35
Mike	Comic	£1
Miller, Hilda T.	Children/Liberty	£15
	Other Pubs.	£8
Milliere, Maurice	Glamour	£15
Millor	Flowers	£1
Millot	Greetings	£1
Mills, Ernest, H.	Animals	£4
Monestier, C.	Glamour	£5
Monier, Maggy	Glamour	£10
Moore, A. Winter	General	£1.50
Moore, F.	Railway	£3
Montague, Love, H	Military	£8
Montague, R.	Shipping	£6
	General	£1.50
Montedoro, M	Art Deco	£50

Moreland, Arthur	Comic	£3
	Political	£5
Morgan, F.E.	Comic	£3
Morris, M.	General	£1.50
Morrow, Albert	Theatre	£12
Moser, Koloman	Art Nouveau	£120
Mostyn, Dorothy	Glamour	£4
Mostyn, Marjorie	Glamour	£4
Mouton, G.	Glamour	£10
Mucha, Alphonse	Art Nouveau	£100+
	Exhibition	£100
	Slav Period	£50
Mulholland, S.A.	General	£1
Muller, A.	Animals	£4
Muller, Valery	General	£8
Muraton, E.	Flowers	£2
Murhaghan		
Kathleen, I.	Children	£4
Mutter, K.	General	£4
Naillod, C.S.	Glamour	£6
Nam, Jacques	Glamour	£10
Nanni,G.	Glamour	£6
Nap	Comic	£2
Nash, A.A.	Children	£4
Nerman	Art Deco	£18
	Theatre	£25
Newton, G.E.	General	£1.50
Ney	Glamour	£10
Nielsen, Harry B.	Comic	£2
Nielsen, Vivienne	Animals	£3
Nixon, K.	Children	£10
Noble, Ernest	Comic	£3
Norfield, Edgar	Comic	£1.50
Norman, Parsons	General	£1.50
Norman, Val	General	£1.50
Norwood, A.Harding	General	£1.50
Noury, Gaston	Art Nouveau	£80
Nystrom, Jenny	Children	£12
	Glamour	£12
O'Beirne, F.	Military	£12
O'Kay	Comic	£1
O'Neill, Rose	Children	£8
Operti, A.	General	£5
Opper, F.	Comic	£1.50

Orens, Denizard	Political	£18
Ost. A.	Art Nouveau	£30
Outcault, R.F.	Children	£8
	Comic	£5
Outhwaite, Ida R.	Children	£25
Overell, J.	Children	£4
Overnell	Children	£5
Owen, Will	Comic	£4
	Theatre	£12
Oyston, George	General	£1.50
Paget, Wal	General	£1.50
Palmer, Phyllis, M.	Children	£5
Palmer, Sutton	General	£1.50
Pannett, R.	Glamour	£8
	Theatre	£18
Parker, N.	Animals	£4
Parkinson, Ethel	Children	£4
Parlett, Harry	Comic	£1.50
Parlett, T.	Comic	£2
Parr, B.F.C.	General	£1
Partridge, Bernard	Political	£4
Parsons, F.J.	Railway	£3
Patek, August	Art Nouveau	£12
Patella, B.	Art Nouveau	£35
Paterson, Vera	Children	£3
Paulus	Military	£3
Payne, Arthur C	General	£2
Payne, G.M.	Comic	£3
	Glamour	£3
Payne, Harry		
/Tuck Early	Horses	£40
/Tuck Early	Military	£40
/Metropolitan Police	General	£40
/Wild West	General	£30
/Coaching	Animals	£30
/Gale & Polden	Military	£15
/Stewart & Woolf	Military	£15
/Badges & Wearers	Military	£12+
/Oilettes	Horses	£6
/Oilettes	Military	£6+
/Military in London	Military	£4
/Rural Life	General	£5
/Other	General	£10+
Pearse, Susan B	Children	£12
Peddie, Tom	Glamour	£3

Pellegrini, E.	Glamour	£18
Peltier, L.	Glamour	£8
Penley, Edwin A.	General	£1.50
Penny, Theo	Comic	£1.50
Penot, A.	Glamour	£15
Pepin, Maurice	Glamour	£12
Peras	Glamour	£8
Percival, E.D.	General	£1.50
Perlberg, F.	Animals	£4
	General	£1
Perly	Comic	£1.50
Person, Alice Fidler	Glamour	£6
Petal	Comic	£1
Peterson, Hannes	General	£2
Pfaff, C.	General	£6
Philippi, Robert	Art Nouveau	£15
Phillimore, R.P.	General	£3
Phipson, E.A.	General	£1.50
Pike, Sidney	General	£1.50
Pillard,	Glamour	£6
	Military	£6
Pinder, Douglas	General	£1
Pinhey, Edith	General	£1
Pinkawa, Anton	Art Nouveau	£30
Piper, George	Children	£3
Pirkis	Comic	£3
Pitcher, Henrie	General	£3
Plumstead, Joyce	Children	£8
Polzin, G.	General	£4
Pope, Dorothy T.	Animals	£8
Popini	Art Nouveau	£30
	Glamour	£5
Poulbot, Francisque	Children	£4
Poy	Comic	£1.50
Praga, Alfred	Shipping	£12
Presland, A.L.	Flowers	£1.50
Preston, Chloe	Children	£9
Prosnocimi, A.	General	£1.50
Purser, Phyllis	Children	£4
Pyp	Comic	£2
Quatremain, W.W.	General	£1.50
Quinnell, Cecil W.	Glamour	£4
	Literary	£4

Quinton, A.R.		
/Salmon J. & Co.	South Africa	£12+
	Ostende	£10+
	General	£3+
	1960/70 Period	.75
	Reprints/7 digit computer nos.	.25
/Tuck R. & Sons	General	£4+

The cards of A.R. Quinton have now been catalogued and priced by Wayne Robbins in 'Quintessential Quinton'.

Quinton, F.E.	General	£1.50
Quinton, Harry	Comic	£2
Quips	Comic	£1.50
A.F.R.	Comic	£1.50
F.A.R.	General	£1.50
J.S.R.	Comic	£1.50
Rackham, Arthur	Children	£25
Raemaekers, Louis	Political	£3
Raimondi, R.	General	£3
Rambler	General	£1
Ramsey, George S.	General	£1
Rankin, George	Animals	£3
Rappini	Glamour	£4
	General	£4
Ratcliffe, W.W.	General	£4
Rauh, Ludwig	Glamour	£15
Raven, Phil.	Comic	£1.50
Read, F.W.	Glamour	£3
	General	£1
Read, T. Buchanan	General	£1
Reckling, L.G.	General	£1
Reichert, C.	Animals	£4
Reiss, Fritz	General	£5
Remington Frederick	General	£8
Renaud, M.	Flowers	£1
Renault, A.	Flowers	£1
Rennie, M.	General	£1.50
Rex	Comic	£1
Reynolds, Frank	Comic	£4
	Literary	£5
Ribas	Glamour	£10
Richardson, Agnes	Children	£5
Richardson, Charles	Comic	£1.50
Richardson, R.V.	Comic	£2
Richardson, R.W.E.	General	£1.50

Name	Category	Price
Richmond, Leonard	Railways	£5
Rickard, J.	Children	£8
Right	Comic	£2
Ritchie, Alick P.F.	Comic	£3
Ritter, Paul	General	£4
Roberts, Howard L.	Comic	£2
Roberts, Violet M	Animals	£20
	Comic	£20
Robida, A.	General	£6
Robinson, W. Heath	Comic	£6
Rodella, G.	Glamour	£5
Rog	Comic	£1.50
Romney, George	Railways	£3
Rooke, H.K.	Shipping	£10
Rose, Freda Mabel	Children	£3
Rosenvinge, Odin	Shipping	£12
Rossi, J.C.	Art Nouveau	£65
Rostro	Political	£15
Rousse, Frank	General	£2
Rowland, Ralph	Comic	£2
Rowlandson, G.	Military	£5
	Comic	£3
	General	£1.50
Rowntree, Harry	Animals	£12
	Comic	£12
Rust, A.	Comic	£1.50
Ryan, F.	Comic	£1.50
Ryland, Henry	Glamour	£8
Rylander	Art Deco	£15
S. (Capital)	Comic	£1.50
S. (Script)	Comic	£1.50
J.M.S.	Comic	£1.50
K.S.	Comic	£1.50
M.S.	Children	£1.50
S.E.S.	Comic	£1.50
Sachetti, E.	Political	£8
Sager, Xavier	Glamour	£15
Salaman, Edith	General	£5
Salmony, G.	Glamour	£5
Sancha, F.	Political	£8
Sand, Adina	Glamour	£54
Sanders, A.E.	General	£1.50
Sanderson, Amy	Children	£3
Sandford, H.Dix	Children	£6
	Comic/Coons	£8
Sarg, Tony	Comic	£2
Sartoi, E.	General	£1
Sauber	General	£6
	Social History	£6
Saville Rena	Children	£1.50
Sayer, Henry	Comic	£5
Schiele, Egon	Art Nouveau	£100+
Schiesl, R.	General	£3
Schonflug, Fritz	Comic	£4
Schonian	Animals	£4
Schubert, H.	Glamour	£5
Schweiger, L.	General	£4
Scottie	Glamour	£6
Scribbler	Comic	£1.50
Scrivener, Maude	Animals	£3
Severn, Walter	General	£1.50
Shand, C.E.	Art Deco	£10
Shaw, H.G.	Animals	£6
Shaw, W. Stocker	Comic	£2
Shelton, S.	General	£1.50
Shepheard, G.E.	Comic	£5
Sherrin, A.	General	£1.50
Sherwin, D.	General	£1
Shoesmith, Kenneth	Shipping	£12
Short, E.A.	Flowers	£1.50
Sikes, F.H.	General	£1.50
Simkin, R.	Military	£15
Simonetti, A.M.	Glamour	£5
Sinty, Juan	Comic	£1.50
Skip	Comic	£1
Smale, B.H.	Comic	£8
	Military	£8
Small, D.	General	£2
Smith D. Carlton	Children	£5
Smith, Edna	Children	£2
Smith, Jessie Wilcox	Art Nouveau	£35
	Children	£30
Smith, May	Children	£8
Smith, Syd	Comic	£2
Smith, W.	General	£1.50
Smyth	Comic	£1
Solomko, Serge de	Glamour	£20
Somerville, Howard	Glamour	£4
	Comic	£2

Name	Category	Price
Sonrel, Elisabeth	Art Nouveau	£60
Sowerby, Millicent	Children/	
	Chromo-Litho	£20
	Other types	£8
Spatz	Comic	£2
Sperlich, T.	Animals	£6
Spindler, Erwin	General	£6
Spurgin, Fred	Comic	£3
	Glamour	£5
	Military	£5
Spurrier, W.B.	Comic	£2
Spy	Political	£15
Stanlaw, S. Penrhyn	Glamour	£4
Stanlaws, Penly	Glamour	£6
Stannard, H. Sylvester	General	£2
Stannard, Lilian	General	£2
Stead, A.	General	£1
Steele, L.	Children	£4
Steinlen, Alexandre	Art Nouveau	£90
Stenberg, Aina	Art Deco	£15
Sternberg, V.W.	Children	£2
Stewart, J.A.	Animals	£5
	Military	£5
Stoddart, R.W.	Comic	£2
Stokes G. Vernon	Animals	£2
Stone, Frederick	Comic	£1.50
Stone, F.	Comic	£2
Stower, Willi	Shipping/	
	Early	£20
	Later	£6
	General	£6
Stretton, Philip	Animals	£5
Strong, G.W.	Comic	£1.50
Studdy, G.E.	Comic/	
	Bonzo	£8
	Others	£5
Syd	Comic	£2
Syllikuss	Comic	£2
Symonds, Constance	Children	£8
Szyk, Arthur	Political	£6/£15
T.	Comic	£1
C.T.	Comic	£1.50
J.T.	General	£1.50
L.B.T.	Comic	£1.50
W.E.T.	Comic	£1.50
Tait	Comic	£1
Talboys, A.	Animals	£3
Tam, Jean	Glamour	£12
Tanquerey, L.	Art Deco	£4
Tarrant, Margaret W.	Children/6	
	Pre-1945	£5
	1945 on	£2
Taylor, A.	Children	£1.50
	Comic	£1.50
Taylor, E.S.	Comic	£1.50
Tempest, Douglas	Children	£1.50
	Comic	£1.50
Tempest, Margaret	Children	£5
Terzi, A.	Glamour	£8
Thackeray, Lance	Comic/	
	Write-away	£10
	Oilettes	£5
Theo	Comic	£1.50
Thiede, Adolf	General	£1.50
Thiele, Arthur	Animals	£15+
	Comic	£15+
	Political	£25
Thomas, Bert	Comic	£5
Thomas, Paul	Animals	£5
Thomas, Victor	Children	£6
Thomas, Walter	Shipping	£10
Thompson, E.H.	General	£1.50
Thorne, Diana	Animals	£1.50
Titicus	Comic	£1.50
Toussaint, M.	Military	£6
Travis, Stuart	General	£1.50
Trick, E.W.	General	£1.50
Tringham, H.	General	£1.50
Trow	Comic	£1
True, W.	Theatre	£12
Truman, Herbert	General	£1
Turner, C.E.	Shipping	£8
Turrian, E.D.	Art Nouveau	£30
Twelvetrees, C.H.	Children	£6
Uden, E.	General	£1
Ullman, Max	Shipping	£15
Underwood, Clarence F	Glamour	£6
Upton, Florence K.	Children	£35
Usabal, Luis	Glamour	£6

60

Name	Category	Price		Name	Category	Price
Utrillo, A.	General	£6			Comic	£2
Valles, F.	Comic	£1.50		White, D.	Comic	£2
Vallet, L.	Glamour	£10		White, Flora	Children	£5
	Military	£4		White, H. Percy	Comic	£2
Valter, Eugenie M.	Animals	£4		Whitehead, Fred	General	£1.50
Valter, Florence E.	Animals	£4		Wichera, R.R.	Children	£6
Vaughan, E.H.	General	£1.50			Glamour	£8
Veal, O.	Comic	£2		Wiederseim, G.G.	Children	£6
Vera	Children	£2		Wielandt, Manuel	General	£8
Vernon, E.	Glamour	£6		Wilcock, A.M.	Children	£4
Vernon, R.W.	General	£1.50		Wilkin, Bob	Comic	£1
Villon Jacques	Art Nouveau	£300		Wilkinson, Gilbert	Comic	£5
Voellmy, F.	General	£8		Wilkinson, Norman	Shipping	£10
Vouga, E.	Flowers	£1		Williams, Madge	Children	£3
F.W.	Comic	£1.50		Williams, Warren	General	£1.50
J.S.W.	Comic	£2		Willis, George	Comic	£1.50
Wain, Louis	Animals/			Wimble, Arthur	Glamour	£2
	Early	£60+		Wimbush, Henry B.	General	£2
	Later	£40+		Wimbush, Winifred	General	£3
	Oilettes	£40+			Glamour	£6
	Advertising	£75+		Wishaw, M.C.	General	£3
Wal.	Comic	£1.50		Wood, Lawson	Comic	£6
Walbourn, Ernest	General	£1.50			Gran'pop	£6
Walker, F.S.	General	£1.50			Prehistoric	£6
Walker, Hilda	Animals	£4			Theatre	£18
Wanke, Alice	Art Nouveau	£20		Wood, Starr	Comic	£5
	Children	£10		Woodville, R. Caton	Military	£6
Ward, Dudley	Comic	£3		Woollett, Cress	Glamour	£3
Ward, Herbert	Military	£5		Woude Sikko van de	General	£2
Ward, Vernon	General	£1.50		Wright, Gilbert	General	£4
Wardle, Arthur	Animals	£8		Wright, Seppings,	General	£2
Warrington, Ellen	General	£1.50		Wuyts, A	Children	£6
Watson, C.M. West	Animals	£5			Glamour	£6
Wealthy, R.J.	Animals	£3		Wyllie, W.L.	Shipping	£8
Weaver, E.	Comic	£1.50		H.Y.	Comic	£1.50
Webb, A.D.	General	£1		Young, A.	General	£1.50
Welzi, A.	Art Nouveau	£30		Young Gwen Hayward	General	£3
Wennerberg, Brynolf	Art Nouveau	£20		Young, Hayward	General	£3
	Glamour	£15		Zandrino, Adelina	Glamour	£10
West, A.L.	Animals	£2		Zirka, C.	Glamour	£6
West, Reginald	General	£1.50				
Weston, Rita F.	Children	£1				
Wheeler, Dorothy	Children	£4				
Whishaw, A.Y.	General	£1.50				
White, Brian	Children	£2				

ARTISTS / COLLECTIONS

The years at the turn of the century saw the production of a number of selected postcard series, now justly celebrated as representing the high-water mark of postcard art and design. In this respect France was very much to the fore, and I give below a list of these series, together with details of other leading European collections. This is almost entirely the province of the European collector, for although these cards do come along from time to time in our Auctions, the interest in Britain is limited to a few people.

Market Report
A highly specialised area which has seen steady interest, mainly at auction.
Not for beginners.
Present price ranges are considered adequate.

AUSTRIA
WIENER WERKSTATTE 1908-1913
Recognised by the title design on the reverse, these cards were produced perhaps as a reaction to the swirling lines of Art Nouveau, being typified by a spare and severe style which gave way to Cubism and Art Deco. Artists include: Mela Koehler and Oskar Kokoschka.
Price Range: £50/750

FRANCE
COCORICO
Probably the most celebrated of all French series. There are 12 designs only. Artists include: De Feure and Steinlen.
Price Range: £150/£750

COLLECTION DES CENT. 1901
A series of 100 cards by leading Artists of the day. Cards have this title printed at the edge. Artists include: Alphonse Mucha, Caran d'Ache, Jules Cheret and A. Steinlen.
Price Range: £50/£500

COLLECTION JOB 1895-1914
There were three series together totalling 78 cards. Reprints of calendars and posters from the period above. Artists include: Angelo Asti, Jules Cheret and Alphonse Mucha.
Price Range: £50/£300

CONCOURS DE BYRHH 1906
A competition held to select advertisements for this aperitif. 113 designs were published as postcards. Artists include: Maurice Denis, Raphael Kirchner and G. Meunier.
Price Range: £50/£300

EDITIONS CINOS 1898
A series of 35 cards by famous artists of the day. Artists include: Alphonse Mucha, Jules Cheret, and Toulouse-Lautrec.
Price Range: £100/750

GERMANY
JUGEND 1899
Three series totalling 75 cards, in the Art Nouveau style. Artists include: Hans Christiansen.
Price Range: £50/£300

BAUHAUS 1923.
This series consisted of 20 designs, with reputedly only about 25 copies of each design printed. Artists include: Paul Klee and Kurt Schmidt.
Price Range: £250/£2500

CHROMO-LITHO

Generally acknowledged as the finest of all colour printing methods. Briefly, the design was etched onto a limestone block and printed in solid colours, as opposed to modern screen printing, where the dots can be seen through a strong glass. Chromo-Litho printing was used extensively for postcards from 1890-1910, particularly in the `Gruss Aus' and `Early Vignette' classifications. The reader is directed to the specialist books in this field which will list many of the hundreds of publishers engaged in this form of printing. The price of any Chromo-Litho card may be found by reference to its subject or artist, but there exist a great many unsigned Chromo-Litho cards of general landscape type.

Early Chromo Litho printed card Gruss Aus der ramsau 1896 £10

ART REPRODUCTIONS

Friezes/Red Border types	£2
Miscellaneous reproductions	£1
Chromo-Litho/Heavy Board	
Misch & Stock/Sborgi/Stengel	£2
Gallery Reproduction Series	
Photochrom Co.	.75

Chromo Litho, . £3

TOPOGRAPHICAL ART

In recent years the collection of chromo-litho topographical art has become popular in its own right. Prominent names in this field include Manuel Wielandt, Michael Zeno Diemer, Raoul Frank, Paul Kley, K. Mutter and A. Prosnocimi. These and others are listed in the main Artist index.

Many cards in this genre however are unsigned, and a guide to the price of these is given below:

French Views	£3
Italian Views	£3
Swiss Views	£3
Other countries	£3

ART TYPES

Colouring Cards/Pairs

Tuck R. & Sons	£2
Miscellaneous Types	£1
Oilfacism	
Tuck R. & Sons	£1.50
Miscellaneous Oil Facsimiles	£1
Hand Painted	
Professional Work	£5
Amateur Work	£1.50
Mass produced	£1

SCULPTURE

Art Sculpture on black card	£1
Gallery/Museum types	.75
Montage scenes	
Mastroianni D.	£2

RAPHAEL KIRCHNER

Kirchner was born in Vienna in 1875 and died in America at the height of his fame in 1917. His work dates from 1897 to 1916 and during this time he produced nearly 800 postcard designs, grouped together in over 120 sets and other issues, published by some 77 separate firms. Kirchner was one of the leading figures in the Art Nouveau movement, although some of his later work lay more in the field of straight Glamour. His cards have been catalogued by Antonio and Pia Dell'Aquila in,"Raphael Kirchner and his Postcards" published in 1996. This magisterial work illustrates every known card and gives a full listing of all known publishers. Readers who wish to look further into the life and work of this great artist can have no better guide. All one can do within the confines of a general catalogue such as this, is give a brief guide to those cards which by reason of publisher or other factors, are most often found on the British market, together with an indication of price. This in itself can only be a very broad assessment, as many of these series were reprinted by other publishers, often in different formats, with added greetings or other variations. It is further noted that certain rare cards not listed here, can be worth anything up to £500+ each. One problem remains with Kirchner in that some of his cards are unsigned. There is not much we can do about this other than refer the reader to Dell'Aquila where every card is identified. What follows is merely a general guide which I hope will be of some help to collectors.

All prices below are for single cards. A complete set may attract a premium over this figure. It must be noted that prices apply to cards in flawless condition, with no marks or damage of any kind. With highly rated cards such as these, condition is everything and those in less than perfect state would be worth considerably less.

'Raphael Kirchner and his Postcards' may be purchased from: Reflections of a Bygone Age, 15 Debdale Lane, Keyworth, Notts. NG12 5HT at the price of £29.95 including postage.

A Quatre Feuilles	Set 6	£65		**Santoy**	Set 6	£60
Girls' heads in clover leaf				Scenes of Japanese Life		
				Demi Vierge	Set 6	£65
				Girls on gold background between		
Enfants de la Mer	Set 10	£65		green borders		
Girls at the Seaside				**Femmes Soleil**	Set 6	£65
				Girls' faces on background of sunrays		
Fruits Douces	Set 6	£65		Same designs on pale blue without sunrays		
Girls with fruit between green borders				**Erika**	Set 6	£65
				Girls' heads on floral background		
Geisha	Set 10	£40		**Marionettes**	Set 6	£65
Scenes of Japanese life				Girls with puppets		
				Bijoux	Set 6	£65
Greek Virgins	Set 12	£65		Girls in goblet/heart shaped panels		
Girls in beige & gold design				**Les Peches Capitaux**	Set 7	£35
See also Tuck Listing				Girl with inset pierrot head		
				Kirchner Girls	Set 24	£25
Les Cigarrettes du Monde	Set 6	£65		Bruton Galleries		
Girls smoking cigarettes				Delta Fine Art Co. EC2		
				Kirchner Girls	Set 12	£25
Maid of Athens	Set 6+			Bruton Galleries		
Studies of young girls				Alphalsa Publishing Co. EC2		
Coloured		£40		**Les Amours de Pierrot**	Set 10	£35
Bw series		£25		Girl with inset pierrot head on titled card		
See also Tuck listing				Reinthal & Newman/New York		
				Librairie de l'Estampe/Paris		£35
Mikado	Set 6	£50		Glamour/WW1 period. 32 cards		
Japanese Girls				Numbered and titled on back		

Cards published in Britain by Raphael Tuck & Sons.

Connoisseur 2555
Salome
Girls' large faces with scenic background
Coloured   Set 6   £60
Black & White   Set 6   £30

Connoisseur 2642
Les Ephemeres   Set 6   £100
Three girls in flowing dresses

Oilette Connoisseur 2709   Set 6   £60
Flashing Motorists

Continental 3002   Set 6   £85
Continental 3003   Set 6   £85
Girls' faces in circle with
mauve background

Continental 3004   Set 10   £85
Continental 3005   Set 10   £85
Girls standing in Flowers

Continental 4002
Continental 4003
Maid of Athens
Coloured   Set 6   £40
Black & White   Set 6   £25

Continental 4008   Set 6   £85
Continental 4009   Set 6   £85
Girls in panels with pink borders

Continental 4016   Set 6   £85
Continental 4017   Set 6   £85
Girls in panels with olive borders

Continental 4024   Set 6   £65
Continental 4025   Set 6   £65
Greek Virgins

Diaphne 3501   Set 5   £200
Diaphne 8902   Set 5   £200
Vitraux d'Art
Girls in stained glass windows

The postcards of Raphael Kirchner can be
divided into three main periods:
The Early Beginnings: 1897 - 1899
The Golden Age: 1900 - 1907
The Glamour Age: 1910 - 1917

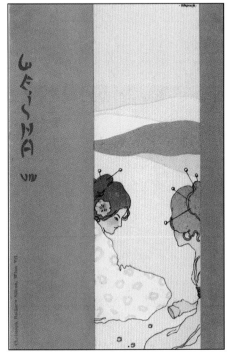

ARTHUR THIELE

Gebruder Dietrich (GDL)
Ser 273.	Ice Sports	£40
Ser 277.	Gentleman & servant	£40
Ser 284.	Whitsun scenes	£40

Friedrich Eyfried (FED)
Ser 474.	Teddy Bears	£50
Ser 486.	Costumes	£50
Ser 525.	Carnival	£30

F&W
Ser 159.	Fantasy Cats	£40

Faulkner C.W.
Ser 1067.	As TSN 1194	£40
Ser 1298.	Musical Cats in Snow	£40
Ser 1373.	As TSN 1423	£20
Ser 1376.	Easter Chicks	£20
Ser 1378.	Springtime in Catland	£40

Klaus & Co.
Ser 474.	The Nursery	£40
Ser 486.	Ladies' Hats	£40

Bruder Kohn (BKW)
Ser 323.	Sporting Types	£40

L&P
Ser 1446.	Kitten Orchestras I	£40
Ser 1447.	Kitten Orchestras II	£40
Ser 1564.	Congratulations	£40
Ser 1566.	Cat Orchestras	£40
Ser 2431.	Du Falsche (1)	£50

Novolito
Ser 476.	Cat Scenes I	£40
Ser 477.	Cat Scenes II	£40

Theo Stroefer (TSN)
Ser 196.	As TSN 1425	£40
Ser 710.	Be-ribboned Cats	£20
Ser 851.	Life at Home	£30
Ser 896.	Cats with Hats	£40
Ser 918.	TheSix Ages of the Cat	£30
Ser 945.	Kittens with Bouquets	£30
Ser 947.	Diabolo	£40
Ser 962.	School Kittens	£20
Ser 975.	Tears and Joy	£25
Ser 995.	Winged Cats	£40
Ser 1010.	Children's Games	£20
Ser 1012.	A Mewsical Party	£20
Ser 1016.	Cats at Play	£40
Ser 1018.	Classic Loves	£40
Ser 1077.	Events at Home	£20
Ser 1113.	Haute Cat-ure	£50
Ser 1194.	Toboggan Rides	£40

Ser 1214.	A Tennis Tournament	£30
Ser 1229.	The Subscription Ball	£30
Ser 1230.	Servants	£40
Ser 1299.	Winter Sports	£50
Ser 1326.	In the Classroom	£20
Ser 1403.	Music in the Snow	£40
Ser 1404.	New Year Greetings	£30
Ser 1405.	New Year Gifts	£40
Ser 1412.	Kittens at Play	£40
Ser 1423.	School Kittens	£20
Ser 1424.	Domestic Service	£30
Ser 1425.	Just like Dad	£40
Ser 1427.	Bowling	£40
Ser 1438.	Spring Scenes	£20
Ser 1468.	Say it with Flowers	£25
Ser 1469.	Fun in Snowland	£30
Ser 1472.	Ice Skating	£30
Ser 1601.	As TSN 1010	£20
Ser 1602.	Street Scenes	£40
Ser 1604.	As TSN 1077	£20
Ser 1646.	As TSN 975	£25
Ser 1667.	As TSN 1010	£20
Ser 1671.	As TSN 1438	£20
Ser 1677.	As TSN 1326	£20
Ser 1703.	As TSN 1424	£30
Ser 1705.	As TSN 1404	£30
Ser 1714.	As TSN 1012	£20
Ser 1726.	As TSN 1423	£20
Ser 1727	As TSN 1077	£20
Ser 1728.	As TSN 1326	£20
Ser 1730.	As TSN 1424	£30
Ser 1789.	As TSN 1468	£25
Ser 1789.	As TSN 1469	£30
Ser 1800.	As TSN 962	£20
Ser 1826.	As TSN 1423	£20
Ser 1827.	As TSN 1077	£20
Ser 1828.	As TSN 1326	£20
Ser 1829.	As TSN 1438	£20
Ser 1830.	As TSN 975	£25
Ser 1852.	As TSN 1012	£20
Ser 1876.	As TSN 1472	£30
Ser 1879.	As TSN 962	£20
Ser 1880.	As TSN 1423	£20
Ser 1881.	As TSN 1077	£20
Ser 1882.	As TSN 1326	£20
Ser 1889.	As TSN 1438	£20
Ser 1892.	As TSN 1424	£30
Ser 1893.	Puppies	£40
Ser 1988.	Kittens at Play	£40
Ser 1989.	Cats at Play	£40
Ser 2030.	As TSN 962	£20
Ser 2031.	As TSN 1326	£20

Tuck R. & Sons		Other Publishers			
Ser 3435. As TSN 1326	£20	Reproductions are known from the following			
Ser 4091. As TSN 975	£25	publishers:			
Ser 8604. As TSN 1468	£25				
Ser 8604. As TSN 1469	£30				
Ser 9782. As TSN 1229	£30	**C.K.M.**	2641	As TSN 710	£20
Ser 9797. As TSN 1012	£20	**H.B.K.**	609	As F&W 159	£40
Ser 9818. Catland	£40	**J.S**	2641	As TSN 710	£20
Ser 9819. Playtime	£40	**K&BC**	3105	As FED 525	£30
Ser 9983. As TSN 1214	£30	**KF**	3076	As TSN 851	£30

Arthur Thiele produced a style of art which proved very popular and many of these series were reproduced both by the original publisher and by others who bought the rights. The same series may therefore be found several times under different imprints. Building on the work of Mr. Gerd Schwartz and Dr. Ronald Hendrickson, I have started listing all known series for future catalogue entry.

All prices above are for single cards. A complete set may attract a premium over this figure. It must be noted that prices apply to cards in flawless condition, with no marks or damage of any kind.

Left: Series 1879 £20

Right: Tuck's 9799
Dogs at school   £20

LOUIS WAIN

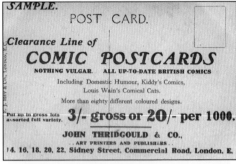

Above Left: Snowball , Faulkner series £35 Above Right: E J Hey series 342 £35. and Middle Right the back of the card, an overprint. Below right: Raphael Tuck card £35. Below Left; Write away series £35.

Above Left: An Intruder £35
Left; Faulkner series £35.
Top: Davidson Brohers 6092 £40.
Middle: Faulkners series £35
Bottom: Write Away series £35.

There is a steady demand for cards by Louis Wain with unusual cards selling well above catalogue.

Top Left: Christmas Card, Tuck1735 priced at £30. Left: Drinking £30.
Top: Cat's singing, Tucks write away £35. Middle Right: Seaside humour £35.
Bottom right: Silhouette £35
All of the above are coloured cards.

Beagles
Coloured & Photographic £35

Boots
Famous Picture Series of 12 £35

Davidson Bros.
Various Cards £40

Dutton/N.Y.
Various Cards £35

Ettlinger & Co.
Series 5226. Father Christmas Cats £80
Series 5376. Father Christmas Cats £80

Faulkner C.W.
Series 182 • 183 • 189 • 190 • 374
453 • 454 • 484 • 485 • 503 • 515
541 • 1596 • plus many others. £35/£50

Gale & Polden
At least 1 design £45

Hartmann
Series 3068. Fluffikins Family £45
Series 3069. Manx Cats £60

Mack W.E.
The Cat's Academy (Not all by Wain) £30

Nister E.
Series 353 • 355 etc. £35
Valentine series £6
Philco series 2093 £35
Salmon series various cards £35

Theo Stroefer
Usually unsigned designs £25

Tuck R. & Sons
Series 130. Black/White und. back £20

Theatre Series 3885 • 3895 B/W £45

Write-Away Series
539 • 956 • 957 • 1003 • 1004 £35

Chromo-Litho Series
1260 • 1261 • 1262 • 1735 • 1748
1749 • 1782 • 5802 • 5892 £30

Chromo-Litho Nursery Rhymes/
Christmas/Pantomime
Series 297 • 298 • 8126 • 8127 £100

Diabolo Series 9563 £45

Dressing Dolls Fairy Tales
Oilette 3385 £100+

Oilette and similar Series
1412 • 3266 • 6075 • 6084 • 6401
6444 • 8515 • 8612 • 8613 • 8614
8615 • 8816 • 8817 • 8826 • 8850
8864 • 9396 • 9540 • 9541 £35

Others/Odd cards/
Part Sets inc. C132/133 £30

Valentine
Coloured Series/Un-numbered £40
Charlie Chaplin cards £100

Wrench
Pantomime/Black Cat Series £50

Anon
Jackson's Hats & Boots/Poster Type £75
WW1 Set including a cat `Kaiser' £75

Many other cards exist, sometimes pirate copies, often with Wain's signature removed. There are also a number of unsigned cards by other artists done in the Wain style. All prices above are for single cards. A complete set may attract a premium over this figure.
It must be noted that prices apply to cards in flawless condition, with no marks or damage of any kind.

Faulkner series 183 £35

Above: Royal Naval
Air Service Silk £50
Left: Grahame-White
at Bournemouth
1910 £12
Below: Parachute
drop £7.50

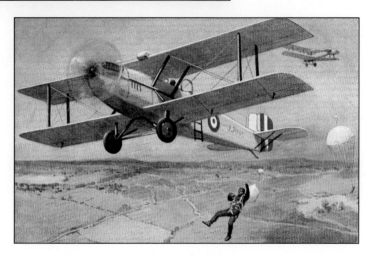

Top: Raphael Tuck Educational Series No.9 Aviation £20
Left: Real Photographic Pilot £15
Right: Royal Flying Corps, Harry Payne £50

AVIATION

The early days of flying presented a challenge which postcard publishers were not slow to take up, with the resulting legacy of a great many fine studies both photographic and artistic on this theme. Postcards cover the whole spectrum of civil and military aviation from the early beginnings, through World War I to the nineteen-thirties and up to the present day. Generally speaking photographic cards are worth more than artistic studies, the former often having some related local history interest. It must be further emphasised that in all cases prices given are for unused cards. If postally used a much higher figure may be expected, depending upon type of postmark, date of flight, clarity of strike etc.

Market Report:
Civil aviation still in demand. Some increases seen in Airships, Balloons and Civil Aviation of all periods. Always a very specialist field with social history connections.

AIRCRAFT

AIRCRAFT Pre-1918
Flying at Hendon Series	£12
Brooklands Aviation	£20
Daily Mail Tour 1912	£10
At named locations	£30
French Aviation	£8
Civil aircraft	£10
Military aircraft	£8

Accidents
Identified	£25
Unidentified	£5

Series
Lefebvre Utile	£35
Lombart	£25

Educational Series
Tuck R. & Sons	£20

The Lightning Series
E. Cook	£15

Famous Aeroplane Series
Tuck R. & Sons	£5

In the Air Series
Tuck R. & Sons	£6

Artist/Derek Bannister
Salmon J. Ltd	£5

AIRCRAFT 1918-1939
Schneider Trophy	£20+
Civil Aircraft	£10-15
Military Aircraft	£5-10
Joy Flights	£6-8

Accidents
Identified	£25
Unidentified	£5

Amy Johnson
England-Australia Flight/Set 6/
Tuck R. & Sons/3867B	£15
Portraits	£15

Imperial Airways
Croydon Airport	£18
Official	£18
Pilots	£20

AIRCRAFT 1939 - 1960
Civil Aircraft	£8-15

Real Photograph Series
Valentine	£3

PILOTS

Pre-1914
With aircraft	£15
Portraits	£12

1918-1939
With aircraft	£15
Portraits	£12

Croydon Airport R/P, £18

British Airways 1939 R/P £15

AVIATION MEETINGS

Blackpool 1909/10	£20
Doncaster 1909	£30
Bournemouth 1910	£25
Burton on Trent 1910	£40
Lanark 1910	£40
Wolverhampton 1910	£40

Doncaster R/P £30

Poster Adverts

Coloured	£85
Black & White	£30

FLOWN CARDS

Beckenham Coronation Balloon/9.8.02
Flown
Unflown

Lifeboat Saturday/20.9.02

Flown	£1,000
Unflown	£100

Lifeboat Saturday/29.8.03

Flown	£1,000
Unflown	£100

Daily Graphic Expedition 1907

Flown	£150
Unflown	£50

First U.K. Aerial Post 1911 (See pg 73)

London-Windsor - Flown	£20/£40
Windsor-London - Flown	£30/£75
Unflown cards	£18

N.B. The value of flown U.K. Aerial Post Cards depends upon which colour type has been used, date of flight, clarity of strike etc. These factors are also relevant to any flown cards.

AIRSHIPS

At named locations	£30
World Flights	£25
GB/Pre-1918	
Barton Airship/Alexandra Palace 1905	£35
Beta/Gamma/Parseval etc.	£18
GB/1918-1939	
R-100/R-101 etc.	£18
French/German	
Pre-1918	£15
1918-1939	£15
Zeppelins	
Early Chromo embossed etc.	£25+
World War 1/ Close-up	£18
/Combat sketches	£5
Wreckage/GB Locations	£10

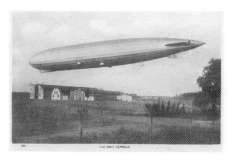

Graf Zeppelin R/P, Price £15

BALLOONS

At named locations	£65
Photographic	£35+
Printed	£20
Military/Printed	£8
Swiss/Meetings Posters	£75+

MISCELLANEOUS

Airfields	£8-12
R.F.C. Interest	£5-8

Commemorative Cards

First/Historic Flights	£25+

Croydon Airport

C.H. Price Series	£20

Royal Air Force

Halton Camp	£8
Airmen/Photographs Identified	£5
/Unidentified	£1.50
Miscellaneous interest	£1.50

CHILDREN

One of the most popular themes for the early publishers of picture postcards, reflecting the tastes of our Edwardian forbears. Cards of Children and related subjects were published by the thousand. Perhaps the best known series is the `Queen's Dolls House', published by Tuck, while many of the early chromo-litho art studies, in their design and execution represent some of the most beautiful cards ever printed.

Market Report

Strong collecting area in which the better artists, particulary those published by Tuck, have moved forward again this year. Early chromos are also in great demand, as are good photographic cards and Teddy Bears.

CHILDREN

Angels

Art studies	£3
Photographic	£1.50

Babies	£1
Perambulators	£5

Fairies

Art Studies	£6

Named artists can command a considerable premium

Photographic	£2

Nursery Rhymes

Art Studies	£4
R. Caldecott	£1.50

Named artists can command a considerable premium

Chromo-Litho studies

These range from quite ordinary types to spectacular cards, again with named artists at a premium.
Price range from £3 - £18

Photographic Studies	£1-£3

Tuck R. & Sons

Fairy Tales/Art Series 3472	£25
Ping Pong in Fairyland/	
Art Series 1156	£30

Frederick Warne & Co.

Caldecott R./8 sets of 6/	
Nursery Rhymes	£1.50

DOLLS

Close-up photos	£6
Greetings type	£2

Mirror Grange

Tuck R. & Sons	£3

Queen's Dolls House

Tuck R. & Sons/Set 48	
Price per card	£1
Complete Set	£60
Wembley Exhibition	£3

Titania's Palace

Tuck R. & Sons/	
Two sets of 8 cards	£3
Gale & Polden	£2

Toy Shop advert   £25

TOYS

Bramber Museum	£1.50
Diabolo sketches	£5
Golliwogs	£15+
Close-up photos	£6
Greetings type	£2

Teddy Bears

Art Studies	£12
Photographic	£8
Pullouts	£15
Roosevelt Cartoons	£30

Alice Marshall £12

Mabel Lucie Attwell £12

Agnes Richardson £5

F.G. Lewin £6

CINEMA

Not a subject much in evidence during the hey-day of the picture postcard, the majority of Film Stars we find today date from the 1920-1939 period. The `Picturegoer' series is very popular, while other collectors look for individual Stars.

Market Report
Plenty of interest in the bigger names (see below), with increases in prices created by high demand. The numbered 'Picturegoer' series remain the most collectable cards here.

FILM STARS

This is a select list of names, whom because of scarcity or demand, are currently fetching prices in excess of Catalogue valuation.

Abbott and Costello	£15
Astaire, Fred	£9
Ball, Lucille	£6
Bergman, Ingrid	£9
Bogart, Humphrey	£12
Brando, Marlon	£10
Brooks, Louise	£35
Cagney, James	£6
Chaplin, Charlie	£8
Comic sketches	£6
Red Letter Stills	£4
Cole, Nat King	£12
Davis, Bette	£9
Dean, James	£12
Dietrich, Marlene	£8
Dors, Diana	£10
Durante, Jimmy	£8
Fields, W.C.	£8
Flynn, Errol	£9
Formby, George	£8
Gable, Clark	£6
Garbo, Greta	£6
Garland, Judy	£9
Betty Grable	£9.50
Harlow, Jean	£9.50
Hepburn, Audrey	£15
Holliday, Judy	£8
Howerd, Frankie	£8
Jolson, Al	£8
Keaton, Buster	£6
Kelly, Grace	£9
Lamour, Dorothy	£8
Lanza, Mario	£6
Laurel & Hardy	£25
Leigh, Vivien	£10
Lloyd, Harold	£5
Lombard, Carole	£6
Loren, Sophia	£8
Mansfield, Jayne	£6
Marx Bros.	£15
Monroe, Marilyn	£25
Presley, Elvis	£12

Paul Robeson	£15
Robinson, Edward G.	£7.50
Rogers Ginger	£8
Temple, Shirley	£6
Valentino, Rudolph	£4
Wayne, John	£7
Welles, Orson	£8
West, Mae	£9.50
Wisdom, Norman	£6

ELIZABETH TAYLOR   METRO GOLDWYN MAYER

Elizabeth Taylor £8

Series

Dave and Dusty	£3
Pictures Portrait Gallery	£2
Cinema Chat	£2
Picturegoer/1921-1939	£3
/1940-1962	£5

The Picturegoer Series ran to 6600 cards, published from 1921 to c.1962.

Film Sets/Stills

Pre-1939	£4
1940 onwards	£6

Picturegoer and other firms also produced six-card sets of scenes from individual films. Prices for the most part follow those of the respective Stars.

Miscellaneous Publishers

Pre-1939	£2
1940 onwards	£4
Continental Stars	£2
Coral-Lee 1980	£1

With all Film Star postcards, the value is determined by the name of the artist. Cards of the 1940's and 1950's are in most demand, and a price of £4 would be realistic for the majority of artists from this period. For cards of the 1920's and 1930's, a corresponding figure would be £2. But there are exceptions as given in our select list, and including certain other names of significance, or with a cult following. As a rule of thumb, the well-known Star is worth more than the unknown.

Please note that plain back cards carry the same value as postcard backs.

Above: Vivien Leigh £10

Below: Marlene Dietrich £8

Gary Cooper £6

Autographs / Ink Signed

Value is determined by the individual Star. Certain names are worth more than others. Advice from a specialist is recommended.

CINEMA

MISCELLANEOUS

Bioscopes	£50
Cinemas	£35
Felix the Cat	£12

Cinema Organists

Dixon, Reginald	£5
Others	£4

Disney

Mickey Mouse/Picturegoer Series Nos.

452, 452a, 452b	£50
Foreign published/France/Holland	£8+
Other Disney issues	£8+

Colourgraph Series, tinted R/P £4

Mickey Mouse, Colour type £12

Bambi £8

Felix the Cat £12

COMIC

T. Gilson £2

Studdy, Bonzo £8

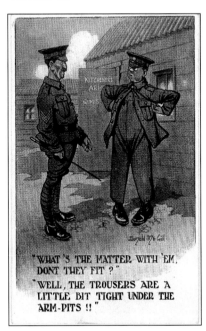

Donald McGill £3

Fred Spurgin £5

COMIC

The Comic postcard is a British institution. It is the yardstick by which most non-collectors judge our hobby! Everyone recognises the Comic card, with its bygone images of hen-pecked husbands, red-nosed drunks, saucy jokes, and embarrassed Vicars! It has been the subject of learned dissertations by authors as varied as George Orwell to Ronnie Barker. And yet, with the exception of a few named Artists or themes allied to other subjects, Comic cards are not as popular today as in former times.

Market Report

A relatively small number of artists have sold well, although there remain few buyers for the great bulk of signed work. Some increases in thematic cards.

SERIES

Bamforth & Co.

Pre 1918	£2
1918-1939	£2
1940 onwards	£1

Tuck R & Sons

Write Away/Early Vignettes	£8
Write Away/Later Issues	£4

Fragments from France/
B. Bairnsfather

Numbers 1 - 48	£3
Numbers 49-54	£10

Sketches of Tommy's Life/
F. Mackain

Set 10/In Training	£3
Set 10/Up the Line	£3
Set 10/Out on Rest	£3
Set 10/At the Base	£3

Black Humour
Happy Little Coons/Tuck R. & Sons/

Oilettes/H.D. Sandford	£10
Other Black Humour	£6

Other Series

Write Off Series/Valentine	£5
Other 'Write-Away' Series	£5

SOMETHING'S COMING YOUR WAY!
Les rencontres imprevues sont souvent
les meilleures!

F.G.Lewin Black Humour £8

Comic £3

GENERAL

All unsigned cards of general interest may be grouped together into the periods listed below, with this suggested price structure.

Pre-1918	£1.50
1918-1939	£1
1940-1960	.50

Early/Chromo-Litho

Undivided back	£8
Divided Back	£3

TYPES

Listed below are suggested minimum prices, bearing in mind that certain Artist signed may be worth considerably more.

Peace is not always found in Solitude

John Hassall £5

Angling	£3
Aviation	£3
Billiards/Snooker	£9
Blacks	£8
Cameras	£8
Card Games	£5
Cats	£2
Chess	£15
Cigarette Packets	£8
Corkscrews	£10
Cricket	£9
Crossword Puzzles	£7
Cycling	£3/£6
Dentistry	£10
Diabolo	£3
Dialect	£1
Erotic	£5
Fleas	£1.50
Football	£6
Golfing	£15
Got Any Cigarette Cards	£12
Gramophones	£5
Hatpins	£1.50
Hunting	£2
Jewish	£25
Lavatorial	£2
Limericks	£4
Maps	£3
Masonic	£15
Match Boxes	£6
Strikers	£15
Military	
Pre-1914	£2
World War 1	£3
World War 2	£5
Miscellaneous	£1.50

Motoring	£6
Obscene/Sexual	£3
Pawnbrokers	£5
Ping Pong	£15
Playing Cards	£5
Police	£4
Postal	£3
Postcards	£5
Postmen	£4
Prehistoric	£2
Pussyfoot	£3
Racing	£5
Railways	£2
Rinking	£3
Rugby football	£6
Scouts	£10
Smoking	£3
Suffragettes	£30/40
Telegrams	£3
Telephone	£3
Television	£4
Tennis	£8
Trams	£3
Wireless/Radio	£6
Irish	£3
Scottish	£3
Welsh	£3

Donald McGill Cycling theme £6

"Lummy, Guv'nor, didn't yer 'ear me 'oller out—port yer 'elm?"

Donald McGill

EARLY CARDS

Postcards were first introduced by Austria in 1869, the first British postcard appearing on 1st October 1870. These were officially issued plain cards with a printed stamp and without a picture, and came to be known as postal stationery. The idea spread rapidly, and within a few years many countries were issuing these novel plain cards. On the Continent, shortly after their introduction, privately issued picture cards came into being, published in varying sizes, but it was not until 1st September 1894 that similar picture cards were permitted in Great Britain, being accepted by the Post Office one month later. These early British cards were known as Court Size. They were smaller and squarer in shape, being issued from 1894-1902, and led to an Intermediate Size from 1898-1902. Until 1902 all cards had to carry the message on the front and the address on the back, thus restricting the design on the card to that of a small picture, or `vignette', with the rest of the surface left free for writing. But on 1st January, 1902, after mounting pressure from commercial interests, Britain became the first country to divide the back, thus permitting both message and address on this side, leaving the front of the card free for a picture. This move saw the adoption of a universal Standard Size of 5.5 x 3.5in, and heralded the real beginning of picture postcards as a major collecting pastime. Other countries quickly followed, and the resultant explosion in picture postcard production world wide lasted until 1914, when the First World War brought an end to this `Golden Age'. This is the most complex heading in Postcards, impossible to catalogue in any depth, covering as it does many millions of undivided back cards published throughout the world from 1869-1907, by which latter date all countries had divided the back and adopted the Standard Size. The entries below will form a general guide to type and price for all Early Cards.

Market Report
These remain the classics of the hobby. Gruss Aus and Early Vignettes. Some of the most beautiful cards ever published, unfortunately rejected by most collectors in their frantic search for Topographical. Still very reasonably priced considering their age and quality.

GREAT BRITAIN
POSTAL STATIONERY/PRE-1894
First Day of Issue Postcard

p.u. 1st October 1870	£400
Unused	£5

Penny Postage Jubilee/Red Card

p.u. May 1890/Guildhall	£50
Unused	£25

Penny Postage Jubilee/& Cover

p.u. July 1890/S. Kensington	£25+
Unused	£8

COURT SIZE/1894-1902
Gruss Aus type

	£25

Early Vignettes

Coloured	£20
Sepia/bw	£12

Postally Used
When the above cards are found postally used before 1897, this consideration of early usage would usually over-ride other factors. The prices given below may be taken as a general guide:

1896	£40
1895	£60
1894	£250
September 1894	£400

With all cards from 1895 onwards, certain rare types may fetch prices in excess of those given above.

INTERMEDIATE SIZE/1898-1902
Early Vignettes

Coloured	£15
Sepia/bw	£6

GB Views

Sepia/bw	£2

STANDARD SIZE/1899-1902
Gruss Aus type

	£20

Early Vignettes

Coloured	£12
Sepia/bw	£4

GB Views

Sepia/bw	£2

If postally used, a small premium may be added to the above prices. It will be seen that some over-lapping occurs in the periods of usage for these cards. This is because there are examples of different sizes known. With regard to the entry for GB Views, it may be added that the majority of these published before 1902, were mass produced common scenes of large cities, towns and holiday areas, and consequently of little interest to Topographical collectors.

FOREIGN
POSTAL STATIONERY/PRE-1894
First Day of Issue Postcard

p.u. 1st Oct. 1869	£400
Unused	£12

Early Constantinople, 1897 £15.

GRUSS AUS/EARLY VIGNETTES

Anniversaries	£25
Festivals	£20
Heraldic	£12
Parades	£18
Souvenirs	£15

Early Vignettes

Coloured	£10
Sepia/bw	£2

For postally used cards a modest premium may be added, in keeping with the scale printed under `Gruss Aus/Topographical'.

Early Tuck Chromo £12

GRUSS AUS/TOPOGRAPHICAL

A difficult area to catalogue, for prices are governed by country of issue, design, condition, and if used date of postmark. The prices given below may be taken as a general indication of value for cards issued in Germany, Austria, Italy and Switzerland, although cards from the smaller towns here are usually worth more than those from large cities.

Fewer Gruss Aus cards were issued by other countries, and as a general rule, the more obscure the country, the higher the value of its cards, with those from places such as the German Colonies, Greece, Palestine, Singapore, and small islands forming the top price bracket of perhaps three times above our base rate.

Prices given apply to postally used cards, although this factor has little significance with later issues from 1896 onwards. Before this date, however, considerations of early usage leading to the field of postcard history may be felt to be of primary importance.

1869-1879	£55
1880-1884	£45
1885-1889	£40
1890-1895	£20
1896-1900+	£12

Early Chromo from Hartlepool £10

Sepia/Black & White
From 1896 onwards the production of Gruss Aus (Greetings From) cards increased dramatically.

Those listed above are usually printed chromo-litho in solid colours from 1896 onwards, and in colour and shades of sepia before this date.

From 1896 we find a great many sepia and black & white cards bearing the legend `Gruss Aus', but these are not worth anything like the superb coloured examples. Their average price would be £1.50.

ETHNIC

Dealing with the races and peoples of the world, this subject was not much in evidence during the early days of collecting, this subject heading covers a fairly broad spectrum of topics mainly showing people in action throughout the world, similar to Social History in Britain. Although before photographic representation of the European Nude became permissible in France during the latter years of World War 1, the many similar studies of native girls offered a culturally acceptable, if hypocritical alternative.

Market Report
Many of the more interesting cards here will be found under 'Overseas Topographical', where they continue to sell well.

ETHNIC GLAMOUR
Cards in this section show girls either topless or semi-clothed.

Ceylon	£8
Ethiopia	£6
South Africa	£3
Sudan	£6
West Africa	£6
India	£10
Japan	£10

Egypt
Tuck R. & Sons/Oilette 7200/

Egypt - The Sphinx	£3
Miscellaneous types	£5

Senegal

Fortier/Dakar	£8

North Africa
The source of the great majority of Ethnic Glamour cards, depicting mainly Arab or Bedouin girls. The leading publisher was Lehnert & Landrock of Cairo and Tunis.

Lehnert & Landrock

Coloured/Numbered on front	£6
/Other series	£6
Sepia/Numbered on front	£3
Real Photographic	£6
Black & White	£3

Other Publishers

ELD/LL/ND/Geiser	£8
Real Photographic	£6
Miscellaneous types	£3

The following cards show girls fully clothed, but are different to the usual National Dress or Trades and Workers types in that they are specifically intended as glamour studies of beautiful girls in the context of their Ethnic background.

Europe	£1.50
Far East	£1.50
North Africa	£1.50

Cards may be found in both categories from certain other countries - Java, Indo China, Japan etc. Depending upon the image, such cards may be rated slightly higher than the above figures.

Ethnic nude £6

Arab ladies R/P   £3

A Matabele in full warpaint £5

MISCELLANEOUS

American Indians	£8
Cannibals	£10
Cowboys	£5
Fakirs/Snake Charmers	£4
Hats	£2
Opium Smokers	£5
Oxford University Robes	£1.50

Contemporary Fashion

c.1910 Family Portraits	£3

Curiosities

Houses/Models etc.	£2
Natural/Trees etc.	£2

Great Britain

Portraits of People/Groups	£2

Ireland

Irish Humour	£3
People/Costume/Life etc.	£3

Japan

Chromo-Litho vignettes	£12
Hand Painted/Black & Gold	£6
/Other types	£4
Art cards	£3
Art Reproductions/Hiroshige etc.	£1.50
Museum cards	£1
Geisha	£4
People/Costume/Life etc.	£1.50
Temples/Cherry Blossom etc.	£1

Jewish Interest

Synagogues/GB	£30
/Foreign	£25
Comic	£20
Jewish New Year	£8+
North African portraits	£3
Palestine Trades/	
Scripture Gift Mission	£2
Rabbis	£5

There are certain very rare 'Types of Life' series from Poland.

Masonic

Are You a Mason?/24 cards	
Millar & Lang	£15
Regalia/Miscellaneous	£8

National Dress

Misch & Stock/Stengel etc.	£1.50
Miscellaneous types	£1

Native Races

South American Indians	
£5	
Other Native Tribes	£5
Local Industries	£2
People/Costume/Life etc.	£1.50

Russia

Types of Russian Life	£10
People/Costume/Art	£3

Scotland

Types of Scottish Dress/Castle Series	£5
Scottish Humour	£2
Highland Washing scenes	£2
People/Costume/Life etc.	£1.50

Wales

Welsh Humour	£2
People/Costume/Life etc.	£2

See also `Ethnic' listing under individual countries.

Zulu women at work R/P £4

EXHIBITIONS

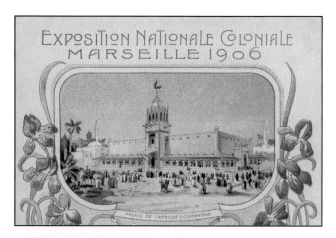

Above: Marseille 1906 £5
Left: British Empire
Exhibition £10
Below: Parisl Exhibition
1900 £10

Above: Brussels 1897 £20
Right: Glasgow Exhibition 1910 £8

OVERSEAS EXHIBITIONS

With hundreds of overseas Exhibitions held world-wide during the past century, it is neither realistic nor practical to attempt to list every single one, let alone give prices for all their cards. Many of these Exhibitions could support their own Catalogue! In last year's edition we listed the most important events as a reference to the cards available.As for pricing, any attempt at this is dependent upon knowing exactly what was published, and this information is not yet in the public domain. As a general guide the following price structure may be of some help:

1881-1895	**£20/£40**
1896-1900	**£10/£20**
1901-1905	**£2/£8**
1906-1918	**£1/£5**
1919 onwards	**£1/£3**

Any pre-1907 card of Gruss Aus design would be worth at least £10, but other early bw or sepia cards such as those from Paris 1900 would be valued at around £1.50. It must be further pointed out that the unusual or spectacular card, such as a Poster Advert, from any Exhibition may be worth considerably more than its range given above while at the same time some Exhibitions may be more popular than others.

For Listings of Foreign Exhibitions see PPV 2003.

EXHIBITIONS

A vast and complex field with many Exhibitions well able to support their own specialised Catalogue. All the events listed below had picture postcards issued, some of which were sold at retail outlets throughout the country, quite removed from the Exhibition itself. All one can do here is to list the main events, and give a suggested minimum price per card, bearing in mind that certain cards may be worth more if depicting Trade Stands, carrying Advertisements, or bearing an Artist's signature. This whole section needs to be re-done by an expert in the field

Market Report
While the better cards will always find a buyer, the great bulk of Exhibitions have few supporters and continue to be offered at very reasonable levels.

GREAT BRITAIN

Royal Naval Exhibition/S.W.
Eddystone Lighthouse
p.u.1891/Violet postmark £75
p.u. 1891/Blue postmark £75

Gardening & Forestry Exhibition
Eddystone Lighthouse
p.u. 1893/Earls Court £150
Unused £75

Victorian Era 1897
Earls Court £50

Women's Exhibition 1900
Earls Court/Dinka Village £5

Glasgow 1901
Cassiers H. £8
bw views £3

Military 1901
Earls Court £5

Cork 1902 £5

Wolverhampton 1902 £5

Highland & Jacobite 1903
Inverness £5

International Fire 1903
Earls Court £5

Scottish Home Industries 1903
Manchester £5

Bradford 1904 £3

International Gas 1904
Earls Court £5

Italian 1904
Earls Court £3

Nottingham 1904
Fire scenes/General views £3

Colonial 1905
Crystal Palace £5

Imperial Austrian 1906
Earls Court £1.50

Balkan States 1907
Earls Court £3

Irish International 1907
Dublin £3

South African Products 1907
Poster Advert Card £12

Crystal Palace 1908 £4

Hungarian 1908 £2

Scottish National 1908
Edinburgh £2

Worlds Mining 1908
Olympia £3

Franco-British 1908
Mucha £125
Woven Silk £50
Trade Stands £6
Hagenbeck Circus/Stadium £5
Comic/Patriotic £3
Views £1

Imperial International 1909
Trade Stands £8
Patriotic/Tartar Camp £5
Views £1.50

C.M.S. Africa & The East 1909
Islington £3

Golden West 1909
Earls Court £3

Japan-British 1910
Trade Stands £8
Comic/Patriotic £3
Views £2

Coronation 1911
Trade Stands £8
White City Views £2

Festival of Empire 1911
Oxo/Patriotic £8
Crystal Palace/Views £3

Scottish National 1911
Glasgow £2

Jubilee International Stamp 1912
Victoria S.W./Ideal Stamp £10

Latin-British 1912
White City £1.50

Shakespeare's England 1912		Fleetway/Sepia	£1.50
Earls Court	£1.50	Other Publishers/RP & Coloured	£1.50
		/Sepia	£1.50

Shakespeare's England 1912
Earls Court £1.50

Building Trades 1913
Olympia £3

Imperial Services 1913
Earls Court £3

Liverpool 1913 £3

Russian Village 1913
Olympia £3

Anglo-American 1914
Band/Patriotic/Wild West £5
White City/Views £2

Anglo-Spanish 1914
Earls Court £3

Bristol International 1914 £3

Newcastle upon Tyne 1929 £3

Empire 1938
Glasgow £1.50

Festival of Britain 1951
Signed Watercolours £8
Far Tottering & Oyster Creek Railway £4
Views £3
Miscellaneous Exhibitions
Daily Mail/Flower Shows etc. £1.50
Cards printed on Stands £8

BRITISH EMPIRE 1924/25
Advertising Cards
Cope Bros/Poster Adverts £50
Tuck R. & Sons by C.E. Flower/
APOC/North British Rubber/
Bryant & May/Sharp's etc. £12
Anchor Line/HMV etc. £12
Court & Pavilion cards
Australia/Bengal/Bombay etc. £3
Falklands Court £30
Exhibition views
Tuck R. & Sons/Coloured £3

Fleetway/Sepia £1.50
Other Publishers/RP & Coloured £1.50
/Sepia £1.50
Colonial views
Tuck R & Sons/RP £3
/Coloured £3
/Sepia £2
Other Publishers/Sepia £1.50
Queens Doll's House
Tuck R. & Sons £3

Liverpool Exhibition 1913 , Priced £3

Imperial Exhibition 1909 £1.50

Festival of Britain, 1951 views £2

PAGEANTS U/K £2
For full listings of UK Pageants see Picture postcard values 2003

PAGEANTS/OVERSEAS
Quebec 1908 £2
Hudson-Fulton 1909 £5
Capetown 1910 £2
National Fetes £3
For full listings of Overseas Pageants see Picture postcard values 2003

EXPLORATION

The explorations and expeditions of the Edwardian Age were well covered by the picture postcards of the time, albeit in smaller production runs than the more popular themes. For this reason the cards which remain are difficult to find and consequently highly priced.

Above left and Left; North Pole Expedition £40

Above: Captain Scott Theatre Poster advert £45

POLAR

1893 Nansen (Norway)
Composite Set 4/Price per Set   £400
On board the `Fram'   £40
Aus Nansen in Nacht und Eis/Set 12/
Meissner & Buch/Series 1016   £15

1897 Adrien De Gerlache (Belgium)
Set 12 / Nels   £50
Expedition antarctique Belge / set 12   £40
Return of Expedition 1899   £40
Various cards   £30

1897 Andree (Sweden)
Hot Air Balloon
Set 25/Bergeret, Nancy   £60
Portraits etc/1930 discovery   £15

1899 'Princesse Alice'
Prince Albert of Monaco etc in
Spitzbergen / set 24   £30

1899 Abruzzi /Cagni (Italy)
On board the `Stella Polare'   £50
Rome Conference 1901/
Subscription Cards   £40
Various cards   £35

1901 Capt. Scott
Wrench Links of empire / set 4 p.u.
from ports of call   £180
  Unposted   £40
  On Board the `Discovery'   £25

'Canterbury Times' / set 24   £45
'Weekly Press' / set 12 (single views)   £50
'Discovery' Antarctic series / set 12   £60
Lansdowne pub 1950s   £8

1901 Otto Sverdrup
Various cards   £40

1901 De Drygalski (Germany)
On board the `Gauss'   £125

1903-1905 Ziegler/`America'
Various cards   £40

1903 Swedish South Polar Expedition
'SY Antarctic' Expedition views / set 12   £60
Argentine rescue pub La Nacion / 16   £40
Various Argentine rescue   £50

1903 J.B. Charcot (France)
Souvenir Card of Subscribers/Tuck   £150

Captain Scott Memorium Card c.1912 £20

Launch of the `Francais' 1903   £40
Set 20/Expedition cards   £50
Various cards   £40

1904 Scottish National
Various cards/Bruce   £40
Set of 12/W. Ritchie & Son   £50

1908 J.B. Charcot (France)
Launch of the `Pourquoi Pas'   £40
Various cards/E.L.D./N.D. etc.   £30
Double picture expedition views / set 12   £50

1908 Shackleton
On Board `Nimrod' 1908   £40

1908 Robert Peary (USA)
N.Pole Gravure /Hampton's mag/ set 13   £10
Kawin & Co./Chicago/Set 50/bw photos   £8
Taggart/Series of sepia photos   £6
Tuck R. & Sons/Oilettes/Operati A.   £6
Ullman North Pole Series 162/Wall B.   £6
S.S. `Roosevelt'/Inset Peary portrait/
Set 3 Official/p.u. 12.9.09   £75
Peary & Cook/Comic sketches   £5

1910-12 Amundsen (Norway)
Artist-drawn; pub Mittet & Co   £40

1910 J.B. Charcot (France)
Various cards/E.L.D./N.D. etc.   £30

1910-13 Captain Scott
Ponting Fine Art series / set 14	£15
Batchelder bros; Rotary Photo	£20
'Terra Nova' in Cardiff or Lyttelton	£30
Advertising cards	£30
In memoriam cards	£20
Memorials and statues	£8

1911 Filchner (Germany)
Views of 'Deutschland', various   £50

Hot Air Balloon/ Princess Alice'
Set 24/Alfonso XIII & Prince of
Monaco etc. in Spitzberg   £30

1914 Shackleton
British Polar expedition	1930
Expedition views/ set 10	£20
With Spratts dogfood advert on back	£30
'Endurance' in harbour	£30

1918 Amundsen (Norway)
Dirigible `Maud'
Various cards   £30

1921-22 Shackleton-Rowett Expedition
Views of RYS 'Quest'   £40

**1925-26 North Pole flights in Airships/
Dirigibles by Amundsen, Bennett, Byrne,
Ellsworth, Nobile**
Various cards   £30

1926 Commander Byrd/North Pole Flight (USA)
Set 18	£12
1928 expedition views pu in 1934 / set 17	£10
'City of New York' at World's Fair	£5

1934 Commander Byrd (USA)
Various cards   £10

1934 J.B. Charcot (France)
Shipwreck 1936	£35
Funeral 1936	£60

1936 J.B.Charcot (France)
Shipwreck 1936	£35
Funeral 1936	£60
1954 Australian Antarctic Bases	
Pub. Seven Seas stamps / set 5	£8
1957 Trans-Antarctic Expedition	
bw photos / set 7	£8

The standard catalogue on Antarctic cards is 'Postcards of Antarctic Expeditions' by Margery Wharton, obtainable from the author.
Email at margery.wharton@tesco.net

EVEREST
1922 Expedition
Group photo/RP   £15
1924 Expedition
p.u. from Rongbuk Base Camp/Set 19   £20

SAHARA
1921 Capt. Angus Buchanan
Set 12/Portraits & Events   £6

*Captain Scott's Ship
Terra Nova £30*

GLAMOUR

One of the stalwarts of the Edwardian picture postcard industry as shown by the great numbers handed down to us. Glamour cards in one form or another are to be found in almost every original album, although the top of the range Artists and photographic Nudes are none too common. These were to be collected mainly in France, or by our troops during the First World War.

Market Report
Photographic Nudes have increased in price in response to strong demand, with the better cards now selling at £15+. French artists have also moved ahead with notable prices being seen at auction. Strong collecting area which will surely repay the attention of informed buyers.

ART STUDIES

Chromo-Litho

Meissner & Buch	£15
Other publishers	£10

Nudes/Semi-Nudes

Pin-up type	£6
French Salon/Coloured	£4
/Sepia/BW	£2
Classical Art	£1

Pretty Girls

Better cards/Pre-1914	£3
Miscellaneous	£1.50

USA Post-War Pin-Ups

Machine cards/Plain back	£5

Bathing Beauties, Photographic study £3

BATHING BEAUTIES

Embossed/Artist drawn

Chromo-Litho	£10
Other types	£5

Photographic/Portraits

Miscellaneous	£3

PHOTOGRAPHIC

Nudes

Prices given both for Nudes and Lingerie apply equally to plain back cards as these formed the bulk of publishers' output during this period.

France c.1916/RP	£15
Germany/Italy etc.c.1916/RP	£12
c.1916/Coloured/Hand Tinted	£18
Printed/Bw & Sepia	£6
Stage Acts/The Seldoms	£8
Couples	£8
Between the Wars	£6
Post-War studies	£3
Body Stocking types	£4
Private photographs	£2
Modern reproductions	£1.50

SM Interest

Numbered RP series c.1920	£20
Bondage/Spanking etc.	£15

Lingerie Studies	£10

Pretty Girls

Better cards/Pre-1914	£3
Miscellaneous	£1

MISCELLANEOUS

Pornographic/Postcard back

Art/Photographic	£18

Plain back cards have no commercial value otherthan curiosity appeal.

Lesbian interest	£18

Erotica

Photographic	£18
Art	£6
Comic Sketches	£6

Bedroom Scenes

Art/Photographic	£4

Miss Europe Competition

RP studies of contestants	£3

Raphael Kirchner £30

Rosy Days by Mary Horsfall £6

Bathing Beauty £8

GLAMOUR

Maurice Pepin £12

Harrison Fisher £10

Mutoscope £5

W. Barribal £12

GREETINGS

Greetings Cards in one form or another provided the bulk of the Edwardian publishers' output. Birthday and Christmas cards of all types were produced in their millions, while the better Embossed cards remain as superb examples of the printer's art. Coin and Stamp Cards were published in long series, although these have never been too popular in today's market. Other themes have been grouped together to make this heading.

Market Report
Top of the range cards in all the categories have sold well this year. The more unusual Father Christmas and other thematics continue to sell at top prices.

COIN CARDS
National Coinage

Embossed	£8
Printed	£5

Banknote Cards

Embossed	£8
Printed	

EMBOSSED

Grade A	£12
Grade B	£5
Grade C	£1

These are as difficult to describe as they are to illustrate! At the top of the range are the superb chromo-litho cards of ornate design, in the middle are the great bulk of nice Embossed, while below these come the common, run of the mill types.

FANTASY

Enlarged Objects	£3
Erotic	£12
Faces in Smoke etc.	£3
Fantasy Maps	£15
Multi-Babies	£1.50

Fantasy Heads

Coloured	£25
Black & White	£10

Faces in Mountains

Pub. Killinger	£12
Later issues	£4

Fantasy Head , Black and White £10

DATE CARDS
Turn of the Century/Postally used

Sent 31.12.99/Received 1.1.00	£30

Year Dates/Up to 1903

Embossed	£10
Printed	£3

Year Dates/1904 onwards

Embossed	£6
Printed	£4

Calendar Cards £4

Embossed , Happy Birthday Teddy £12

FATHER CHRISTMAS
Hold to Light type	£85
WWI Silk type	£20
Tuck Oilette	£8
Coloured	£6
Photo type	£3
Snowmen	£3
Early embossed	
Red robes	£15
Other Coloured Robes	£16

Prices are for good full-length or full-face Santas. Small designs or those with Santa forming part of a larger picture are worth less.

LANGUAGE
Deaf and Dumb Alphabet	£5
Language of Fruit	£2
Language of Stamps	£2
Language of Vegetables	£2
Esperanto	
Tuck R. & Sons/Oilette series	£8
Miscellaneous issues	£3/£5
Language of Flowers	
Welch J & Sons	£1.50
Miscellaneous issues	£1.50

A.M.Bowley, Happy Christmas, £12

RECREATIONAL
Casinos	£1.50
Playing Cards	£8
Roulette Wheel Cards	£2
Romance	
Cupid's Darts/Welch J. & Sons	£1.50
Proverbs/Welch J. & Sons	£1.50
Miscellaneous Comic Types	£1.50
Greetings/Sentimental/Lovers	£1

LARGE LETTER
Names of People	£2
Names of Places	£2
Numbers	£2

Cherubs
Tuck R. & Sons	£12
Other series Embossed	£8
Printed	£4

Initials
Colour embossed	£8
Coloured	£4
B/W & Sepia	£1.50

Large Letter, colour photographic £4

SEASONAL GREETINGS
Christmas	£1
Decoration Day	£6
Easter	£1
Halloween	£6
Independence Day	£4
New Year	£1
Poisson d'Avril	£1
St. Patrick's Day	£3
Thanksgiving Day	£4
Valentine's Day	£5

These are prices representing the average card found in any section, but the spectacular item will fetch considerably more.

Birthday
Deckle-edge c.1930	.50
Miscellaneous	£1

Flora White £5

STAMP CARDS

Embossed	£8
Printed	£5

Certain countries, e.g. Canada, realise a considerable premium.

MISCELLANEOUS

Champagne Bottles	£5
Davis Message Cards	£1.50
Fireworks	£6
Flowers	£1
Fruit	£1
Hands Across the Sea	£1
Lincoln Abraham	£4
Moonlight	£1
Mottos/Sayings	£1
Rough Seas	£1
Swastikas/Greetings type	£1

Faith, Hope and Charity

Set 3	£5
Single cards	£1.50

Silhouettes

Camp Silhouette Series/ 25 cards/Photochrom Co.	£3
Cut-out types	£6
Printed types	£2

Smoking

Cigarette Card Comics	£20
Cigarettes/Pipes/Tobacco	£4

Miscellaneous Greetings

Better cards/Pre-1914	£3
General Types	£1

With the lower value Greetings cards, Christmas and Birthday etc., anything Embossed, or printed Chromo-Litho, or carrying an unusual design, would certainly be worth more.

Christmas greeting Pauli Ebner £8

Valentine message, Art Nouveau £30

HERALDIC

Originally far more popular than they are now, Heraldic cards of all kinds were published in profusion by the Edwardians. Perhaps the sense of identity with a particular town or city was stronger then than it is now, certainly this would account for the enormous numbers of cards left to us.

Market Report
This area remains a slow seller with the exception of the early Chromo-Litho cards.

FULL OUT CRESTS

Faulkner C.W. & Co.	£3
Ja-Ja- Heraldic Series	
Stoddart & Co.	£2
School/University Arms	
Robert Peel Postcard Co	£1.50
Reliable Series	
W. Ritchie & Sons	£1.50
Multi-crest cards	£1
Special Crests	
Sports/Occupations	£1.50
Miscellaneous Publishers	
Better cards/Pre-1914	£2
General issues	£1

CRESTS WITH VIEWS

B & R's Camera Series	
Brown & Rawcliffe	£1.50
Faulkner C.W. & Co.	
Cathedrals/Stately Homes	£1.50
Favourite Series	
W.E. Byers	£1
F.S.O. Heraldic Series	£2
Ja-Ja- Heraldic Series	
Stoddart & Co.	£3
Jarrold's Series	£1
Robert Peel Postcard Co.	£1.50
Reliable Series	
W. Ritchie & Sons	£1
Tuck R. & Sons	
Heraldic Series	£12
Heraldic View	£2
Valentine's Series	£1
Miscellaneous Publishers	£1

MISCELLANEOUS

Papal Series	
Ferloni L.	£5
FLAGS/NATIONAL ARMS	
Aristophot Flag Series	£1.50
E.F.A. Series	
Excelsior Fine Art	£1.50
Faulkner C.W. & Co.	
Early series	£6
Arms of the Nations	
Kohl/Tuck R. & Sons	£12
Flags of the Nations	
Valentine & Sons	£4

Miscellaneous Publishers	
Embossed/Chromo-Litho	£8
Printed/Coloured	£1.50

TARTANS

B.B.	
Tartan View Series	£1
Brown & Rawcliffe	
Arms, Views & Tartans	£1
B & R's Camera Series	£1
Cynicus Co.	£1
Johnston W. & A.K.	
Tartan & Arms Series	£3
Stoddart & Co./Ja-Ja	
Clan Tartan Heraldic Series	£3
Tuck R. & Sons	
Scottish Clans Series	£3
Valentine & Sons	
Tartan Series	£1.50
Valentine's Series	£1
Wildt & Kray	
Badge & Tartan	£2
Miscellaneous types	£1

MAP CARDS

Early Chromo /Embossed	£6/ £25
Mountain Charts	£1
Romantic/Comic types	£1
Walker John & Co.	
Geographical Series	£6

Full Out Crest, Faulkner & Co. £3

HARROGATE.

LITERARY/MUSIC

Judging from the diverse range and numbers remaining, cards of Literary and Musical interest would appear to have been quite popular in the pre-television days of our forebears. A good subject to collect, reflecting as it does, a wide spread of artistic endeavour.

Market Report
Certain cards in this section have shown signs of movement, notably early Tucks , Opera, and a few other desirable themes.

DICKENS

Cassell & Co./Barnard F.
Character Sketches from Dickens   £4

Chapman & Hall
Dickens Novels/Set 13   £6

Faulkner & Co.
Pickwick Series/244   £4

Hildesheimer/Manning E.F.
Dickens Characters   £4

Jones A.V.N./Reynolds F.
Dickens Characters   £5

Stewart & Woolf/Crowquill A.
Dickens Characters/3 sets   £4

Tuck R. & Sons
Early Numbered Series   £12
Dickens Postcard Series/Kyd   £12
Dombey and Son/
Set 6/Oilette 6050   £3
Nicholas Nickleby/
Set 6/Oilette 6052   £3
With Famous Authors & Painters   £4
In Dickens' Land/Oilettes   £2
Dickens Characters   £4

Valentine
Dickens Characters   £4

Portraits/Sites/Events   £1.50

MISCELLANEOUS

Alice in Wonderland
Nixon K./Set 6/
Faulkner & Co./Series 1819   £12
Tenniel/Set 8/
Fuller & Richard   £12
Folkard C./Set 6/
A&C Black/Series 80   £12

Literary Personalities
Early Chromos   £8
Later Portraits   £1.50

Lorna Doone
Scenes from Lorna Doone/
Set 12/Photochrom Co.   £1.50

Early Chromo Litho £8

Characters from Lorna Doone/
Valentine   £1.50
Poetry
Patience Strong cards   £1
Verses/Miscellaneous   £1

Sherlock Holmes   £10

SHAKESPEARE

Ackermann/Munich
Silhouettes/Set 12   £5

Faulkner & Co.
Shakespeare Series   £5

Hildesheimer/Carter S.
Sketches from Shakespeare   £2

Nister E.
Scenes from Shakespeare/ub   £8
Later series/Divided back   £2

Tuck R. & Sons
Early Numbered Series   £12
Hamlet/Set 12/Copping H.   £5
Merry Wives of Windsor/
Series 466-477   £5
In Shakespeare's Country/Oilettes   £2

Valentine
Characters from Shakespeare   £2

Portraits/Sites/Events   £1

BANDS

Brass Bands	£6
Dance Bands	£10
Military Bands	£6
Pipe Bands	£5
Dagenham Girl Pipers	£3
Champion Bandsmen	£4
Band Leaders	£5

OPERA

Gilbert & Sullivan

Savoy Co.	£12
Other Publishers	£8

Breitkoff & Hartel/Set 60

Wagner Series	£12

Faulkner & Co./Series 1401

Wagners Operas/Set 12	£15

Meissner & Buch

Wagner series	£18

Ricordi

Chromo-litho ub/Japanese style	£18
Madame Butterfly	£18
Tosca	£18

Tuck R. & Sons

Wagner series	£18

Opera Houses	£5

Opera Singers

Butt Clara	£5
Caruso Enrico	£20
Chaliapin	£20
Melba Dame Nellie	£10
Patti Adeline	£10
Tetrazzini	£10
Other Singers	£6

POP STARS

Beatles	£7.50
Others	£1.50
Modern	.50
Elvis	£9

SONG CARDS

BAMFORTH

Set 3	£4.50
Set 4	£6

Prices are for complete sets

Odd cards	£1.50

OTHER TYPES

Miscellaneous Types	£1

Tuck R. & Sons

Illustrated Songs Series	£1.50

The Beatles £7.50

MISCELLANEOUS

Bandstands	£5
Bells	£1.50
Bellringers	£8
Hymns	£1
Musical Instruments	£3
Advertised by musicians	£6
Musicians	£3
Orchestras	£6
Singers	£3

Composers

Art Studies	£3
Photographic	£2

Gramophones

Art/Photographic	£8
Comic types	£5

Jazz

Bands/Groups	£12
Instrumentalists/Singers	
£12	

Organs

Church	£2
Cinema/Theatre	£5

Song Cards/Musical Notation

Embossed	£5
Printed	£1.50

MILITARY

The Military conflicts of history from the Boer War to the present day have always been covered by the picture postcard. In a variety of styles ranging from actual battle scenes to the personalities, patriotic and propaganda issues of the period, the postcard was not slow to reflect current tastes and national sentiment. The many issues relating to the First World War form the largest catalogue.

Market Report
Very strong collecting field with prices in all areas holding up well. More interest this year in good quality photographic plus Military Art and almost anything of unusual interest.

For Political Cartoons in all sections please see POLITICAL classification.

SPANISH AMERICAN WAR 1898
Miscellaneous types   £25

BOER WAR 1899-1902
Jamestown Raid	£40
St. Helena/Camps etc.	£20
War Photographs	£15
Sites & Events/Historic	£5

City Press
C.I.V./bw Vignettes	£15

Collectors Publishing Co.
Personalities/Photographic	£15

Koumans P.J.
Personalities/Photographic	£15

Picture Postcard Co.
War Sketches/Caton Woodville etc.	£20
Personalities/Vignettes	£20

Tuck R. & Sons
Peace Card/Coloured Vignette	£25
Souvenir of 1900	£25
Empire Series/Art Sketches/bw	£18
Overprinted for Victories	£30

Other Publishers
Early Vignettes/Coloured	£18
Early Vignettes/bw	£15

GRUSS VOM KRIEGSSCHAUPLATZ

Telegramm, 30. Oktober 1899.
Während der Nacht gingen 1000 Maultiere mit ihren Geschützen durch.
General WHITE.

Boer War cartoon £20

BOXER REBELLION 1900-1901
War Photographs   £25

RUSSO-JAPANESE WAR 1904-1905

Military Review 1906
With Kobe Handstamp	£10
With Tokyo Handstamp	£8
Without Handstamp	£6

Japanese Official
Post Office 1904 issue	£8
Photo montage/Art Borders	£8
Communications Dept/Post War issue	£5

Peace Conference
Knight Bros./Multi-view	£8
Miscellaneous issues	£5

Russian Outrage on Hull Fleet
Real Photographic	£5
Valentines/Other Publishers	£3

Tuck R. & Sons
Real Photographic Series 5170	£8
Russo-Japanese Series 1330	£8
Russo Japanese War Photographs/ Set 6/Silverette 6534	£8
The Russo-Japanese War/ Set 6/Oilette 6484	£6

WarPhotographs/Sketches
Hildesheimer/War Series 5224	£6
Other Publishers	£5

ITALIAN-TURKISH WAR 1911-1912
War Photographs
Traldi/Milan	£12
Miscellaneous issues	£8

CHINESE CIVIL WAR 1911-1917
War Photographs	£15
Art Studies	£8

BALKAN WARS 1912-1913
War Photographs	£12

WORLD WAR 1 1914-1918
FUND RAISING CARDS

Anglo-Russian Hospital Fund	£3
Asiles de Soldats Invalides Belges	£2
Belgian Relief Funds	£3
Bovril/Lord Roberts	£5
British Ambulance Committee	£3
British Committee of the French Red Cross	£3
British Gifts for Belgian Soldiers	£3
National Egg Fund	£5
National Fund for Welsh Troops	£2
National Institute for the Blind	£1.50
National Relief Fund	£3
Performer Tobacco Fund	£6
Red Cross	£3
War Bond Campaign/Set 12	£3
Y.M.C.A. Hut Fund	£2

National War Bond Tank

Trafalgar Square	£5
In G.B. locations	£15

General Joffre WW1 £6

War Bond Campaign Postcard

Trafalgar Square	£5
In G.B. locations	£15

Weekly Dispatch Tobacco Fund

`Arf a Mo' Kaiser/Thomas B.	£4

War Loan/Patriotic Designs

France	£5
Germany	£6
Italy	£5
Russia	£8

NAVAL ACTIONS

Bombardment of Britain 1914	£12

Scapa Flow

German Fleet/Sinking etc.	£8

Zeebrugge

WW1 Actions/Interest	£1

OFFICIAL STATIONERY/ FIELD SERVICE CARDS

Great Britain	£2
France	£2
Germany	£3
Other Countries	£3

PATRIOTIC
Admirals of the British Navy

Francis Dod	£3

Britain Prepared Series

24 cards/Photochrom Co.	£3

Butterfly Girls

Published Geligne/Marotte	£8

Generals of the British Army

Francis Dodd	£3

Heroes of the War

Cuneo, Cyrus	£10

Leurs Caboches/Nos Allies/Nos Poilus

Dupuis Emile	£5

Les Femmes Heroiques

Dupuis Emile	£5

Out for Victory

Hill L. Raven-	£4

Series 1021

Vivien Mansell	£4

The Allies Series

James Henderson	£4

United Six Series

Inter-Art Co.	£4

Types

Bulldogs	£6
Comic	£3
Flags	£3
Poems	£1.50
Royalty	£3

Miscellaneous types

Great Britain	£3
France	£3
Germany	£6
Other Countries	£3

PERIOD SENTIMENT

Great Britain	£1.50
France	£1.50
Germany	£2
Other Countries	£2

PERSONALITIES

France	£2
Other Countries	£3

WW1 photographic card £12

Germany
Generals/RP Portraits	£8
Art Studies	£5
Other Generals/Leaders	£3

Great Britain
Kitchener Memorial Card	£3
Other Generals/Leaders	£1.50

PRISONERS OF WAR
Allied in German Camps
Art sketches	£10
Photographic	£5

German in Allied Camps
Photographic	£6

WELFARE ORGANISATIONS
Church Army	£3
Salvation Army	£3
St. Dunstans	£3
Y.M.C.A.	£3

Red Cross
There are many cards issued by Red Cross Organisations dealing with aspects of WW1 in their respective countries,
A guide to price may be inferred by reference to similar themes in the WW1 section and a premium added for the presence of the Red Cross symbol. We would suggest £5 as a basic price.

WAR PHOTOGRAPHS
Chicago Daily News	£4
E.L.D/N.D. etc.	£4
Hildesheimer & Co.	£4
Imperial War Museum	£2
In the Balkans/E.L.D.	£3
L.V. Cie	£3
Official Photograph/Censored at GHQ	£3
Photochrom Co.	
Bw series	£4

On Active Service/Set 48	£3
Sketch The	£4
Sphere The	£4
French Edition	£4
Sport & General Press Agency	£3
Tit-Bits	£3
War Photogravure Publications	£3
The War Series	£3
World War Series	£3
Yes or No	£3
Special Cards	£5

Daily Mail Battle Pictures
Numbers 1 - 96	£2
Numbers 97-144	£2.50
Numbers 145-160/Anzac Series	£6
Numbers 161-176	£4

This famous series was published in 22 sets of 8 cards each.
Real Photographic series	£6

Daily Mirror
Canadian Official Series/RP	£5
Coloured	£3
Sepia	£3

Newspaper Illustrations
	£3
Black & White series	£3
Coloured series	£3
Sepia series	£3
Shell damage Series	£1

Regent Publishing Co.
The War Series	£3

Tuck R. & Sons
At the Front	£4
The European War 1914	£3
Types of Allied Armies	£4

Miscellaneous
Great Britain	£3
France	£3
Germany	£5
Other Countries	£5

London Buses arriving with wounded at Ghent, printed card, £12

WW1 Nurses £6

Any cards from the above series which are particularly interesting or depict an unusual facet of the War can be individually priced..

MISCELLANEOUS WORLD WAR 1

Allied Occupation/Germany 1919	£4
Armoured Cars	£6
Campaign Maps	£5
Cemeteries/Memorials	£1.50
Conscientious Objectors	£20
German proclamations issued in French towns	£4
Greetings Cards/Regimental	£6
Mesopotamia Campaign	£4
Palestine Campaign	£8
Recruiting Parades/Departures	£25
Refugees in G.B.	£25
Salonika Campaign	£3
Shell Damage/Foreign	£1
Tanks	£4

Christmas Cards

From POW Camps	£8
Miscellaneous	£3

Dardanelles Campaign
Gallipoli/Anzac Cove/Suvla Bay etc.

Troops/Action	£12
RP Landscapes	£6

Dogs

Major Richardson's War Dogs	£8
Red Cross War Dogs	£8

Victory Parades

GB	£1.50
Paris 1919	£1.50

War Wounded

Brighton	£5
Miscellaneous	£3

Women on War Work

For the Cause/Tuck R. & Sons	£8
La Femme et La Guerre/Leroy	£8
Our Own Girls/Arthur Butchur	£8
Miscellaneous	£8

There are many other photographic cards, particularly those issued by Germany, France and Belgium depicting different aspects of World War 1, including Troops in Action,At Rest, Ammunition Transport, Convoys,Gun Crews, Machine Gun Nests,Vehicles etc.
One may use a guide price of around £5 for such cards, bearing in mind that some will be worth more, some less.

RUSSIAN CIVIL WAR 1917-1921

Allied Expeditionary Forces	£15
Red Propaganda	£18
White Russian Propaganda	£20
Miscellaneous Issues	£10

GRAECO-TURKISH WAR 1919-1923

War Photographs

Smyrna	£15
Miscellaneous issues	£8

SPANISH CIVIL WAR 1936-1939

Gen. Franco	£15
Republican Propaganda	£20
War Photographs	£20
Military Personalities	£15

ITALIAN-ABYSSINIAN WAR 1938

War Photographs	£12

WW1 Women workers, real photo £6

WORLD WAR 2/1939-1945

OFFICIAL STATIONERY/FIELD SERVICE CARDS

Germany	£3
U.S.A.	£3
Other Countries	£2

PATRIOTIC

Great Britain	£8
France	£5
Germany	£12
Netherlands	£5
U.S.A.	£8

PERSONALITIES

France	£4
Germany	£10
U.S.A.	£4
Gen. Eisenhower	£5
Other Countries	£4

Great Britain

Churchill	£4/£8
Gen. Montgomery	£5
Other Leaders	£3

WAR PHOTOGRAPHS/SKETCHES

Photochrom Co.

Britain Prepared	£3

Salmon

Aviation sketches/A.F.D. Bannister	£5

Valentine

Real Photograph series/Aviation	£2
Aircraft Recognition silhouettes	£2

MISCELLANEOUS WORLD WAR 2

Prisoners of War	£10
Tanks/Guns/Vehicles	£5
V2 Rocket on display	£8
With The W.A.A.F./Set 24	
Sepia photos/Tuck R. & Sons	£20
Women on War Work	£12

Comic Sketches

Bizeth/Sets of 6/Price per set	£36
Dutch Troops	£4
U.S.A.Troops	£4
Maneken-Pis	£3
Tuck R. & Sons	£4

Germany

Erich Gutjahr Series	£10

This is an extensive numbered series of superb RP studies of the Germany Army in WW2.

Germany/6x4 size

Generals/RP Portraits	£12
Patriotic Posters	£12

Hitler/Portraits	£12
Luftwaffe propaganda	£10

Peace Celebrations
Amsterdam Victory Parade 1945

6x4 size	£5
VE Day	£6
VJ Day	£6

Red Cross

As with WW1 there were many cards issued by Red Cross Organisations in WW2 dealing with aspects of war in their respective countries,A guide to price may be inferred by reference to similar themes in the WW2 section and a premium added for the presence of the Red Cross symbol. We would suggest £5 as a basic price.

Shell Damage

London Blitz	£4
Foreign	£1.50

USA

Troops/Action	£5
Pre-war Camp Life	£3

There are many photographic cards, particularly those issued by Germany, France and Belgium depicting different aspects of World War 2, including Troops in Action, At Rest, Anti-Aircraft emplacements, Ammunition Transport, Convoys, Gun Crews, Machine Gun Nests,Vehicles etc. One may use a guide price of around £5 for such cards, bearing in mind that some will be worth more, some less

17th Lancers, Harry Payne £15

Royal Horse Guards, Harry payne £30

MILITARY ART
Gale & Polden
History & Traditions	£10
History & Traditions/Rates of Pay	£18
Regimental Badges	£6
Miscellaneous Coloured	£6

Knight Bros.
	£3

Lavauzelle C./Paris
Early Vignettes	£8

Valentine
The Kings Army	£3

Italian Regimental
Chromo-Litho	£12
Sepia/Black & White	£4

Miscellaneous Art/Coloured
Early Vignettes	£12
Later Issues	£3

Photographic Studies
Coloured	£3
Black & White	£1.50

Tuck R. & Sons
Oilette Series

3100 Cavalry on Active Service/ Harry Payne	£18
3105 Our Fighting Regiments/ The RoyalArtillery/Harry Payne	£12
3113 Comrades/ Harry Payne	£25
3159 The US Army on the Western Front /Harry Payne	£25

3160 Colonial Badges and their Wearers/ Harry Payne	£15
3163 Our Fighting Regiments/ 1st LifeGuards/Harry Payne	£15
3165 Our Fighting Regiments/ 1st Dragoon Guards/Harry Payne	£15
3204 Badges and their Wearers/ Harry Payne	£75
3205 Badges and their Wearers/ Harry Payne	£75
3546 Military in London/ Harry Payne	£5
3642 Scots Pipers/ Harry Payne	£8
6412 Military in London/ Harry Payne	£4
8491 Badges and their Wearers/ Harry Payne	£50
8625 The Scots Guards/ Harry Payne	£12
8635 The 21st Lancers/ Harry Payne	£12
8637 17th Lancers/ Harry Payne	£15
8731 Our Territorials/ Harry Payne	£12
8732 Wake up England/ Harry Payne	£15
8738 Types of the British Army Harry Payne	£30
8761 Defenders of the Empire/ Harry Payne	£12

Gale & Polden, Harry Payne £12

8762 The Red Cross Series/ Harry Payne	£30	**Army Camps**	
8763 The Royal Horse Artillery/ Harry Payne	£12	Field Camps/Named	£8
		Field Camps/Un-named	£3
8770 Regimental Bands/ Harry Payne	£5	Hut Camps/Named	£5
		Hut Camps/Un-named	£2
8807 16th Lancers/ Harry Payne	£15	Barracks	£5
8831 1st Royal Dragoons/		**British in India**	
Harry Payne	£15	Military Life/Sites etc.	£4
8835 1st Life Guards/ Harry Payne	£15	**Italian Regimental**	
8848 11th Hussars/		Menus/Patriotic/Seals etc.	£4
Harry Payne	£15	Chromo-Litho designs	£12
8871 Badges and their Wearers/ Harry Payne	£15	**Life in the Army**	
8890 6th Dragoon Guards/		Gale & Polden	£3
Harry Payne	£10	Star Series	£1.50
9081 Military in London II/		Miscellaneous photographs	£3
Harry Payne	£5	**Medals**	
9132 Deeds of British Heroism	£8	Present Day War Ribbons/Rees H.	£4
9134 British Battles	£8	V.C. Winners/Various issues	£10
9139 Military Life & Military Tournaments/		Daring Deeds	£3
Harry Payne	£5		
9478 The British Army	£5	**Military Tattoos/Displays**	
9527 Life at Aldershot/		Aldershot	£1.50
Harry Payne	£15	Royal Tournament	£1.50
9587 Military in London III/		Miscellaneous Events	£1.50
Harry Payne	£5	**Uniforms/Dress**	
9762 Scotch Pipers/		Mrs. Albert Broom series/Guardsmen	£8
Harry Payne	£8	Regimental photographs	£3
9883 Queens Own Cameron Highlanders/		Identified	£3
Harry Payne	£12	Unidentified	£1.50
9884 Gordon Highlanders/ Harry Payne	£12	**Unknown Warrior**	
9885 Seaforth Highlanders/		Cenotaph Services/Parades	£2
Harry Payne	£12		

9934 For Home and Empire/ Harry Payne £15

9937 Argyll and Sutherland Highlanders/ Harry Payne £12

9980 Royal Scots Greys/ Harry Payne £12

9993 Coldstream Guards/ Harry Payne £12

9994 Black Watch/ Harry Payne £12

There are many photographic cards depicting aspects of pre-war Military Life in different countries, including Troops on exercise, Parades,Training etc. One may use a guide price of around £3 for such cards,bearing in mind that some will be worth more, some less.

Tuck R. & Sons

Military in London/Oilettes £2
Unsigned Oilettes £3

MISCELLANEOUS

Artillery £2
Battlefields/Historic £1.50
Battle of Waterloo £1
Beefeaters £1
Joan of Arc £2
Napoleon £3

German machine gun R/P £12

MILITARY AIRCRAFT

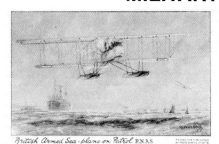

Royal Naval Air Service, Algernon Black £8

Aircraft aboard HMS Courageous £12

Airships

Nulli Secundus Pr.Photo c.1907	£6
Beta/Gamma	£12/£15
Zeppelins Close-up	£12
Combat sketches	£3/5
Wreckage/GB Locations	£8

Aircraft

Royal Flying Corp 1912-18
Royal Naval Air Service 1914-18

Pilots/Machines	£10/12
Groups/Machines named Sqdn.	£15/20
Aces/Machines	£20
Portraits	£12/15

R.F.C. & R.N.A.S. amalgamated in 1918 to become the Royal Air Force.

1918-1939	£5
1939-1960	£3

Miscellaneous

Airfields/Hangers	£8
Bombers/Fighters	£3
Flying Boats	£5
Gliders	£3

Captain Leefe Robinson V.C. £12

HMS Evolution hoisting the plane inboard.

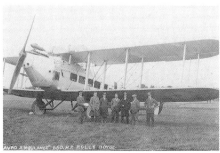

Avro Ambulance R/P £12

NAVAL

A vast and complex section where we will attempt to give some idea of the types of Warships in H. M.'s service.
Publishers produced large quantities of cards relating to capital ships where crews often numbered 1000-1200+. These are common and so priced. Other R/P's of named ships in exotic ports and harbours are of more interest and priced according to location.
Market Report: Always plenty of cards to see in most dealers stocks, but still sells well when keenly priced.

BATTLESHIPS/CRUISERS
Tuck R. & Sons
Empire Series	£20
Oilette Series	£3/5
Artist drawn	£3/5

Foreign Types
Early Vignettes	£15
Visit of US Fleet to Melbourne	
1908 / Embossed / Inset Ship	£18
Japanese Official/Inset Ship	£10/15
Pre - 1939	£3/10
1939 Onwards	£3/5

HMS dreadnought, Tuck Oillette £5

Gale and Polden £3

A shell for 'Lizzie's big 'un' £2

LIFE IN THE NAVY
Gale & Polden	£2/3
Nelson Victory Cards	£2/5

Miscellaneous
Shotley Barracks/HMS Ganges	£4
Ships moored off-shore	£4
Other Barracks etc.	£4
Wooden Walls (Training Ships)	£4
Fleet Reviews/Displays	£3
Naval Engagements/Sketches	£6/£8
Personalities	£2
Sailor's Photographs etc.	£2
Graf Spee sinking set of 12	£6

The Imperial British Navy

Battleships	£3
Dreadnought Cruisers	£3
Battlecruisers	£3/5
Cruisers	£3
Aircraft Carriers	£5/6
Sea Plane Carriers	£6
Flotilla Leaders	£3/4
Destroyers	£3/4
Torpedo Boat Destroyers	£4
Submarines	£4/6
Sloops	£5/6
Mine Layers	£3
Mine Sweepers	£3

Battleship H.M.S. London   £3

Small Craft & Auxiliaries

River Gunboats	£6+
Monitors	£5+
Patrol Boats	£4
Motor Torpedo Boats	£3/5
Depot Ships	£4/£5
Repair Ships	£3
Hospital Ships	£10/12
Surveying Ships	£3
Yachts.	£3/4
1939-1950 R/Ps	£2/5

HMS resolution at Algiers   £5

Others Include :-

Drifters	£4
Ice Breakers	£5
Target Ships	£3
Troopships	£3

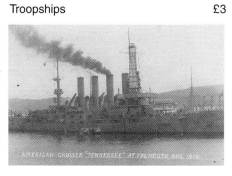

American cruiser "Tennessee" £3

The Fleet in the Thames R/P £6

Cruiser "Frobisher" £3

Torpedo Boat Destroyer "Lance" £4

Aircraft Carrier "Ark Royal" £5

Submarine "Sturgeon" £6

Sea Plane Carrier "Ark Royal" £7

Sloop "Odin" £6

Flotilla Leader "Codrington" £3

Minelayer "Adventure" £3

Destroyer "Walrus" £3

Minesweeper "Hussar" £3

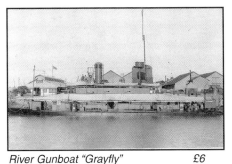

River Gunboat "Grayfly" £6

Depot Ship "Cyclops" £5

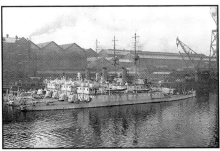

Monitors "Mersey, Humber & Severn" £8

Repair Ship "Resourse" £5

Patrol boat "P.59" £4

Hospital Ship RFA "Maine" £12

Motor Torpedo Boat £4

Surveying Ship "Gleaner" £3

NOVELTY

Today, as in the past, a strong collecting area, where the original publishers vied with each other to produce the exotic and unusual cards which now make up this category. Novelty cards are those which do something, or have things attached to them, or which deviate in any way from the norm.

Market Report
As in previous years the prices in this area have not moved much at all. As always it is the more spectacular items, Hold to light Santa's and good mechanicals for example, which have been selling.

APPLIQUED MATERIALS

Dried Flowers	£2
Feathered Birds	£10
Feathered Hats	£6
Glass Eyes	£5
Glitter Cards	£1.50
Jewellery	£3
Lace	£6
Matchbox Strikers	£12
Material	£2
Metal Models	£10
Mirror Cards	£2
Photo Inserts	£1.50
Real Hair	£10
Sand Pictures	£4
Seeds	£2

HOLD TO LIGHT

Exhibitions	£15
Father Christmas	£85
Flames	£18
Gruss Aus type	£12
Greetings/Churches etc.	£6
G.B. Views/W.H. Berlin	£4
Large Letter/Date cards	£15
Better Designs	£15

"Bearly" time to write, but here's some lovely Views of BRIGHTON

I am a "beater" of wishes, And if you'll look behind, Some lovely spots You're bound to find

Pull Out Teddy £12

COMPOSITE SETS

Animals/Set 3/5	£30/£50
G.P. Government Tea/Set 6	£120
Jeanne d'Arc/Set 10/12	£75
Jesus Christ/Set 10/12	£75
Nansen/Set 4	£400
Napoleon/Set 10/12	£75
Samurai Warriors/Set 8/10/12	£96/£144
Albert Memorial/Set 15	
F.G.O. Stuart	£60
Map of London/Set 6	
Tuck R. & Sons/Series 9352	£75

MATERIALS

Aluminium	£3
Celluloid	£3
Leather	£3
Panel Cards	£1.50
Peat	£3
Rice Paper/Oolong Tea	£10
Wood	£3

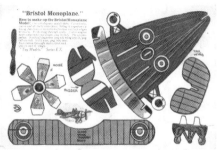

Push out £20

MECHANICAL

Blow Up	£20
Heat-activated	£6
Invisible Picture	£6
Kaleidoscopes	£30
Lever Change	£8
Moveable Hats	£5
Paper Chains	£15
Perfumed	£4
Push-Out Models	£20
Reversible Bottle/Sand etc.	£8
Squeakers	£5
Venetian Blinds	£6
Wagging Tails	£3

Cut-out Models

Tuck R. & Sons	£45+
Mack W.E./Henderson J.	£40
Star Series/Animals	£20
Later issues/Salmon J	£10

Gramophone Records

Ettlinger	£8
Tuck R. & Sons	£8
Other Publishers	£8

Jigsaw Puzzles

Tuck R. & Sons	£20
Other publishers	£12

Roller Blinds

Early type	£25
Later issues	£5

Rotating Wheels

Early type	£25
Later issues	£3

Stand-up Models

Exhibition types	£75

PULL OUTS

Animals	£3
Artist/signed	£5
Beer Bottles	£5
Buses	£6
Cats	£6
Comic	£3
Dogs	£5
Father Xmas	£10
Fortune Telling	£6
Hop-Picking	£8
Irish Subjects	£4
Mail Vans	£4
Military	£3
Motor Cars	£6
Postmen	£5
Railway Tickets named	£6
Shamrocks	£3
Teddy Bears	£12
Town views/multi-view fronts	£3
Trams	£8
Welsh Ladies	£3

SIZES

Folded	£3
Giant	£5
Midget	£3
Panorama	£5

Book Marks

Art type	£3
Actors/Actresses	£2
Egyptian Scenes	£1.50
Other types	£1.50

TRANSPARENCIES

Angels/Greetings	£6
Continental subjects	£10
Exhibitions	£15
Father Christmas	£12
GB Views/Hartmann	£8
GB Views	£3
Meteor	£10
Puzzle Type	£5

MISCELLANEOUS

Bas Relief	£3
Puzzle Cards	£4
Stamp Montage	£6

Shapes

Circular/Leaf etc.	£6

Three Dimensional

Pre-1914/With eye-piece	£6
Modern/Nudes etc.	£1

POLITICAL

A great many Political cards were published in the early days, reflecting perhaps a greater awareness of current affairs at the time. This is a major collecting area, covering Wars, Political and Social events, Suffragettes and Strikes, etc.

Market Report
A subject with a limited number of collectors, but one where some very fine cards may be found. Prices for Suffragettes have slowed this year, while other better cards will always sell to the right buyer. Social History and photographic events remain very popular.

L.Raemaekers
World War One
cartoon £6

Boer War £18

CARTOONS/WAR
BOER WAR 1899-1902

Antiquariat Bremen	£18
Bruno Burger	£18
Friedello	£18
Kunzli Freres/Thiele A	£25
Regel & Krug	£18
Ropke & Woortman	£18
Vlieger J.G.	£18
Zieher Ottmar/Thiele A	£20

BOXER REBELLION 1900-1901

Bruno Burger	£25
Kunzli Freres	£20

RUSSO-JAPANESE WAR 1904-1905

Hildesheimer/Hardy D	£15
P.L. Paris/Muller E.	£15
M.M. Paris	£15

Russo-Japanese, Tokyo Printing Co. £10

WORLD WAR I/1914-1918
Great Britain

The Hun/E. Sachetti/	
Set 6/Geo. Pulman & Sons.	£8
Davidson Bros./Ludovici A.	£5
Jarrold & Sons/Punch Cartoons	£3
Tuck R. & Sons/Aesop's Fables	
Set 6/Oilette 8484	£8
Miscellaneous Publishers	£4

France

Les Monstres des Cathedrales	£6
Miscellaneous Publishers	£4

Germany	£6

Italy

Sculpture Montage types	£5
Miscellaneous Publishers	£5

Edith Cavell

Corbella T.	£10
Mourning Cards	£6
Portraits	£3
Grave	£2

See also Silk Cards

Other Types

Human Butterflies/WWI Leaders	£10
Raemaekers, L	£6

WORLD WAR 2/1939-1945
Anti-Nazi	£12
Miscellaneous Cartoons	£8
Hitler portraits	£10-15

OTHER CAMPAIGNS
Alsace Lorraine
Hansi	£15
Miscellaneous Cartoons	£5
Bulgaria 1903	£12

Anti-Nazi cartoon by Low £12

CARTOONS/SOCIAL
GREAT BRITAIN
Anti-Semitic	£20
National Insurance Acts	£5
Shops Act	£5
Worker's Compensation Acts	£4

Fiscal
Tuck R. & Sons/Game Birds	£8
Bradshaw P.V.	£7

Masonic
Are You a Mason?
24 cards/Millar & Lang	£15
Miscellaneous Publishers	£8

Tariff Reform
Free Trade/Family in Kitchen	£1
Other Types	£6

Other types
Westminster Cartoon Series	£6
Davidson Bros/Ludovici A.	£5
Faulkner & Co./Moreland A.	£5
Walker J. & Co./Furniss H.	£5
Wrench E./Punch Cartoons 1901	£5
Miscellaneous Publishers	£4

FRANCE
Anti-Royalty/KE VII Debauchery	£10
Russia/Czar Nicholas etc.	£15

Orens D./le Burin Satirique

ITALY
Fascist Cartoons	£12
Mussolini/Portraits	£10
/Hanging	£8

DREYFUS AFFAIR
Miscellaneous issues	£10

ELECTIONS
Candidates	£8
Canvassing Cards	£8
Poll Declarations	£10

IRISH HOME RULE
ULSTER CAMPAIGN
Sir Edward Carson/Portraits	£15
Meetings/U.V.F.	£25
Political Cartoons	£12/ £30

EIRE CAMPAIGN
Easter Rising 1916	£12
Gun Running	£30
Leaders	£25
Mourning Cards	£25
Troubles 1920	£25

1916 Irish Rebellion, £10

East End Siege £8

NATIONAL SOCIALIST PARTY
This highly specialised subject has been researched and catalogued in depth by Willi Bernhard in his work BILDPOSTKARTEN SPEZIAL-KATALOG NATION-SOZIALIS-MUS 1933-1945 published Hamburg 1975.

Nationalist Socialist Party	£15
Hitler portraits	£10-15
Mosley period	£25

PERSONALITIES

Tuck R. & Sons/Empire Series	£20
Sir Winston Churchill	£8/12
Lloyd George	£5
Prime Ministers	£3/5
Cabinet Ministers	£3
Governor Generals	£3
M.P.'s Memorial Cards	£6
Foreign Personalities	£2 / £5

Faulkner C.W./Series 41

British Statesmen	£15

Great Britain

Early Vignettes	£15
Portraits/Art	£3
Portraits/Photographic	£2
House of Commons/Lords	£1.50

Herbert Henry Asquith, became Prime Minister in 1908. Photographic Card, £5

General strike R/P £25

POLITICAL EVENTS

Meetings/Treaties	£6/10
Mourning Cards	£6
Funerals	£6

Visits

Czar Nicholas to France 1896	£30
Miscellaneous visits	£6

SUFFRAGETTE CAMPAIGN

Events/Demonstrations	£85
Leaders/Portraits	£75
Publicity Cards	£75

Cartoons

Davey Geo/Suffragette Series	£30
Valentine & Sons	£30
Nat Union of Women's Suffrage Soc.	£40

STRIKES/MARCHES/UNREST

Seathwaite Navvy Riot 1904	£20
Leicester March to London 1905	£20
Belfast Strike 1907	£25
Laxey Miner's Strike 1907	£50
Winchester Riots 1908	£30
South Wales Coal Strike 1910	£35
Liverpool Strike 1910/11	
Carbonara Co.	£25
W. & Co.	£25

For full details on this series please refer to PPV 2003

Cardiff Strike 1911	£35
Llanelly Strike/Riots 1911	£35
Thirlwell Strike 1911	£55
Ilkeston Strike 1912	
Coal Picking Scenes	£75
Sydney Street Siege 1911	£8
Smethwick 1913	£50
Tonypandy Riots 1913	£30
General Strike 1926	£25
London Dock Strike	£35
Worcester Railway Strike	£50
Demonstrations/Meetings	£20

POSTCARD INTEREST

This is the study of the hobby itself, and a theme which unfortunately has very few supporters. What this does mean, of course, is that a fine collection of these cards may be built up today at nominal cost.

Market Report
One or two cards in this classification will sell, but regrettably, the majority are of interest only to the true collector of postcard history. No significant movement this year.

POSTCARD CATCH-PHRASES

Are we downhearted? No!	£1
My word! If I catch you bending	£1
My word! If you're not off	£1
On the knee	£1
We are seven	£1
When father says `turn'	£1
When shall we three meet again?	£1

POSTCARD CLUBS

International Post Carte Club	£100
Association of Picture Postcard Collectors	£25
Les Maitres de la Carte Postale	£25
Clubs & Societies/Modern	£1.50

POSTCARD COMMEMORATIVE

Besnardeau	
Published 1903	£75
(1870/71 cards are not genuine)	
Dr. Emanuel Hermann	
Postcard Jubilee 1894	£100
Signed by him	£300
Anniversary 1952	£20
German Anniversary 1939	
70 years of the Postcard	£20

POSTCARD COMPETITIONS

Faulkner C.W.	
Place in order	£5
St. Paul's Hospital/Set 12	
£1000 Competition	£1
Shurey's Great Prize Competition	£1.50
Tuck R. & Sons	
1900/Largest collection	£12
1902/Largest collection	£12
1904-5 Place in order	£6
1909/in two parts	£3
1914/Largest collection	£3
Father Tuck's Painting Book	
Colouring Cards/Pairs	£3

POSTCARD EXHIBITIONS

1894-1896	£150
1897-1899	£100
1900-1920	£50
1921-1969	£15
1966/Friendly Cities	£20
1970/Century of British Postcards	£5
1970/V & A Museum	£8

POSTCARD RESEARCH

Advert Cards/Poster type	£50
Bray Cards	
From the W.R. Bray collection	£5
Cards featuring Publishers' Offices/Adverts etc.	£8
Different Captions to same postcard	£1.50
Incorrect spelling	£1.50
Packets/Lists	
With details of contents	£1.50
Photographer's Holes	£1
Postcard Displays	
Collections/Indoors etc.	£10
Postcard Shops/Displays	£30
Postcards featuring or mentioning postcards	£4
Postcards used as trade calling cards	£3
Proofs/Trials	
Plain back	£1.50
Publisher's specimens	
With prices	£3
Without prices	£1.50
Re-entries/Up-dating	
Motor Cars added etc.	£3
Shorthand/Code messages	£1.50
Souvenir Cards	
Lands End cachet	£2
Snaefell Summit cachet	£2
Snowdon Summit cachet	£2
Other locations	£2

RAILWAYS

As the dominant mode of transport in the Edwardian years, this subject was very well covered by the publishers of the time. The Railway Companies themselves led the way with a great number of sets and series extolling the virtue of travel on their own particular lines, and here the less common cards, or those from the smaller Companies, are highly sought after. As well as the correspondence cards listed here, many ordinary set cards were overprinted for correspondence or advertising use. These command a premium of no more than a couple of pounds.

OFFICIAL CARDS

A term used to describe postcards issued/sold by railway companies to gain revenue and to promote all aspects of their business. Subjects depicted include Hotels, Ships and Buses.

PRE-1923 COMPANIES

BARRY
Paddle Steamers	£10
Barry Island/Coloured view	£30
Barry Docks/Correspondence	£40

BELFAST AND COUNTY DOWN
Slieve Donard Hotel/Jotter	£10
Hotels/bw	£12

BIDEFORD, WESTWARD HO AND APPLEDORE
Views/Trains	£25

CALEDONIAN
Engines/Rolling Stock
Sepia	£4
Coloured	£5

Hotels
General views	£5
Interiors/bw	£6
Interiors/Coloured	£8
Poster Adverts	£20

Views
Coloured/ Valentines	£4
coloured/ other	£6
Black/White	£10
Tartan Border	£8
Clyde Steamers/Clyde views	£10
Vignette/Multi-view/Pic both sides	£20
Green or Brown artwork/1903	£30

Poster Adverts
Shipping/Coloured	£30
Other types	£75

CALEDONIAN AND LNW
West Coast Joint Stock/Coloured	£8
Sleeping Car/Reservation card	£40

Royal Mail Route
Coloured	£15
Black/White	£15

CALLANDER & OBAN
Ballachulish Hotel	£10
Views/Booklet sepia	£15

CAMBRIAN
Views	£6
Holiday Advertising/Correspondence	£12
Maps	£22
Vignette/PicturePostcard Co.	£25

CAMPBELTOWN & MACRIHANISH
Advertising	£80

CENTRAL LONDON
Celesque Series	£8
Maps/Rolling Stock	£20
1911 Strike	£50
Poster Adverts	£40

Exhibitions
Pillar Box Pullout	£35
Blow Card	£75

CHESHIRE LINES
Views/Correspondence	£30

CORK BANDON & SOUTH COAST
Views/Oilettes	£4

CORK BLACKROCK & PASSAGE
Paddle Steamer `Audrey'	£40

CORRIS
Views
Corris Railway Series/Photographic	£8
/Printed	£12
As above but Georges	£5

DISTRICT RAILWAY
Vignettes
Court size/Pictorial Postcard Syndicate	£40
Intermediate/Pictorial Postcard Company	£35

DUBLIN & SOUTH EASTERN
Hotel/Jotter	£10
Views/Correspondence	£30

DUBLIN, WICKLOW & WEXFORD
Peacock Series/Correspondence £35
Views/Undivided Back £35

DUMBARTON & BALLOCH JOINT LINES
Views
Black/White £10
Coloured £12

EAST COAST ROUTE
Flying Scotsman/Hildesheimer £4
Views/Rolling Stock/Stations £12
Vignette/Write Away £10

FESTINIOG
Views/Photochrom £8
Views/Valentines £10
Poster Adverts £90

FRESHWATER YARMOUTH & NEWPORT
Vignette/Picture Postcard Co. £40

FURNESS
Engines & Rolling Stock/Series 18-19 £6
G. Romney Art/Series 12-13 £24
Exhibitions £45
Poster Adverts/Series 21 £90
Views
Furness Abbey/Series 14-15 £1.50
McCorquodale £4
Tuck/Series 1-7 £3
Tuck/Series 8 £4
Furness Abbey Hotel/Series 16-17 £6
HHH Series £15
Sankey/Tours through Lakeland £25
Vignettes/McCorquodale £40
Steamers
Lake Steamers/Series 9-11 £5
Barrow & Fleetwood Steamers/Ser. 20 £15

GLASGOW & SOUTH WESTERN
Poster Adverts £75
Steamers
McCorquodale £3
Other publishers £10
Hotels
General views £4
Multi-view £6
Tuck/Chromo-litho £10
Views
Oilettes £5
Vignettes £20

GREAT CENTRAL
Immingham Docks £4
Hotels £6
Engines/Rolling Stock £18

Restaurant Car £15
Poster Adverts £65
Perforated Engine Card/
Central Advertising Co. £90
Shipping
Overprints on other company cards £20
Printed £14
Photographic £16
Turner C.E. £12
Steam Ship Department £40
Tuck £30
Views
Faulkner Series 545 & 546 £8
as / panel cards £4
HHH Series £20
Vignettes/Picture Postcard Co. £30

GREAT EASTERN
Stations./Trains £6
Hotels £7
Underground Railway Maps of London £6
Southwold Bus £15
Poster Adverts £90
Views
Crest on Picture/Oilettes £3
Crest on Picture/bw £4
Shipping
Black & White £8
Coloured £10
Black & White/Correspondence £12
Correspondence
General types £25
Jarrold £35
Oilette type £25
Vignettes
Greetings from Harwich £12
Tuck cathedrals £75
Cathedrals
Faulkner/Series 118 £60
Faulkner with crest £75

GREAT NORTH OF SCOTLAND
Views/Porter £25
Cruden Bay Golf Tournament £80
/Named Players £100
Hotels
Palace Hotel Series £15
Multi-view £25
Multi-view/Pictures both sides £30

GREAT NORTHERN
Hotels £6
Correspondence £25
Panoramic/Skegness & Sheringham £30
Poster Adverts £90

123

Engines

Photochrom	£2
Locomotive Publishing Co.	£5

Views2 Photochrom/Coloured

£3	
Black & White	£30

Vignettes

London views/Picture Postcard Co.	£25
Coloured	£40
Intermediate/Picture Postcard Co.	£35

GREAT NORTHERN & CITY

Views/bw Poster style	£35
Map	£50

GREAT NORTHERN/IRELAND

Correspondence	£15
Views/Overprint on picture	£25
Hotels/Multi-view	£18
Milroy Bay Motor Bus	£40

GREAT NORTHERN PICCADILLY &BROMPTON

Railway scenes	£8
Map	£25

GREAT SOUTHERN/IRELAND

Hotels	£6

GREAT SOUTHERN & WESTERN/ IRELAND

Views/Oilettes	£4
Joint with MGW/Wembley 1924	£25
Parknasilla Hotel/Motor Bus/ Stage Coach Tours	£15
Poster Adverts/Parknasilla/	£70

Hotels

Jotter	£6
Lawrence/Correspondence	£12
Hotels in the Kingdom of Kerry	£20

GREAT WESTERN

Docks Series	£10
Fishguard Harbour/Route	£8
Motor Bus/Slough	£12
Restaurant Car/En Route	£18
Maps/with GWR crest	£40

Engines

Series 6	£2
Others	£4

Shipping

Photographic	£5
Coloured	£12

Views

Coloured or Sepia	£4

Hotels

General types	£4
Vignette	£8

Correspondence

General	£20
Wyndhams	£18

Poster Adverts

General types	£50
Series 3	£90

Vignettes

Intermediate/Picture Postcard Co.	£22
/London views	£30
Court Size/London views	£30

HAMPSTEAD TUBE
Views

Last Link	£6
Multi-view/Map on reverse	£12

HIGHLAND

Map/Correspondence	£75

Hotels

Inverness	£5
Others	£10

Views

Circular crest/bw	£12
Straight line inscription	£15
Highland Railway photos	£25
Early coloured/Red circular crest	£40

HULL & BARNSLEY

Scenes at Alexandra Dock etc.	£35
Views	£35
Train	£40

INVERGARRY & FORT AUGUSTUS

Views/Highland Railway series	£30

ISLE OF WIGHT

Vignettes/Picture Postcard Co.	£35

ISLE OF WIGHT CENTRAL

Vignettes/Picture Postcard Co.	£35
Views	£40

JOINT SOUTH WESTERN & BRIGHTON

Vignettes/Picture Postcard Co.	£35

KENT & EAST SUSSEX

Engines/Correspondence	£8
Views/1-6	£7
Other Correspondence cards	£35

LANCASHIRE & YORKSHIRE

Correspondence	£30
Vignettes/Picture Postcard Co.	£25

Engines/Rolling Stock

General issues	£3
Overprinted French	£6

Views

1905 &1907 series	£3
New series	£4
Overprinted French/All series	£5

Shipping

1907 series	£4
New series	£6
Overprinted French/All series	£7
Liverpool and Drogheda Steamers	£35

LIVERPOOL OVERHEAD

Dock views	£25

LONDON, BRIGHTON & SOUTH COAST

Correspondence	£40
Poster Adverts	£90

Views

Waterlow/Series 1-6	£4

Vignettes

French vignettes/Red overprint	£15
Picture Postcard Co.	£25

LONDON, CHATHAM & DOVER
Vignettes/Court Size

Black/White	£25
Coloured	£35

LONDON & NORTH WESTERN
McCorquodale

Engines/Rolling Stock	£2/£4
Views	£2
Hotels	£4
Shipping	£3
Buses/Lorries etc.	£10
/Horse drawn	£6
Exhibitions	£20
Poster Adverts	£80
Maps/Correspondence	£80

Tuck

Coloured/Royal Trains etc.	£1
Engines/Rolling Stock	£2
Views	£3
Shipping	£4
Hotels	£4

St. Louis Exposition/Undivided back

Exhibits/Multi-view	£6
Tuck/bw	£10
Tuck/Coloured	£15

LONDON & SOUTH WESTERN

Orphanage	£4
View with crest/Correspondence	£40

Shipping

Black/White	£6
Coloured/Early	£18

Poster Adverts

Southampton Hotel	£45
Other Posters	£80

Vignettes

Pictorial Postcard Syndicate	£35
Intermediate/Picture Postcard Co.	£22
London views/Picture Postcard Co.	£22

LONDON UNDERGROUND ELECTRIC
Poster Adverts

W.H.S.	£15
London Nooks and Corners	£40
Other types	£40

LONDONDERRY & LOUGH SWILLY

Map/Correspondence	£60

LYNTON & BARNSTAPLE

Views/Stations/Trains	£18

MARYPORT & CARLISLE

Map/Correspondence	£90

MERSEY

Views/Stations/Lifts/Trains	£12
Poster Advert	£80

METROPOLITAN

Correspondence	£15
Maps	£15

VIEWS

Sepia/1-30	£5
Black/White	£15

METROPOLITAN DISTRICT

Engines/Rolling Stock	£6

MIDLAND

Engines	£3
Rolling Stock	£8
Midland Express/St. Pancras	£5
Ships	£6
Carriages	£10
Exhibitions	£18
Maps	£20
Heysham Electric Train	£25

Views

Photochrom	£4
Nearest Station/Coloured	£12

Hotels

General types	£4
Vignettes/Coloured	£6
/Travel & Entertainment	£30
/BW & Sepia	£18
Midland Grand Hotel/Business Lunch	£90

Vignettes

Black/White	£15
Coloured/Andrew Reid	£20

Poster Adverts

General types	£25
Series	£75

MIDLAND & GREAT NORTHERN JOINT

Views/Correspondence	£40

MIDLAND GREAT WESTERN

Hotels	£6
Wembley Exhibition/Trade Stand	£18

MIDLAND/NORTHERN COUNTIES COMMITTEE

Trains	£12
Views/Correspondence	£35

NEWPORT GODSHILL & ST.LAWRENCE

Vignette/Picture Postcard Co.	£35

NORTH BRITISH

Ships/Coloured	£6
Ships/BW with crest	£12
Scottish Exhibition/Poster overprint	£40

Hotels

General types	£3
Poster Adverts	£8

Views

NBR Series/Caledonia 129	£3
Black/White & Coloured	£12
With crest	£14
Photo/White or decorated border	£15

NORTH EASTERN

Hotels/ York & Newcastle	£2
Hotels/ Others	£5
Riverside Quay/Hull	£5
Newcastle Electric Trains	£6
Brussels Exhibition	£12
Steam Goods Lorry	£50

Views

Photo Panoramic/1-40	£20
/Maps below picture	£30

Poster Adverts

General types	£75
Industrial Poster Reproductions	£90

NORTH STAFFORDSHIRE

Correspondence	£15

Views

McCorquodale/W&K	£4
W&K and W&TG/White border	£7
Golf	£30
Glossy anon.	£15

PORTPATRICK & WIGTOWNSHIRE JOINT

Ships	£18
Views	£35

SNOWDON MOUNTAIN RAILWAY

General types	£4
Snowdon Series/1-90	£8
Maps	£40
Poster Adverts	£60

Court Cards

Advertising/Hotel & Railway	£65

SOMERSET & DORSET JOINT

Views/Correspondence	£60

SOUTH EASTERN AND CHATHAM

Views/McCorquodale	£3
Engines/Rolling Stock	£3
Stations/Trains	£4
Hotels	£6
Ships	£4
London-Paris/English or French	£12
Bologne views/Stevenard	£12
Exhibitions	£8
Views/Correspondence	£25
Maps	£22
Poster Adverts	£90

SOUTH EASTERN & CHATHAM & DOVER

Vignettes

London views/Picture Postcard Co. etc.	£20
Intermediate/Picture Postcard Co.	£25
Pictorial Postcard Syndicate	£35

STRATFORD-ON-AVON & MIDLAND JUNCTION

Poster Advert	£100

VALE OF RHEIDOL

Views/Advertising overprints	£15

WEST CLARE

Views	£25

WEST HIGHLAND

Views	£6

WESTON, CLEVEDON & PORTISHEAD LIGHT

Train	£35

WICK AND LYBSTER

Views/Highland Railway Series	£35

WIRRAL

Views/Correspondence	£60
Map/Correspondence	£80

POST - 1923 COMPANIES

GREAT WESTERN

Engines	£3
Views	£4
Hotels	£4
KGV/Folded locomotive card	£75
Poster Adverts	£60

LONDON MIDLAND & SCOTTISH

Engines	£3
Hotels	£4
Ships	£6
Camping Coaches	£12
Views/Holiday tickets	£12
Container services/Removals	£35
Poster Adverts	£30

LONDON & NORTH EASTERN

Engines/Trains	£4
Hotels	£4
Ships	£8
Views	£8
Camping Coaches	£10
Paddle Steamers	£6
Poster Adverts	£90

Northern Belle Cruise Train

Unused	£25
Used on Train with Cachet	£75

SOUTHERN

Engines/Trains	£3
Ships	£5
Poster Adverts/LBSCR	£90

Views

Coloured/L. Richmond	£25
Correspondence	£35

POST-1947/BRITISH RAILWAYS

Hotels	£3
Ships	£3
Trains	£3
Gleneagles/Turnberry Golf Courses	£10
Seaspeed/Hovercraft	£1.50
Birmingham/New St. Station	£4
Correspondence	£4
Kyle of Lochalsh Station	£5
Poster Adverts	£15

NON-OFFICIAL CARDS

ACCIDENTS

Cudworth	£6
Grantham 1906	£4
Shrewsbury 1907	£6
Salisbury 1906	£6
Witham1905	£4
W. Gothard/In Memoriam type	£15/£75
Miscellaneous	£15+

OVERSEAS RAILWAYS

Engines	£3

FRENCH POSTERS/OFFICIAL ISSUES

Orleans post-1920	£8
Artist signed	£12
Chemins de Fer de l'Quest	£8
Chromo-litho/Undivided back	£25

FUNICULAR & CLIFF RAILWAYS/LIFTS

Lynton-Lynmouth	£2
Other UK	£5
Overseas	£3

LOCOMOTIVES

Oilettes	£3
OJ Morris	£3
E.Pouteau	£4
Locomotive PublishingCo./ F.Moore	£2.50
Real Photographic	£2
France/F. Fleury	£3
Other Artist Drawn cards	£2.50

MINIATURE RAILWAYS

Ravenglass & Eskdale	£5
Romney, Hythe & Dymchurch	£3
Volk's Electric Railway	£3
Other Railways	£6

MISCELLANEOUS

Animated Scenes	£10
Bridges/Tunnels/Viaducts	£4
Level Crossings	£20
Locomotive Works	£12
Locomotive Sheds	£6
Motor buses/ road vehicles	£20
Railway Staff	£8
Signal Boxes	£15
Trains on the Line	£3

Locomotive Publishing Co.

Vignettes/Coloured	£30
Vignettes/Monochrome	£25

MOUNTAIN RAILWAYS

Snowdon/Non-Official	£1.50
Overseas	£2

NARROW GAUGE

Vale of Rheidol	£3
Others	£6

RAILWAY STATIONS

Large City Stations

Interior	£8
Exterior	£4

Others

Interior	£40
Exterior	£20

UNDERGROUND RAILWAYS

London Transport	£10
Foreign/U. Bahnes/Metros	£6

RAILWAYS

Railway signal man £8

Southern Railway, Golden Arrow £3

Locomotive at Victoria station R/P £10

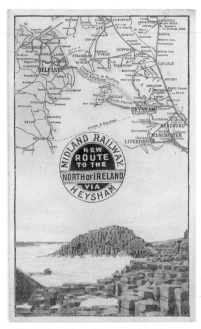

Midland railway Map card £18

Miniature Railway, Hythe £3

MEMORIES
THE COLLECTORS SHOP
130 Brent Street Hendon, London NW4 2DR
OPEN MONDAY TO SATURDAY, 11.00am - 5pm
(Postcard appraisals Thurs-Sat 11-5pm)
HUGE STOCKS OF POSTCARDS FOR SALE,
PLUS CIGARETTE CARDS & EPHEMERA.

MEMORIES Photography and Framing David Smith

Real photographic reproductions from your originals or negatives. 25 years experience in black and white and sepia photography. We Also offer a full framing and mounting service.Trade terms available

Sporting Memories
Philip Smith offers large stocks of Sporting collectables. We also pay Top prices for sports postcards and ephemera

ROAD TRANSPORT

The majority of these cards were the work of the town or village photographer and produced for the local topographical market. Consequently they were never issued in any great number, which is why they are so highly rated today. Many are now finding their way to auction, being sold as single cards at prices ranging up to £75 each.

London Horse drawn Bus £10

It is pointed out that for all relevant entries e.g. Buses, Lorries, Traction Engines, Trams etc. the stated prices are for cards, either RP or Printed, fully identified and showing a 'Close-up at a named location' with real photographic cards being the most desirable. Unlocated cards and middle or far-distance views would be priced accordingly.

BUSES

Steam	£40
Horse-drawn	
Real Photographic (close up)	£30/£50
Printed	£15
London horse-drawn/Coloured	£10
Motor	
Real Photographic	£40
Printed	£25
Charabancs	

Trolleybuses

Pre-1939	£30
1940 onwards	£15

Trolleybus in street scene £10

Coaches/Single-deck £12/£20
There are in circulation many privately produced, postcard-size, plain back photographs of Buses and Trams.
Most of these have been printed in quantity from an existing negative and consequently have only a nominal value.

Gillingham Bus depot R/P £25

Whole Vehicle	£8
Part Vehicle	£3

Girl's friendly society caravan £35

LORRIES

Petrol Tankers	£30
Vans	£25
Coachbuilders' advertising cards/	
RP studies of Lorries/Removal Vans	£6

Steam

Commercial	£40
Military	£20

Motor

Lorry Fleets/Groups/RP	£50
Commercial	£30
Military	£20

Advert Cards

Poster Type	£35
Other Adverts	£12

Where applicable, prices are for trade vehicles sign-written with company name and location.

Real Photo horse Box advert card £30

Three wheel delivery van £25

MOTOR CYCLES

Close-up	£20
With Sidecar	£20

Advert Cards

Poster Type (Colour)	£35
Other Adverts	£12

TRACTION ENGINES

Showmans	£50
Commercial	£30
Agricultural	£30
Military	£20
Steam Rollers	£30
Repair Gangs	£25
Accidents	£50

Real Photo Agricutural. Traction Engine £30

Motor Cycle Club meet, Norwich £20

Motor Cycle R/P £20

MOTOR RACING
MOTOR CYCLE RACING
SEE SPORT PAGES 158-163

MOTOR CARS

Pre-1918	£12
1918-1939	£8
1940 onwards	£5
Garages	£30
Exhibitions/GB and Foreign	£6
Factories and Works/Interiors	£12
Celebrities of the Motoring World/	
Set 6/Tuck Oilette 9017	£6

Advert cards

Poster Type	£35
Other Adverts/Pre-1939	£15
/1940 onwards	£5

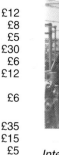

Interior of Vauxhall factory R/P £10

Motor Garage   £25

Caravan and car, Advert Cosby £20

Left hand drive ford model T £30

Real Photo Early Motor car £15

Car outside mews garage £10

Modified cars at Pontefract   £15

TRAMS

Steam Trams	£35
Electric Trams	£35
Horse-drawn Trams	£35
Track-laying/Removal	£35
Trials	£30
Opening Ceremonies	£35
First Tram	£35
Last Tram	£20
Commemorative Cards	£25
In Memoriam Cards	£15
Tram Graveyards Early	£35

Decorated Cars	£8
Depots	£35
Works Vehicles	£30
Douglas S.E. Tramway	£6

OTHER TRANSPORT

Ambulances

Horse-drawn	£35
Motor	£20

Fire Engines

Hand Drawn	£40
Horse Drawn	£40
Motor	£40

Royal Mail Vans	£35

There are in circulation many privately produced, postcard-size, plain back photographs of Fairground and Showman's engines.
Most of these have been printed in quantity froman existing negative and consequently have a nominal value of maybe £5

Pontypridd R/Photo £35

Bristol tramway centre R/P £25

Trams, Five Lamps Waterloo £35

Paddington Fire Station Pr. £30

Middlesbrough decorated car £8

133

ROYALTY

I think the British Royal Family, and the many European dynasties at the turn of the century, must have been looked upon as a commercial goldmine by the Edwardian publishers. The vast numbers of cards handed down to us bears adequate testimony to their popularity at the time, when all types of Royal personages and Events both British and Foreign were subject to volume output by the picture postcard industry. I suppose the same is true today, as interest in this field has continued unabated through the years. And yet, it is perhaps fair to say that the wide public interest in Royalty and their doings, is not reflected in current price levels for historical picture postcards, for while the more unusual Portraits and Events will always sell, as will the many superb chromo-litho foreign commemorative issues, the bulk of the catalogue consisting of the more common GB types has always proved difficult.

Market Report
There have always been buyers for the more unusual cards in this field, there has been little movement in the more common british Royals and dealer's boxes are still full of this type of material which nobody seems to want. Overseas Royals have shown an increase in popularity.

GREAT BRITAIN
QUEEN VICTORIA
Diamond Jubilee 1897

p.u. 1897	£150
Unused	£75

Mourning Cards 1901 £20

Portraits £8

KING EDWARD VII
Royal Tour 1901/'Ophir'
Wrench/Links of Empire/Set 20

p.u. from Ports of Call	£30
Unposted	£15

Queen Victoria R/P £15

Royal Tour 1901 / 'Ophir'
Tuck R. & Sons/Empire Series 1649

p.u. from Ports of Call	£30
Unposted	£15

Coronation 1902
Tuck R. & Sons/Coronation Series/

Embossed	£12
Stewart & Woolf/Set 10	£10
H.Cassiers/London View Series	£8
Other Souvenir Cards	£8
Coronation Souvenir/bw£4	
Coronation Procession	£2

Visits to Paris 1903

Tuck R. & Sons/Set 10	£8
Voisey Chas./Set 15	£8

Death 1910

Mourning Cards	£3
Funeral Procession	£1

Visits

GB	£12
Foreign	£8
Portraits	£1.50

KING GEORGE V
Coronation 1911

Souvenir Cards	£3
Coronation Procession	£1

Delhi Durbar 1911 £2

Silver Jubilee 1935

Souvenir Cards	£4
Procession	£1.50

Death 1936

Mourning Cards	£4
Funeral Procession	£1.50

Visits

GB	£12
Foreign	£8
Portraits	£1.50

KING EDWARD VIII

Investiture as Prince of Wales 1911	£3
Coronation Souvenir	£6
Wedding Souvenir	£35

		OVERSEAS

		OVERSEAS
With Mrs Simpson	£40	*It will be seen that an equivalent list to the*
Visits		*foregoing could be produced for every coun-*
GB	£20	*try in the world which has had a Monarchy at*
Foreign	£15	*any time since 1869! This remains a vast,*
Portraits	£3	*uncharted field, where much research is yet*
		to be done. I give below a general guide to
KING GEORGE VI		*price for the Commemorative Souvenir cards*
Coronation 1937		*already known.*
Souvenir Cards	£6	
Coronation Procession	£2	**ROYAL EVENTS**
Visit to France 1938	£10	**1888-1891**
Victory Celebrations 1945	£5	**1892-1895**
Mourning Cards 1952	£10	**1896-1899**

ROYAL EVENTS

1888-1891	£50
1892-1895	£35
1896-1899	£25
1900-1902	£20
1903-1907	£15
1908-1914	£10
1915 onwards	£5

Visits

GB	£12
Foreign	£8
Portraits	£1.50

PORTRAITS

Balkans/Eastern Europe	£8
Belgium/Spain	£2
Other Countries	£6
Weddings	£6

QUEEN ELIZABETH II
Marriage 1947

Souvenir Cards	£5
Betrothal Souvenir Cards	£3

Russia

Continental Publishers	£30
Cartoons	£30
British Publishers	£25

Coronation 1953

Souvenir Cards	£4
Coronation Procession	£1

Prince of Wales Investiture 1969	£1.50
Silver Wedding 1972	£1
Silver Jubilee 1977	£1

Visits/Pre-1970

GB	£6
Foreign	£4
Portraits	£1/£4

MISCELLANEOUS EVENTS

Coronation Bonfires	£18
Proclamations	£10
Royal Gatherings	£3
Royal Weddings	£3

N.B. Portraits include family groups. Less photographed members of the Royal Family, e.g. Prince John, together with other examples of minor Royalty, would be worth around £1.50+.

SERIES
Kings & Queens of England
Tuck R. & Sons/Set 42

Price per card	£12
King Insurance Co.	£6
Faulkners Series	£8

THE NEW KING AND QUEEN OF BULGARIA

King Ferdinand of Bulgaria with his 2nd wife Princess Eleonore von reuss Kostritz. R/P £8

SHIPPING

R. M. S. "AQUITANIA".

MAIN STAIRCASE. R.M.S. AQUITANIA.

R.M.S. "AQUITANIA." Grill Room.

CUNARD LINE. R.M.S. "AQUITANIA". PALADIAN LOUNGE.

Cunard Line's Aquitania was built by John Brown & Co., Ltd., Clydebank. Her maiden voyage across the atlantic, took place in May 1914. She was requisitioned by the government and converted to a troop ship during World War One. In 1919 she returned to civilian duties and finally finished service in 1949.
Top: FGO Sttuart card R/P £10 . Interiors showing the opulent designs R/P £5 each.

The 'Titanic' was one of three sister ships for the White Star Line. Olympic and Britannic being the other two, Built by Harland & Wolff Ltd in Belfast. She famously 'went down' in 1912, before many cards were produced. The majority of cards being 'in memorium' and cards showing the Olympic.
Top: Quite scarce Black and white printed card £100+ Middle Left: Olympic LL card £20
Middle right: French card £35 Bottom: This is one of the most common, it actually shows the 'Olympic' R/P £45

SHIPPING

A great number of cards were issued during the early years of the century, and indeed later, perhaps reflecting the dependence which an island nation placed upon the sea. Always a popular theme with collectors, there has been a steady supply of new cards issued on this subject, thanks largely to the many Shipping Companies, who continued publishing through-out the depressed inter-war years, when the flow of more general cards abated.

With the expert knowledge of Tom Stanley, we have once again, reviewed this section.

ADVERTISING

1. This listing is not definitive, and never can be until all cards published by the Shipping Companies are fully known and understood.

2. A certain difficulty exists in defining exactly what constitutes an Advertising card. It could be argued that all cards issued by the Companies are Advertising Cards, since the reason for their issue was to gain publicity.

3. Not only is the life of a ship a factor, but also its role, as many ships were subject to considerable modification at different stages in their career. Number of funnels may change, or the ship may have been pressed into hospital ship service. Some companies issue pictures of their ships in war-time dazzle painting for example, and there are many other changes to which a ship could be subject to.

Liverpool & North Wales Advertising £25

Hamburg-Amerika Line Advertising £27

S.S. Solent Queen. advertising at £15

4. A true Shipping catalogue should ideally also list every ship, but this is a daunting, if not impossible task. Some ships lasted for forty years while others sank on their maiden voyage.

5. The number of ships owned by any one company, when multiplied by several hundred Shipping Companies, gives some idea of the difficulties to be faced when attempting anything like a comprehensive listing. For example, between 1890 and 1960 the Hamburg America Line commissioned no less than 600 ships! P&O 180, Royal Mail 160, and Cunard and Union-Castle 100 each! And these are approximate figures!

*Such is the complexity of this whole section, it must be clearly understood that even within the stated price ranges, the quoted figures represent no more than a general guide. It is not possible to be specific when the individual ship, i.e. `Titanic' or `Carpathia', may be worth far more than the figure given for its Shipping Line. On the one hand, cards of certain ships are very common indeed, while for other ships no card is known to exist!

Aberdeen & Commonwealth Line (GB)
Ships £5
Aberdeen Direct (Rennie) Line (GB)
B&W ship vignettes £10
Ships £3/£8
Aberdeen Line (GB)
B&W ship vignettes £10
Ships £5/£10

Aberdeen Line £10

Aberdeen, Newcastle & Hull (GB)
Ships £12
Aberdeen Steam Navigation (GB)
Ships £5/£10
Adelaide Steamship (Australia)
Ships £10
Adler Line (Germany)
Cable laying scenes £8/10
Adriatica Line (Italy)
Ships/Photographs/Printed £3/5
Ships/Coloured impressions £2/6
Affreteurs Reunis, Cie. De. (France)
Ships £4/5
Alaska Steamships (USA)
Ships £5
Alcoa (USA)
Ships £3/5
Allan Line (Canada)
Adverts/Chromo-Litho £20/30

AllanLine £8.

Adverts £12/£18
Ships £8
Deck views etc./Coloured £5
American Banner Line (USA)
Ships £5
American Export Line (USA)
Ships £5
American Hawaiian Line (USA)
Ships £4
American Line (USA)
Adverts/Chromo-Litho £25
Coloured ship vignettes £18
Ships £3/£6

American Mail Line (USA)
Ships £2/5
American President Lines (USA)
Ships £2/5
Anchor Line (GB)

Anchor Line ship card £6

Adverts £15/£20
Coloured ship vignettes £15
Ships £3/£8
Anglo-American Nile & Tourist Co.
Ships £10

Anglo-Egyptian Mail Line (GB)
Ships £6
Poster Ads £20
Arosa Line (Panama)
Ships £3
Associated Humber Lines (GB)
Ships £5
Atlantic Transport Lines (USA)
Adverts £12/£15
Adverts.Chromo-Litho £20
Ships £3/£8
Australasian United S.N. (A.U.S.N.)
Ships with flag £10

Australian Commonwealth Line (Australia)
Ships   £5

Australind Steam Navigation Co. (GB)
Ships   £4/£10

Aznar Line (Spain)
Ships   £2/£5

Baltimore Mail Line (USA)
Ships   £1.50/£5

Bank Line (GB)
Ships/Passenger   £5

Barry & Bristol Channel(GB)
Paddle Steamers   £10

Bateaux "Moulettes" (France)
River steamers   £3

Belfast Steamship Co. (GB)
Adverts   £22
Coloured ship vignettes   £15
Ships   £2/£5

Belle Steamers (GB)
Paddle steamers   £8

Bennett Line (GB)
Adverts   £20
Ships   £10

Bergen (inc. B&N) Line (Norway)
Ships   £1.50/£10

Bibby line ship card £7.50

Bibby Line (GB)
Adverts   £12/£30
Ships   £3/£10
Deck games   £3
Views   £2.50

Bland Line (Gibraltar)
Adverts   £30
B&W ship vignettes   £8
Ships   £1.50/£5

Blue Funnel Line (GB)
Adverts   £10/£20
Ships   £1.50/£8

Blue Funnel Line Coloured cards £8

Blue Star Line (GB)
Ships   £3/£10

Bombay Steam Navigation Co. (India)
Ships   £4

Booker Line (GB)
Ships   £1.50/£10

Booth Line (GB)
Adverts/Chromo-Litho   £22
B&W adverts/Ships   £8/£14
/Interiors etc.   £4
Ships   £4/£10
Coloured views   £2/£5

Bore Line (Finland)
Chromo-Litho Adverts   £20
Ships   £1/£4

Bornholm Line (Denmark)
Ships   £1/£3

Bournemouth & South Coast S.P. Co. (GB)
Adverts   £30
Paddle Steamers   £12

British India Line (GB)
Adverts   £20
Ships/Coloured impressions   £10
Ships   £1.50/£5

British & Irish S.P. Co. (GB)
Adverts   £25
Ships   £5/£12
Interiors   £2

Brugge-Sluis (Holland)
Ships/timetables   £10

Bucknall Steamship Lines (GB)
Adverts   £28
Coloured ship vignettes   £20

Bull Lines (USA)
Ships   £5

Burns & Laird Lines (GB)
Ships   £5/£10

Burns Line (GB)
Adverts   £30
Ships   £5

Burns Philp (Australia)
Ships £10

Caledonian Steam Packet (GB)
Adverts £20
Paddle steamers/Ships £4/£12

Campbell P&A, (GB)
Paddle steamers £4/£12

Canada Steamship Lines (Canada)
Ships £4
Views £1

Canadian Australasian Line (Canada/NZ)
Advert vignettes £15
Ships £5

Canadian National Steamships (Canada)
Ships £2/£10

Canadian Pacific Steamships (Canada)
Adverts/Chromo-Litho £20/£30
Adverts/Poster Type £20/£28
Ships/Ocean Passenger £2/£10
Ships/Lake £1.50/£4
Interiors £2/£4
Views £2/£4

Canadian Pacific Ocean passenger £7.50

Carron Line (GB)
Adverts £30

Castle Line (GB)
Adverts £35

Cawston (GB)
River steamers £5

Central Hudson Steamboat (USA)
Ships £4
Interiors £2

Chandris Line (Greece)
Ships £1/£4

Chargeurs Reunis, Cie. Des. (France)
Ships/Coloured £10
Ships/Sepia £2/£5
Interiors £2

Chemin De Fer Du Congo Superior (Belgium)
Ships £15

Chicago-Duluth Trans. Co. (USA)
Ships £10

China Navigation Co. (GB)
Adverts £22
Ships £1.50/£10

City Line (GB)
Adverts £25

City of Cork Steam Packet (GB)
Adverts £20
Ships £3/£6

City of Dublin Steam Packet Co £15

City of Dublin Steam Packet (GB)
Adverts £22
Coloured ship vignettes £20
Ships/Chromo-Litho £15

City Steamboat Co. (GB)
Paddle steamers £10

Cleveland & Buffalo Line (USA)
Ships £2/£5

Clipper Line (Sweden)
Ships £4

Clyde Line (USA)
Ships £3/£12

Clyde-Mallory Lines (USA)
Ships £4

Clyde Shipping Co. (GB)
Adverts £15/£22
Ships £3/£7

Coast Lines (GB)
Ships £1.50/£10

Cogedar Lines (Italy)
Ships £1.50/£3

Colonial Navigation Co. (USA)
Ships £10

Colonial De Nav., Chia., (Portugal)
Ships £1.50/£4

Colwyn Bay & Liverpool SS Co. (GB)
Adverts £30
Paddle steamers £8

Constantine Line (GB)
Ships   £1.50/£5

Cook's Tourist Steamers (GB)
Nile steamers   £4/£7

Cosens & Co. (GB)
Paddle steamers   £4/£15

Costa Line (Linea "C") (Italy)
Ships   £1/£5

Cunard Line (GB)
Adverts   £15/£30
Ships   £1.50/£10
Cunarder at ...   £5
Interiors/Coloured   £1.50/£5
Interiors   £3

Cunard Line, Photo card   £6

Currie Line (GB)
Ships   £1.50/£5

Cosulich Line (Italy)
Ships   £3/£10

Dairen K.K. (Japan)
Ships   £10
Ships inset into views   £10

Dansk-Statsbaner (Denmark)
Ships   £1.50/£3

DFDS (Denmark)
Ships   £2/£5

Detroit & Cleveland Line (USA)
Ships   £5

Deutsche Ost-Afrika Line (Germany)
Ship vignettes   £20
Ships   £4/£10
Interiors   £4

Dollar Steamship Lines (USA)
Adverts   £25
Ships   £10
Views (coloured)   £2

Dominion Line (GB)
Ships   £5

Dominion & Commonwealth (GB)
Ships   £5

Donaldson-Atlantic Line, ships   £8

Donaldson Line (GB)
Adverts (B&W)   £20
Ships   £1.50/£10

Dublin & Manchester Line (GB)
Ships   £10

Dublin & Silloth Line (GB)
Ships   £10

DubrovackaParobrodska Plovidba (Yugoslavia)
Ships   £10

Dundee, Perth & London (GB)
Ships   £4

East African Railways
Lake ships   £5

Eastern & Australian Line (GB)
Adverts   £18
Ships   £1.50/£10

Eastern Shipping Corporation (India)
Ships   £5

Eastern Steamship Lines (USA)
Ships   £2/£5

Egyptian Mail Steamship Lines (GB)
Ships   £10

**Elder Dempster Lines (GB)
(includes Africa Steamship Co. & British & African S.N. Co.)**
Adverts   £10/£30
Ships   £3/£8

Ellerman & Bucknall Steamships (GB)
Adverts   £22
Ships   £3/£10

Ellerman & Papayanni Lines (GB)
Adverts   £30

Ellerman's City Line (GB)
Adverts   £22

Ellerman's Hall Line (GB)		**Grand Trunk Pacific SS (Canada)**	
Adverts	£22	Ships	£5
Chromo ship views	£15/£20	**Greek Line (Greece)**	
Ellerman Lines (GB)		Ships	£3/£5
Ships	£3/£10		
Ellerman's Wilson Line (GB)		**Hamburg-Amerika Line (Germany)**	
Ships	£3/£10	Adverts	£15/£30
		Ships/Chromo-Litho	£15
Empresa Insulana De Nav. (Portugal)		Ships	£3/£10
Ships	£2/£5	Interiors/Chromo-Litho	£10
Enkhuizen-Stavoren (Holland)		Interiors	£3/£5
Ships	£4	Views	£1.50/£10

Ellerman's Hall Line (GB)
Adverts £22
Chromo ship views £15/£20
Ellerman Lines (GB)
Ships £3/£10
Ellerman's Wilson Line (GB)
Ships £3/£10
Empresa Insulana De Nav. (Portugal)
Ships £2/£5
Enkhuizen-Stavoren (Holland)
Ships £4
Erste Donau (Austria)
Danube steamers £4/£10
Euxine Shipping (GB)
Ships £3
Everard (GB)
Ships, yachts, barges, etc. £3/£10
Fabre Line (France)
Ships £5
Fall River Line (USA)
Ships £5
Farrell Lines (USA)
Ships £3/£5
Finska Angfartygs Aktiebolaget (Finland)
Adverts £18
Ships £1.50/£10
Fraissinet, Cie (France)
Ships £3/£5
France, Fenwick & Co. (GB)
Adverts £20
French Line (CGT) (France)
Adverts £15/£30
Ships £1.50/£10
Interiors £3/£5
Views £3/£10
Furness Bermuda Line (GB)
Ships £3/£10
Furness Line (GB)
Adverts £30
Ships £3/£10
Furness Prince Line (GB)
Adverts £12
Fyffes Line (Elders & Fyffes) (GB)
Ships £3/£18
General Steam Navigation Co. (GB)
Ships (inc. paddle steamers) £5/£10
Interiors £2
Glen Line (GB)
Adverts £30
Ships £1.50/£3
Grace Line (USA)
Ships £3/£5

Grand Trunk Pacific SS (Canada)
Ships £5
Greek Line (Greece)
Ships £3/£5
Hamburg-Amerika Line (Germany)
Adverts £15/£30
Ships/Chromo-Litho £15
Ships £3/£10
Interiors/Chromo-Litho £10
Interiors £3/£5
Views £1.50/£10

Hamburg-Amerika Line   £20

Hamburg-Atlantic Line (Germany)
Ships £3/£5
Hamburg-Sudamerika Line (Germany)
Adverts £20/£30
Ships £12
Menus £10
Harrison Line (GB)
Ships £2/£6
Hellenic-Mediterranean Lines (Greece)
Ships £2/£5
Henderson Line (GB)
Adverts £12/£22
Holland-Amerika Line (Holland)
Ships £2/£10
Interiors £3
Views £2

Holland-America Line   £7.50

Holland Steamship Co. (Holland)
Adverts £18

Holland-Veluwe Line (Holland)
Ships £3

Home Lines (Panama)
Ships £2/£6

Horn Line (Germany)
Ships £4/£12

Hough Line (GB)
Ships £4/£12
Interiors £5

Houlder Line (GB)
Adverts £22
Ships £5

Hong Kong, Canton & Macao Steamboat (GB)
Ships £15

Howard Smith Co. (Australia)
Ships £4/£15

Huddart Parker (Australia)
Ships £3/£10

Hudson Navigation Co. (USA)
Ships £5

Hudson River Day Line (USA)
Adverts £16
Ships £4

Imperial Direct West India Mail (GB)

Imperial Direct West India Mail £8

Adverts £18/£22
Ships £3/£10
Ships inset into views £8

Incres Line (Panama)
Ships £2/£5

Indiana Transport (USA)
Ships £5

Instone Line (GB)
Ships £5

Irrawaddy Flotilla Co. (GB)
Ships £12

Islands Steamship (Iceland)
Ships £2/£10

Isle of Man S.P. Co. (GB)
Paddle steamers £10
Ships £2/£8

Isles of Scilly Steamship (GB)
Ships £2/£5

Italia (Flotta Riunite) (Italy)
Ships £2/£5

Italia (Soc. Di Nav. A Vapor.) (Italy)
Ships £10

Italnavi (Italy)
Ships £5

Jadranska Plovidba (Yugoslavia)
Ships £3/£10

Jamaica Banana Producers
Ships £2/£6

Jardine Mathison (GB)
Ships £10

Johnson Line £6

Johnson Line (Sweden)
Ships £2/£6

Jugoslavenski Lloyd (Yugoslavia)
Ships £10

Khedivial Mail Line (GB)
Adverts £28
Ships £4/£12

Koln-Dusseldorfer (Germany)
Adverts £15/£28
Ship and view vignettes/Coloured £10
Ship and view vignettes/B&W £4
Ships (inc. paddle) £1.50/£10

Kon. Hollandsche Lloyd (Holland)
Ships £3/£10

Kon. Java-China-Paket (Holland)
Ships £2/£5

Kon. Nederlandsche Stoomboot (Holland)
Ships £2/£5

Kon. Paketvaart Mij. (Holland)
Ships £2/£10
Viewsk £2/£5

Kon. Rotterdamsche Lloyd (Holland)
Ships £2/£10
Interiors £2
Views £2

"Kosmos" Line (Germany)
Adverts £28
Ships £10

"La Veloce" (Italy)
Adverts £20
Ships £10

Laeisz (Germany)
Sailing ships /Chromo-Litho £15
Ships £3/5

Lamport & Holt (GB)
Adverts £18
Ships £3/£10
Interiors £3/£5
Views £3

Langlands & Sons (GB)
Ships £5
Views £2

Lassman (Russia)
Ship vignette/Advert £30

Lauritzen, J., (Denmark)
Ships £3/£5

Lauro Lines (Italy)
Ships £1/£4

Leyland Lines (GB)
Adverts £10/£22

Liverpool & North Wales Steamship (GB)
Adverts £30
Paddle steamers £4/£6
Ships £3/£5

Leyland Line £10

Lloyd Austriaco (Austria)
Ships £10

Lloyd Brazileiro (Brazil)
Ships £5

Lloyd Italiano (Italy)
Ships £10
Interiors £2

Lloyd Latino (Italy)
Ships £10

Lloyd Royal Belge (Belgium)
Ships £8

Lloyd Sabaudo (Italy)
Adverts £18/£30
Ships £3/£10
Interiors & deck views £1.50/£4
Interior details £3

Lloyd Triestino (Italy)
Ships £3/£10

London County Council (GB)
Paddle steamers £10

London & Edinburgh Shipping (GB)
Ships £10/£18

Los Angeles Steamship Co. (USA)
Ships £4

Lund's Blue Anchor Line (GB)
Ships £4/£15

MacAndrews Line (GB)
Ships £2/£5

MacBrayne, David, (GB)
Adverts £20/£30
Ships £3/£10

McIlwraith, McEacharn Line (Australia)
Ships £10

MacIver Line (GB)
Ships £10

Maritime Belge Du Congo. Cie., (Belgium)
Adverts £15/£22
Months of the Year £12

Maritime Belge Du Congo, adverts £20
Ships £3/£10
Views/Coloured £3/£6
Interiors £3

Matson Line £5

Matson Navigation Co. (USA)
Ships £4/£12

NGI Shipping Co £8

Messageries Maritimes (France)
Adverts £8/£20
Ships £3/£10
Views £5
Interiors £3

Messina & Co. (Italy)
Ships £3/£5

Mitsui Line (Japan)
Ships £3

Mixte, Cie. De Navigation, (France)
Ships £3/£10

Mogul Line (India)
Ships £3/6

Morgan Line (USA)
Ships £3/£6

Moore-McCormack Line (USA)
Ships £4/£10

Morocco, Canary Islands & Madeira Line (GB)
Adverts £22

Muller (Batavier Line) (Holland)
Ships £5

Munson Steamship Co. (USA)
Ships £5
Interiors £3

Nacional De Nac., Chia. (Portugal)
Ships £3/£10

Natal Line (GB)
Ships £3/£10

National De Navigation, Cie. (France)
Ships £5

Navigation Nationale de Grece, Cie. (Greece)
Ships £10

Navigazione Generale Italiana (Italy)
Adverts £15/£30
Ships £3/£12
Interiors £3/£5

Navigazione Libera Triestina (Italy)
Ships £10
Interiors £3

Nederland Line (Holland)
Adverts £8/£18
Ships £4/£10

Nelson Line (GB)
Adverts £20
Ships £4/£10

New Bedford, Martha's Vineyard etc. (USA)
Ships £4

New Medway Steam Packet Co. (GB)
Paddle steamers £10
Ships £5

New Palace Steamers (GB)
Ships/Chromo-Litho £18
Paddle steamers £3/£10

New York & Cuba Mail (USA)
Ships £10

New Zealand Shipping Co, £8

New Zealand Shipping Co. (GB)
Ships £1.50/£10
Deck Views etc. £2/£5

Niederland Dampfs. Rhederei (Holland)
Paddle steamers/Chromo-Litho £18
Paddle steamers £5

Niagara Navigation Co. (Canada)
Ships £5

Nicholson Erie-Dover Line (Canada)
Ships £5

Nippon Yusen Kaisha (NYK) Line (Japan)
Adverts Chromo Litho £20
B&W ship and view vignettes £10/£15
Ships £2/£10
Deck views etc./Coloured £3/£5

Nomikos Line, Greece   £4

Nomikos Lines (Greece)
Ships £2/£5

Norddeutscher Lloyd (Germany)
Advert views/Chromo-Litho £8/£15
Ships £3/£12
Menus £10
Ships with inset captains £10
Interiors £3/£10

Nordenfjeldske (Norway)
Ships £3/£10
Views £3

Nordsee Line (Germany)
Paddle steamers/Chromo-Litho £12
Deck views £4
Ships £3/£4

Norske-Amerika Line (Norway)
Ships £3/£10

North Coast S.N. Co. (Australia)
Ships £10

North of Scotland, Orkney & Shetland (GB)
Ship with view vignettes £30
Ships £3/£10

Northern Michigan Transportation (USA)
Ships £10

Northern Navigation Co. (Canada)
Ships £5

Northern Steamship Co. (New Zealand)
Ships £5
Views £3

Oceanic Steamship Co. (USA)
Ships £5/£10
Views/In ovals £3/£5

Olsen, Fred. (Norway)
Ships £3/£10

Oresund, Svenska Rederi-Aktiebolaget (Sweden)
Paddle steamers £10
Ships £3/£5

Orient-Pacific Line (GB)
B&W ship vignettes £10
Orient-Royal Mail Lines (GB)
Ships £10
Orient Steam Navigation (GB)
Ships £2/£10
Interiors £3/£6
Oilette views £3/£6

Orient Steam Navigation RMS Orsova £7.50

Osaka Shosen Kaisha (Japan)
Ships inset into views or maps £10/£15
Ships £3/£10

Osaka Shosen Kaisha ship into view, £12

Ostasiatiske Kompagni (Denmark)
Ships £3/£10
Ostend-Dover Line (Belgium)
Adverts £28
Paddle steamers/Chromo-Litho £12
Paddle steamers £3/£12
Ships £3/£8
Ozean Line (Germany)
Ships £10
Pacific Coast Steamship (USA)
Ships £5
Pacific Mail Line (USA)
Ships inset into flag £12
Ships £3/£10
Views £4

Pacific Steam Navigation Co. (GB)
Adverts/Chromo-Litho £20/£35
Ships/Chromo-Litho vignettes £20
Ships/Chromo-Litho £15
Ships £3/£10
Deck views/Interiors/Chromo-Litho £20
Panama-Pacific Line (USA)
Ships £3/£5
Paquet, Cie. De Navigation (France)
Ships £3/£5
Peninsular & Occidental Steamship (USA)
Adverts £20
Ships £3
Peninsular & Oriental S.N. Co. (P&O) (GB)
Coloured vignettes of named ships £15/£20
Coloured vignettes £15
Ships £3/£10
Deck games, interiors £3/£5
Views £3

P&O Colour ship £7.50

P&O Branch Service (GB)
Ships £3/£8
Pinillos Line (Spain)
Ships £4/£12
Polish Ocean Lines (Poland)
Ships £3/£5
Polytechnic Cruising Association (GB)
Ships £3/£6
Port Line (GB)
Ships £3/£5
Powell Line (GB)
Adverts £22
Ships £10
Prince Line (GB)
Ships £1.50/£3
Provinciale Stoomboot (Holland)
Paddle steamers £10
Ships £3/£5
Puget Sound Line (USA)
Ships £3/£5

Russian Steam Nav & Trade £15

Rankine Line (GB)
Ships   £5
Red Star Line (USA/Belgium)
Adverts   £12/£20
Ships/Cassiers   £12/£20
Ships   £3/£6
Views   £3/£6

Red Star Line Advert   £12

R&O Navigation (Canada)
Ships   £3/£5
Rickmers Line (Germany)
Shipyard advert   £35
Sailing ships/Coloured   £20
Ships   £10
Roumanian State Service (Roumania)
Ships   £10
Royal Hungarian River & Sea Navigation (Hungary)
Maps   £22
Paddle steamers   £4/£10
Views   £2
Royal Line (Canada)
Adverts   £15/£28
Ships   £3/£8

Royal Mail Steam Packet/Lines (GB)
Early small size advert/view   £22

Ships/Chromo-Litho   £15
Ships   £3/£15
Interiors/Chromo-Litho   £10
Interiors   £3/£5
Views/Shoesmith   £12
Views/Oilettes   £3/£5
Russian-American Line (Russia)
Ships   £8
Russian Steam Navigation & Trade (Russia)
Ships   £15
Sachsisch-Bohmischen Damps.Ges. (Germany)
Paddle steamers   £10
Saltash, Three Towns & District Steamboat (GB)
Paddle steamers   £10

Salter River Steamer   £5

Salter (GB)
River steamers   £5
San Francisco & Portland Steamship (USA)
Ships   £5
Savannah Line (USA)
Adverts   £20
Scandinavian American Line (Denmark)
Ships   £4/£10
Scottish Shire Line (GB)
Ships   £5
Seas. Shipping (USA)
Ships   £5
Sessan Line (Sweden)
Ships   £3/£5
Setsuyo Shosen Kaisha (Japan)
Ships   £15
Shaw, Savill & Albion Line (GB)
Adverts   £18/£22
Coloured ship views   £4/£10
Ships   £3/£10

Sidarma Line (Italy)
Ships £3/£5

Siosa Line (Italy)
Ships £3/£5

Sitmar Line (old company) (Italy)
Ships £3/£10
Views £2

Sitmar Line (later company) (Italy)
Ships £3/5

Sloan & Co. (GB)
Adverts £8/£25

Soc. Anon. Di Nav. "San Marco"
Ships £5

Soc. Di Nav. "Puglia"
Ships £5

S.G.T.M. (France)
Ship vignettes £5/£10
Ships £3/£5
Interiors £1.50/£3

Soc. Misr De Navigation (Egypt)
Ships £4

Soc. Partenopea (Span) (Italy)
Ships £3

Southampton, Isle of Wight & South of England Steam Packet (Red Funnel) (GB)
Paddle steamers with corner views £15
Paddle steamer vignettes £12
Paddle steamers £3/£10
Ships £3/£5

Southern Pacific Railroad (USA)
Ships £3/£5

Southern Pacific Steamship (USA)
Ships £3/£5

Standard Fruit (Vaccaro Line) (USA)
Ships £3/£5

Stettiner (Germany)
Ships £3/£6

Stinnes, Hugo, (Germany)
Ships £4/£10

Sud-Atlantique, Cie De Navigation £10

Sudan Government Steamers (Sudan)
Nile steamers £10

Sud-Atlantique, Cie De Navigation. (France)
Ships/Coloured £10
Ships £3/£10
Interiors £3/£5

Svea Line (Sweden)
Ships £3/£5

Svenska-Amerika Line (Sweden)
Ships £3/£10

Svenska Lloyd (Sweden)
Ships £3/£10

Tasmanian Steamers (Australia)
Ships £10

Taya Line (Spain)
Ships £12

Tintore Line (Spain)
Adverts/Coloured £40
Adverts/Sepia £20
Ships £10

Toyas, John (Greece)
Ships £4/£6

Toyo Kisen Kaisha (Japan)
Ships £4/£12
Japanese style/life £10
Interiors £4

Transatlantica Italiana (Italy)
Ships £4/£10
Interiors £3£5

Trasatlantica Espanola advertising £20

Trasatlantica Espanola (Spain)
Adverts £12/£20
Ships £3/£10
Interiors £3/£5

Trasmeditaerranea (Spain)
Ships £3/£10
Interiors £3/£5

Turkish Maritime Lines (Turkey)
Ships £3/£5

Tyne General Ferry (GB)
Adverts/Chromo-Litho £15/£20

Tyne-Tees Shipping Co. (GB)
Advert Chromo-litho £25
Advert views £12
Ships £10

Typaldos Lines (Greece)
Ships £3/£5

Ullswater Navigation Co. (GB)
Ships/Chromo-Litho £18
Views/Coloured £4
Views/Photographic £2

USSR
State Shipping Company's £3/£10

Union Castle Line £5

Union-Castle Line (GB)
Adverts £15/£30
"Dunottar Castle" cruise cards £4/£10
Ships £3/£10
Interiors/Chromo-Litho £10/£15
Interiors £3

Union Steamship Co. of New Zealand (GB/NZ)
Adverts £20/£30
Ships £3/£10

United American Lines (USA)
Ships £3/£10

United Baltic Lines (GB)
Ships £3/£5

United Fruit Lines (USA)
Ships £3/£5

United States Forces (USA)
Transports £3/£6

United States Lines (USA)
Ships £3/£6
Interiors £3/£5

Uranium Steamship Co. (GB)
Ships £10

Vereenigde (Holland-Africa) (Holland)
Ships £3/£5

Villain & Fassio (Italy)
Ships £3/£10

Virginia Ferry (USA)
Ships £3

Warren Line Advert £22

Warren Line (GB)
Adverts £22

Warnemunde-Gedser (Germany)
Ships £3

White Star Line (GB)
Ships/Chromo-Litho £8/£20
Ships £5/£20
Menus £10/£20
Interiors/Coloured £5/£20
Interiors/Photographic £5/£10

Wilson Line (GB)
Ships/Coloured £5/£10
Ships/Photographic £3

Woermann Line ships £12

Woerman Line (Germany)
Adverts/Chromo-litho £20/£30
Ships £4/£12

Ybarra (Spain)
Ships £3/£10
Interiors £1/£3

Yeoward Line (GB)

Adverts	£20
Ships	£5

Zeeland Line (inc. Queensboro & Flushing Line) (Holland)

Early small size adverts	£30
Adverts	£15/£22
Paddle steamers/Chromo-Litho	£10
Paddle steamers	£10
Ships	£2/£5

Zim Lines (Israel)

Adverts	£12
Ships	£3/£10

Lusitania R/P £15

FAMOUS LINERS

Lusitania R.M.S.

Sketches of Disaster	£8
Art/Photographic	£6/£15
In Memoriam	£15

Celebrated Liners/Tuck R.

Oilette Series/20+ Sets	£6/£12

Miscellaneous Liners

Pre-1939	
/Coloured	£5/£20
/Real Photographic	£4/£15
1940 onwards	£4/£10
Interiors	£3/£10
Hoffman C./Southampton	£5/£10
F.G.O. Stuart	£5/£10

Titanic R.M.S.

Building/Harland & Woolf	£100+
Ship's anchor in transport	£100+
Leaving Southampton 1912	£90+
Passengers in `Carpathia' lifeboats	£150+
Other related pre-disaster cards	£90+
'Nearer my God to Thee'/Set 3/4.	
Pub. Bamforth. Price per card	£18

The cards listed above are all genuine

`Titanic' and mainly real photographic in style. As such they are worth considerably more than other `Titanic' cards listed below, which are usually re-titled versions of her sister ship `Olympic', often overprinted with details of the disaster. The reason for this is that the `Titanic' went down before the majority of publishers got round to photographing her, so they substituted existing pictures of the almost identical `Olympic'. One can tell the difference in that the real `Titanic' had a closed superstructure while that on the `Olympic' was open.

Titanic printed card £35

In Memoriam/Bragg E.A.	£50
National Series	£50
RP/Printed Photographic	£35
Art Types	£30

Associated Ships

Britannic (Sister ship/4 funnels)	£40
Carpathia	£50
Olympic	£15

MISCELLANEOUS PHOTOGRAPHIC

Cable Ships	£5/£10
Cargo Ships	£5/£10
Hospital Ships	£12/£25
Houseboats	£5
Icebreakers	£10
Launchings	£10/£20
Lightships	£12
On-board-ship scenes	£3/£5
Pleasure Boats	£3/£5
Speedboats	£6
Tankers	£5/£8

Princes Pier, Port Melbourne R/P £8

Troopships	£8

Convict Ships

At named locations	£15
Unlocated	£6
Interior Studies	£5

Divers

Naval	£5/£15
Civilian	£15
Winchester Diver	£18

Docks/Harbours/Ports

Construction/Southampton	£40
Construction/Immingham	£20
Spectacular RP Views	£30
General scenes	£3/£10

Ferries

Cross Channel	£3/£10
Steam Ferries	££3/10
Floating Bridges	£8
Rowing Boats	£5

Japanese Shipping

Inset types	£15
Launch Souvenirs	£20

Launching the Lifeboat at Southend R/P £25

Lifeboats

`Inland Launchings'	£35
Advertising Posters RNLI	£35
Lifeboat Saturday Parades	£35
Close-up Studies	£20
Crews/Portraits	£18
Parades	£28
Coastguards/Stations	£10

Lighthouses

GB Locations	£2/£10
Foreign Locations	£3/£5

Paddle Steamers

GB	£4/£10
Overseas	£4/£8
Rhine Steamers	£3/£10
Swiss Lake Steamers	£2/£5

Royal Yachts

GB	£2/£5
Foreign	£2/£6

Sailing Ships

Barges	£5/£15
Coastal	£5/£10
Ocean	£5/£8

Shipyards

Cammell Laird	£8
Harland & Woolf	£5/£10
Ship under construction	£10/£20
Yards miscellaneous	£5/£20

Tugs

Paddle	£7/£12
Officials	£8/£20
Others	£5/£10

Whaling Industry

Hebrides/Factory scenes	£45
Ships/General Views	£10/£25
Stations/Factory Scene	£25
Washed up/Stranded	£5/£18
Ships	£18

Wrecks

HMS Montagu	£5/£25
Submarine at Hastings	£10/£15
SS Mahratta	£5/£15
Other Wrecks .	£10/£20

Yachts

Americas Cup	£5/£10
Racing	£2/£6
Private/Powered	£6

SILK CARDS

The earliest cards of this type were Woven Silks which originated in Germany in 1898. The main manufacturers were H.M. Krieger and Rudolf Knuffman. Shortly afterwards in 1903 the Coventry based firms of Thomas Stevens and W.H. Grant began making similar cards in this country, while at around the same time Neyret Freres commenced manufacturing Woven Silks in France.

Embroidered Silks first appeared in 1900, although it was not until the First World War that they reached the height of their popularity. The basic difference between the two types is that Woven Silks were machine made, and consequently of uniform finish, whereas Embroidered silks were mainly produced on hand looms, leaving a raised surface where the threads may be clearly seen, with often irregular variations in design from card to card.

The RF Catalogue 1985 contains a comprehensive listing by Chris Radley of all the main Woven and Embroidered Silk card types.

Market Report

Certain very rare Regimental Silks are now fetching prices up to £250 at auction. It is difficult to list these individually as the price may change considerably the next time the card comes up for sale, but attention should always be paid to anything unusual, away from the standard Regiments.

Further information may be sought from Ken Lawson, who runs *Specialised Postcard Auctions*. (Szee his advert on the inside front cover for further details)

WOVEN

STEVENS T.

Experimental Types	£90
Portraits	£60+
Religious Subjects	£50
Views	£25+
General Subjects	£25+

Ships

Titanic	£750
Battleships	£90+
Transports	£60
Liners, Steamers and Landing Stages	£40+
Hands Across the Sea	£30+

HANDS ACROSS THE SEA.

WOVEN IN SILK

R.M.S. EMPRESS OF BRITAIN.

'Hands Across the Sea' woven £30

Britons all £8

Royal Engineers £15

Alpha Series
(Designs produced by Stevens for Alpha Publishing Co.)

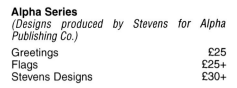

Greetings	£25
Flags	£25+
Stevens Designs	£30+

Ships and Greetings	£35+
Greetings from	£30+
Greetings, Songs and Hymns	£35
Views	£20+

FRANCE
A. Benoiston

GRANT W.H.

Exhibitions	£40+
Portraits	£40+
Subjects	£35+
Hands Across the Sea /	

Paris Exposition 1900	£150
Others	£40

Army Service Corps £15.

Queens Royal Lancers £60

Neyret Freres	
1903-1904	
Art Nouveau/Paintings/Portraits	£50+
1905-1914	
Art Nouveau/Portraits/Views	£50+
1907-1918	
Religion/Paintings	£30+
1915-1917	
WW1 Patriotic/Portraits	£25+
1917-1918	
WW1 Patriotic/Portraits	£25+
1916-1919	
Flames	£20+
1917-1918	
Sentimental Greetings	£25
Bertrand and Boiron 1915-1916	
WW1 Portraits/Religion	£50+
Others 1930-1945	£12+
GERMANY	
H.M. Kreiger	£30+
Rudolf Knuffman/1898-1905	£30+
Nazi Interest/1936-1938	£50+
Others/1899-1915	£25+
OTHER EUROPEAN	
Austria/1900-1939	£25+
Switzerland/1900-1910	£25+
Czechoslovakia/1916-1938	£12+
JAPAN	
Views and Portraits	£40
With Copy of Grant Mount	£50
U.S.A.	
1904 Exposition	£200
Set 14	£2000
Others	£30+

PRINTED SILK/SATIN

Flames//Edition Gabriel	£20
Kitchener Lord	£20
Stewart & Woolf Series	£15
Regiments/Countries	£15
Miscellaneous	£8
H.M. Krieger	
Four Seasons Set	£200
Others	£30
Cavell Edith	
In original D.M. envelope	£6
Card only	£4
Cinema Stars/Plain Backs	
Transatlantic Films	£3

FAB PATCHWORK CARDS

W.N. SHARPE/BRADFORD

Actresses	£15
Royalty	£15
Views	£12
Heraldic	£12
Flowers	£12
PAT.735 (Gaunt Armley)	£12

'Flame' Albert 1914   £25

EMBROIDERED/WW1

REGIMENTAL BADGES

Household Cavalry	£40
Cavalry of the Line	£60
Cavalry Special Reserve Units	£60
Yeomanry Regiments	£60
Royal Regiment of Artillery	
British Regiments	£35
Overseas Regiments	£50
Foot Guards	£50
Infantry of the Line	£50
Territorial Force	
Independent Units	£50
London Regiments	£40

Expeditionary Forces

Britain/France	£40
Australasia	£40
Canada/USA	£50

Divisional Corps £40

British Army Corps

British Corps/ASC.RE.RFA, etc.	£15
Overseas Corps	£40

Overseas Regiments £75

Royal Navy

Units	£50
Ships	£50
Royal Navy	£40
Royal Naval Air Service	£50

Royal Air Force

Royal Flying Corps	£45
Royal Air Force	£45

Independent Organisations

Red Cross/.Salvation Army etc. £50

The whole field of WW1 Embroidered Silk Cards is vast and complex, with literally thousands of different designs covered under the three columns of this listing. Many of these cards are very scarce, in some cases only one copy being known. This catalogue can only offer a general guide to type and price. For further information you are referred to the standard work on the subject by John Westland: 'The Concise Catalogue of Embroidered Silk Postcards', obtainable from:

Michael Cox.
7 Collingwood Rd.
Woodbridge. Suffolk, IP21 1JL

LEADERS/STATESMEN/ROYALTY

Inset Photos/Single	£20
Inset Photos/Doubles	£25
Names/WW1 Leaders	£25

HERALDIC

Overseas Towns	£40
Overseas Countries/Islands	£25
European Towns	£15
European Countries	£15
English Towns	£30
England/Scotland/Wales	£25
Ireland/Eire/Shamrock Isle	£25

Birn Brothers/With Printed Title

Overseas Towns	£25
European Towns	£20
English Towns	£20

YEAR DATES

1914-1919	£10
1920-1923	£15
1925-1939	£18
1940	£10
1945	£15

SENTIMENTAL GREETINGS/ HEARTS & FLOWERS TYPE

Flag/Patriotic £8

Sentimental Greetings £5

Many cards of this type were made in the form of an Envelope. If such a card still contains its original insert, the following premium may be added to the prices above:

Silk Handkerchief	£3
Artist signed	£1
Celluloid	£1
War Scenes	£1
Perfumed	£1

BETTER DESIGNS

Advertising	£40
Aircraft/Guns etc.	£15
Army Camps	£25
Buildings	£20
Cartoons	£18
Cathedrals	£20
Cathedrals in Flames	£15
Cats	£15
Colonial Exhibition	£40
English Buildings	£30
Father Xmas/Girls etc	.£25
Flower Baskets	£8
Pan-Pacific Exhibition 1915	£40
Personal Names	£15
Saints	£15
Soldiers/Sailors/Medals etc	.£25
War Destruction	£15
Zeppelins	£20

To qualify for listed price the image must be the dominant feature of the card. A tiny Cat or small Building will not do!

EMBROIDERED/ MISCELLANEOUS

Birn Bros.

Printed Regimental Badges	£20
Flowers	£8

Tuck R. & Sons

Broderie D'Art series £6

Spanish Embroidery

Early cards	£6
Later	£3
Modern	£1.50

SPORT

One of the subjects which enjoys a popularity today at least equal to that of the Edwardian period, when Sporting cards filled every album. Always a good collecting area with a very wide variety of cards, where prices have been subject to continued and steady growth over the years.

Market Report

Football Teams prices may soon peak, although the top clubs are still in high demand. Golf comic has slowed, but high quality identified players continue to rise in value, mainly due to a short supply and high demand. Tennis and Horse Racing are still very popular whilst Cricket and Boxing have been quiet again this year.

ANGLING
Comic Sketches	£3
Miscellaneous	£4

ARCHERY
Miscellaneous	£5

ATHLETICS
Meetings	£12
Athletes/Named	£12
Stadiums	£8

BADMINTON
Miscellaneous	£3

BASEBALL
Players	£5/£15
Comic Sketches	£10/£18
Stadiums	£5/ £12

BASKETBALL/NETBALL
Miscellaneous	£3

Billiards comic sketch £10

BILLIARDS/SNOOKER
Players/Named	£20
Players/General	£10
Billiard Halls	£6
Comic Sketches	£8-£12

BOARD GAMES
Chess	£15
Other games	£3

BOWLS
Miscellaneous	£4

BOXING
Famous Boxers/Beagles Ltd.	£15
Professional Boxing	£15-£25
Amateur Boxing	£5

BULLFIGHTING
Art Studies	£2
Photographic	£3

CAVES/CAVING
Miscellaneous	£2

Early Comic cricket £10

CRICKET
Players	£15
W.G.Grace	£25
Donald Bradman	£25
Signed	£25/£100
County Grounds	£15
Comic Sketches	£8/£15

Teams
County Teams	£20
International Teams	£15/£20
Star Series	£6

Dainty series, Sussex X1   £20

Amateur Teams/ Identified   £4

CROQUET
Miscellaneous   £6

CURLING
Miscellaneous   £2

CYCLE RACING
Tour de France/Portraits   £15
Tour de France/Pre 1939   £20
Personalities/Events/Pre 1939   £15
 /Post 1939   £6

FENCING
Miscellaneous   £4

Commemorative cards similar to this are very sought after, expect to pay up to £60 for this type of card.

FOOTBALL
LEAGUE TEAMS
Series
Rapid Photographic series   £50
Famous Football Teams/
Wrench Series 107...(Names)   £50
Oxo Advertising Cards   £50

Football, Faulkner series, priced at £45

London Football Teams/
B&B Series G11/Coloured   £40
Ozograph Series/Bristol   £40
Rotary Photographic/Series 3844 £50
Health & Strength   £40
Misch & Co "Football Teams"   £40

Miscellaneous
Football League/Bw photographic £45
 /Bw printed   £40
Olympic Teams   £15/£30
Prices for League Teams are governed largely by the status of the team itself. e.g. Man. Utd. is worth more than Barnsley.

Players
Wrench Series 21../29../c.1903   £45
Benefit Cards/Football League   £40
Bw photographic   £30
Tuck Famous football players   £40

Football stadiums similar to this fetch up to £45

Amateur football team R/P £6

Birmingham Novelty Co 'Football' series £50
C.W.Faulkner &co £45
"Herriot" series £45

MISCELLANEOUS

Wembley Cup Final 1923/Campbell Gray/	
Commemorative Set 3/With Packet	£120
/Without packet	£80
Arsenal Cartoon/Kentish Independent	£50
International Teams	£40
Football Series 940/c.1903	
Tuck R. & Sons	£40
In Memoriam Cards/In Memory of/	
b/w Comic Sketches	£30
Football League Stadiums	£45
Football Stadiums Overseas	£15
Football Colours/Frank Reynolds/	
Comic Sketches	£15
Non-League Teams/Semi-Pro	£15
Amateur Teams/Identified	£6
/Unidentified	£4
Crowd scenes/Brighton/F. Wiles	£12
/Miscellaneous	£10
Comic Sketches	£8

Golf Comic,
Artist Tom Browne, priced at £12

GOLF

Wrench Series/Players/ (**See page 164**)

Bw undivided back	£100+
Players/Named	£70
Tournaments	£75
Club Houses	£8/£15
Championship Courses	£18
Courses	£5/£8
Comic Sketches	£12/£15

Golf course R/P

Advert Cards

Poster Type	£60
Product Advertising	£30

The leading specialist dealers for Football
and Golf cards are: Sporting Memories,
130, Brent Street, Hendon NW4 2AD.

GYMNASTICS

Miscellaneous	£3

HOCKEY

International teams	£10
Miscellaneous	£3

HORSE SHOWS/JUMPING

Int. Horse Show/Product Advert	£8
Show Jumping/Riders	£5
General Scenes	£3

HORSE RACING

Jockeys	£8
Race Horses	£5

Race Courses

Doncaster/York etc./	
Printed multi-view type	£3
In current use	£3

Wrench series, derby Winners, £10

Photochrom colour printed £6

Pre-1939

Gatwick	£50
Lewes	£50
RP studies	£20
Printed/Goodwood etc.	£5
Abandoned	£12

Courses where Racing was abandoned long ago are worth more than those in current use.

Series

B & D/Kromo Series	£12
Bird H./Everett's Series	£12
Meissner & Buch Series 1003	£15
Tuck R./Derby Winners	£12
Tuck R./Popular Racing Colours	£12
Walker J./Celebrated Racers	£12
Wildt & Kray/Racing Colours	£12
Wrench Series	£12

MOTOR RACING

L'Hirondelle Series	£20
Peking-Paris	£15
French Drivers c.1905/ Pub. J. Bouveret/Le Mans	£15
European Circuits	£8
Valentine's R/P racing car series	£8

Brooklands

Action/Portraits	£20
Track Construction	£20

Gordon Bennett Races

Coloured	£18
RP/Printed	£10

Isle of Man

Motor Cars/RP Close-up	£50
Action/RP Middle distance	£25

Valentine & Sons

Autocar Series	£7

Action/Portraits

Pre-1939	£15

Valentines, Racing Car series, £8

1940 onwards	£6
Art Studies	£6

MOTOR CYCLE RACING

Isle of Man

Pre-1939	£25
1940 onwards	£10

Racing/Other Circuits

Pre-1939	£18
1940 onwards	£10

Action/Portraits

Pre-1939	£18
1940 onwards	£8

MOUNTAINEERING

Everest	£8
Miscellaneous	£3

OLYMPIC GAMES

SUMMER GAMES

1896 Athens	£10/£80
1900/04/08 Expos	£1/£8
1906 Athens	£1/£60
1912 Stockholm	£5/£30
1920 Antwerp	£8/£40
1924 Paris	£8/£30
1928/1956	£2/£15

1912 Stockholm Olympics, £12

See PPV 2005 for further information on Olympic cards

1960/1968	£2/£7
1972/1988	£1/£7
1992/2012	£1/£2

WINTER GAMES

1924/1928	£10/£50
1932/1936	£3/£12
1948/1956	£3/£10
1960/1968	£2/£8
1972/1988	£1/£2

Ancient Olympia	£2
Empty Stadiums	£1/£2
Crowded Stadiums	£3/£7
Torch Ceremony	£2/£5

POLO

Miscellaneous	£3

ROWING

Named Crews	£6
Oxford Eights etc.	£6
Henley Regatta	£4

Rowing, Cambridge crew 1931 £6

RUGBY FOOTBALL

International Teams	£20
League/Union Teams	£30

Rugby league side £25

Players/Named	£25
Amateur Teams/Identified	£4

SAILING/YACHTING

Admiral's Cup	£5
Racing	£5
Kirk of Cowes/RP studies	£5
Powered Yachts	£5
General scenes	£3

SHOOTING

Bisley Scenes	£12
General Shooting	£5

SKATING / RINKING

Miscellaneous	£3
Professional	£5

SPEEDWAY

Riders/Pre-1939	£18

Sailing, Racing £5

Riders/Post-War £12

SPORTS DAY/LOCAL SPORTS
Miscellaneous £6

SWIMMING
Channel £6-£12
Miscellaneous £3

TABLE TENNIS
Players/Competition £18
Players/General £6
Comic/Early £25

Channel Swimmer Wolffe. £12

Table Tennis: R/P £18

Comic Sketches £15

TENNIS
Wimbledon scenes (early) £15
Wimbledon scenes £12
Tournaments/Miscellaneous £5/£10
Courts £3
Comic Sketches £6/£12

Players
Portraits/E.A. Trim early period £18
Portraits/E.A. Trim pre 1939 £12
Competition/Pre-1939 £12
   /1940 on £6
Wimbledon series/c.1960 £4

WALKING
London-Brighton £10
Other Races £6
Comic £3
Mountain Walking £1

WATER POLO
Miscellaneous £3

WINTER SPORTS
Skating £1.50
Skiing £1.50
Tobogganing £1.50
Art types £3

WRESTLING/BODY BUILDING
Miscellaneous £12/£20
Sandow £18
Hackenschmidt £12

Tennis: Comic sketch £6

Health & Strength Body Building £12

GOLFING POSTCARDS PUBLISHED BY WRENCH

The Wrench series.
These all depict scenes at St Andrews

No.	CAPTION ON CARD
1979	A.Herd (Champion 1902) / Andrew Kirkcaldy
1980	A.Kirkcaldy / Willie Park (Champion 1887,1889)
1981	Archie Simpson / A.Kirkcaldy / Ben Sayers / A.Herd (Champion 1902)
1982	The late Mr F.G.Tait Breaking the record for Medal Play
1983	Mr John Ball Jnr. / The late Mr.F.G. Tait
1984	Mr.Mure Fergusson / Mr J.E.Laidlay
1985	Mr J.Graham / Mr.J.L. Lowe
1986	Mr Leslie Balfour Melville Amateur Champion 1895 / Mr P.C.Anderson Amateur Champion 1893
1987	Tom Morris / Mr. J.E.Laidlay / Mr Scott
1988	Laidlay / Muir Fergusson*
1989	Rt.Hon. A.J.Balfour M.P. / Rt. Hon. H.H.Asquith M.P.
1990	Rt.Hon. A.J.Balfour M.P. / Graham Murray Esq
1991	Mr Leslie Balfour Melville Amateur Champion 1895 / L.Auchterlonie
1992	Mr H.G. Hutchinson Amateur champion 1885. 1887.
1993	Tom Morris / Mr. H.H.Hilton / Mr. J.Lowe
1994	D.Simpson / Mr. John Ball Jnr.
1995	Unknown
1996	The Late Mr F.G. Tait Amateur champion 1896 and 1898
1997	A.Kirkcaldy / James Braid champion 1901
1998	Ben Sayers / W.Auchterlonie Champion 1893
1999	Simpson / Kirkcaldy / sayers / Herd*
2000	J.H.Taylor Champion 1900
2001	Kirkcaldy / Fernie*
2002	Tom Morris / Harry Vardon Champion 1896. 1898. 1899 / A.Herd Champion1902 NOTE: This is an incorrect caption. It actually depicts Tom Morris, Harold Hilton and John Lowe, as No. 1993
2003	Harry Vardon Champion 1896. 1898. 1899
2004	J.H.Taylor*
2005	Mr.R.Maxwell
2006	Tom Morris Champion 1861.1862.1864.1867.
2007	Andrew Kirckaldy
2008	Unknown
2009	Wm. Auchterlonie Champion 1893

The following cards are views of St Andrews:

2039   St Andrews from the Links
2042   St Andrews The Golf Club House

The above sequence of numbers would suggest they are from a set of six.
The following, still called The Wrench series, are printed in a
different style, with a plate mark surrounding the image.

3829   Mr. Horace Huthinson
3830   Unknown
3831   Rt.Hon. A.J.Balfour M.P.
3832   Hon.A.Lyttleton M.P.
3833   Mr Lewis Waller

Again, the sequence of numbering above, suggests a set of six.

Mr. H. G. Hutchinson.   Mr. Charles Hutchings
                               (Amateur Champion 1902).

All information kindly supplied by Philip truett
*Cards not in the Truett collection

THEATRICAL

Part of the staple of the old publishers. Theatrical cards of all kinds filled the Edwardian albums, and have retained their popularity to the present day.

Market Report
A good collecting field with wide appeal. This subject gives huge scope for investment at all levels, with prices ranging from £1 to £60.

ACTORS/ACTRESSES

Baker, Josephine	£60
Bernhardt Sarah	£10
Coward Noel	£10
Duncan Isadora	£25
Hari Mata	£30
Irving Henry/Memorial Card	£6
Langtry Lily	£12
Portraits/Miscellaneous	£1.50
Play Scenes	£1.50
Embossed/Applique	£1.50

*Edwardian
Actress
Gertie Millar
£1.50*

The predominant theme in this category is Edwardian Actors and Actresses of which vast quantities exist. Formerly little collected, they have now started to attract buyers, often looking for one or two named stars. In the circumstances a price of £1.50 is considered reasonable for one card, but they can be picked up in bulk at auction, or from a dealer, at less than this figure.

ADVERTISING
POSTER TYPE

Coloured	£15+
Black & White	£6

Miscellaneous

Comedians/Performers	£5
Playbill Reproductions	£10
Play Scenes/With Advert	£3

Where applicable, the value of Poster Type cards is determined by the name of the Artist. See main Artist Index.

BALLET
Artistes

Fonteyn, Margot	£10
Genee, Dame Adelina	£10
Markova, Alicia	£10
Nijinsky	£50
Nureyev, R	£22
Pavlova	£15
Other Artists	£6
Companies/Troupes	£6
Post-war	£3

THEATRES

Music Hall/Variety	£25
Opera Houses	£4
Piers/Winter Gardens	£3
Interiors	£4
London West End/Coloured	£4

Prices for Theatres are for good, close-up mainly photographic studies and not for middle or far-distance views. Theatres forming part of a standard Street Scene are classed in that category

Mr A. Clifton Alderson a in Othello   £5

CIRCUS

ADVERTISING

Barnum & Bailey
Poster Type	£40
Others	£20

Buffalo Bill's Wild West
Poster Type	£25
Others	£15

Miscellaneous
Poster Types	£30
Others	£15

MISCELLANEOUS
Acts/Performers	£8
Animals Caged	£6
Bands	£8
Circus Sites/Identified G.B.	£40

Clowns
Early/Chromo Litho	£20
Photographic Performers	£15

Freaks
Animal	£10
Human	£6
Giants	£6
Midgets/Troupes	£4

VARIETY ARTISTS
Bard, Wilkie	£6
Chevalier, Albert	£6
Chirgwin	£6
Elliott, G.H.	£6
Forde, Florrie	£6
Formby, George	£12
King, Hetty	£6

Gerald Du Maurier £9

Lauder, Harry	£6
/Comic	£6
Leno Dan	£6
Lloyd Marie	£9
Miller, Max	£8
Robey, George	£4
Stratton, Eugene	£6
Tate, Harry	£6
Tich, Little	£8
Tilley. `Vesta	£6

RADIO/TELEVISION
Children's Programmes/Radio	£6
Radio Celebrities	£4
Studios	£6
Transmitting Stations	£5
Wireless Sets	£8
QSL Cards/Radio Amateurs	£1
Comic Sketches	£6
Children's TV/Sooty etc.	£3
Brooke Bond Chimps	£3
Radio Pictorial Series	£5

MISCELLANEOUS
Amateur Dramatics	£1.50
Escapologists/Stuntmen	£20
Harry Houdini	£60
Magicians/Conjurers	£25
Speciality Acts	£6
Ventriloquists	£25
Drag Artists	£4

Autographs
Known Stars	£3+
Unkown Artists	£1

Prices quoted are for Autographs signed in ink. Printed Autographs have no value above that of the subject.

Cabaret
French Skeletons	£1
Other Acts	£3

Concert Parties
Named Troupes	£4
Un-named	£1.50

Dancing
Ballroom/Stage etc.	£2
Greetings/Romance	£2

French Showgirls
`A Travers Les Coulisses'	£12
Moulin Rouge/Coloured	£12
Portraits/Miscellaneous	£3

TOPOGRAPHICAL

The most popular and eagerly sought after cards in the hobby, the finest of which have again seen a dramatic rise in price. Yet herein lies the enigma of Topographical cards, because it could be argued that the great majority of them are virtually unsaleable! As has often been said before, the problem with Topographical cards is that there are a great many very common cards of any particular area. These include the standard High Street views, local buildings of interest, the church and the park etc.; originally produced in vast quantities by regional and national publishers. And once the collector has obtained these common views he does not buy them again. They remain in the box, as any postcard dealer will testify, for possibly years! And being so common they keep turning up over and over again in the dealer's current buying.   I

siastic collector no more than six months to assem-
h as these. But then he joins the rest of us in seek-
ting back streets and scenes of local social history
ema, Theatre, Shop Fronts, Delivery Vehicles,
Disasters, Post Offices, Public Houses, Windmills,
very nature were invariably produced in relatively
and today, some ninety years later, allowing for nat-
he ground. So as ever more collectors come to the
er cards, the prices go up and will continue to go
ard trade that you can sell cards like these but you
ly superb street scenes are now so highly saleable
that they often don't get as far as the dealer's box or album, but are offered privately to the collector of that particular town at a negotiated price!

So this is the Topographical market we are at present faced with. There is nothing we can do about it, save to re-double our efforts to find the cards which collectors want.

If I may now look briefly at the production of Topographical cards and at the methods involved, the following notes may be of interest to collectors. These are based on a paper I wrote in conjunction with Brian Lund and which was published in `Picture Postcard Monthly' in June 1982. We looked at the accepted definitions of `Real Photographic' and `Printed' cards, and suggested a more clearly defined structure, offering some thoughts toward a re-assessment of the Topographical nomenclature. To briefly summarise our conclusions, they were as follows:

Postcards were finished in two basically different methods:

1. By a photographic process.   **2. By a Printing Machine process.**

PHOTOGRAPHIC
Local Photographers
By small, local firms producing each photograph individually, or in very small batches onto an existing postcard back, and hand-cutting or guillotining the batches, possibly four at a time. The style of finish varies widely, from the superb clarity of the very best examples, to the image which has almost faded away, according to the skill of the photographer in the developing process. The caption was often hand-written, with the photographer's name or initials often appearing on the front of the card. These may be styled as the best examples of `Real Photographic' cards, and the work of photographers such as Bragg, Gibson, Garratt, Wellsted, Ross, Braddock, Perkins and Daniell, immediately spring to mind as pre-eminent in this zfield. There are of course many other local photographers who produced superb work, and where there is a great deal of research yet to be done. These men concentrated upon their own immediate locality, and as a result it is in this work that you will find the fascinating cards of local history interest referred to above, and thus it follows that in these cards we are now seeing the most significant advance in price.

Regional Publishers

Postcards were produced in quantity by larger companies who covered a wide circulation area. They probably used a mass-production technique involving contact printing from a negative on to machines which could produce copies in large numbers. Many of these cards are designated `Real Photographic' on the back, and are often found with a white border framing the picture. They are characterised by a uniform, glossy finish, the machine controlled output being less susceptible to variations in tone. Leading firms who worked in this style include Sankey, Camburn and E.T. Bush, covering the areas of Cumbria, S.E. England and South Wales respectively. The subjects depicted tend to be High Street and main street views, the Railway Station, Cinema, Theatre, Post Office, and other views of immediate local interest, although you will not find cards here, showing a line of barefoot children queueing up at a soup kitchen, this being essentially the province of the local man. Cards in this section do not generally command such high prices, partly because they are more readily available, being produced in larger quantities, and also because the scenes they depict tend to be more `standard' than the offbeat work of the local photographer.

National Publishers

Also involved in postcard production, but this time on a national scale were big publishing houses such as Frith, Valentine, Davidson Bros, W.H.S. Kingsway Series and many others. Their work was machine produced and similar in all respects to that of the Regional Publishers both in style and content, but the difference lay in the fact that these were national publishing concerns who produced cards covering the length and breadth of the country. Prices here would fall into the same range as those for the Regional Publishers.

PRINTED

Without getting into a complex and perhaps misleading explanation of all the different printing techniques employed here, it is enough to state that if a card was not produced by one of the Photographic methods given above, in other words if it does not have a glossy finish, then it must have been produced by one of the many printing processes available at the time. Basically the method employed involved splitting the original photographic image into dots, or what is known as the screen process, and then transferring this on to a printing plate. While this method enabled mass produced copies of quite appalling definition to flood the market, the finest printed cards are the equal of the finest photographics. Here again we have three main areas of commerce.

Local Publishers

Many local photographers produced cards in a variety of printed formats, and some may have combined these with their own original photographic work. Many local shops and stores had their names overprinted on to the backs of cards produced for them by the Regional Publishers. The content of these cards, while being essentially local in character, does fall into the same style as that of the Regional Publishers above, and prices would be at approximately the same levels.

Regional Publishers

The work of Charles Martin in London and the South East perhaps most clearly illustrates the very high standard to which many Regional Publishers aspired. If we may include Lucien Levy also in this classification, some of his work is certainly the equal of anything in the entire Topographical field. Subjects depicted were again similar to those of the Regional Publishers of Photographic cards, the `line of hungry children' being always the work of what has been termed `the back-street photographer'. Prices for these cards fall into line with the other regional photographic work above.

National Publishers

Here we come to those cards which today form the great bulk of stock to be found in any dealer's box. Endless mass-produced stereotyped views by Frith, Judges, Valentine, Tuck, Stengel and many other substantial publishing corporations. Printed in a wide variety of styles, with many cards coloured, and nearly all of them depicting the standard views and tourist areas of any town or city, as well as incalculable numbers of Churches, Cathedrals, Seasides, Scottish Lochs and Welsh Mountains! Some, of course, are more interesting than others, but overall, these are the cards which the collector soon obtains. Prices for the majority of them are at the lower end of the price scale.

Market Report

Continued demand for the rare card, or the spectacular RP street scene, has again seen prices surge ahead. These days, if you have something really special, then catalogue price becomes irrelevant, leaving the purchase to be negotiated between buyer and seller.
We have placed some examples over the next few pages which we hope will help you.

VILLAGES

Spectacular animated street scenes	£30+
Animated street scenes	£20
Other street scenes	£10
Empty streets	£6
Common Views/Landscapes	£2
Modern views/1945-1970	£3

COUNTRY TOWNS

Spectacular animated street scenes	£30+
Animated street scenes	£18
Other street scenes	£10
Empty streets	£6
Common views/Town Hall etc.	£2
Modern views/1945-1970	£3

INDUSTRIALISED TOWNS AND CITIES

Spectacular animated street scenes	£28+
Animated street scenes	£18
Other street scenes	£10
Empty streets	£6
Common Views/City Centres etc.	£2
Modern views/1945-1970	£3

LONDON SUBURBAN

Spectacular animated street scenes	£30+
Animated street scenes	£20
Other street scenes	£10
Empty streets	£6
Common Views/Parks etc.	£2
Modern views/1945-1970	£3

LONDON CENTRAL

Spectacular animated street scenes	£20
Animated street scenes	£15
Other street scenes	£8
Empty streets	£6
Oxford St./Regent St. etc.	£1.50
LL Published	£5
Common Views/Trafalgar Square etc.	.50
Modern views/1945-1970	.50

N.B. This is a new-style listing of Topographical cards, which I have now sub-divided into six separate classifications, with a price representing an average figure for that type. Within these classifications many anomalies exist. For example, there are some superb animated LL cards of London Central, which at the same time are very common! With these, and similar examples, only knowledge and experience can be your guide. I have not tried to be too specific and break this down even further into considerations of `RP, Printed, Coloured, Local and

National Photographers etc.', as this would only lead to confusion. I have not even tried to separate Real Photographic from Printed cards because, as we all know, there are some awful RPs, and some very fine Printed types. I have, however, given the main category to those superb Topographical views of both kinds which stand out in any collection.

* Animated Street Scenes: A card which is full of activity, life and movement, or which depicts a scene of particular relevance to that area, or is otherwise of unusual interest. These cards are very much the exception, often being produced by the local photographer. The majority of street scenes in any dealer's stock would be classified as `Other street scenes'.

MISCELLANEOUS

Abbeys/Convents/Priories	£1.50
Aerial Views	£5
Archaeological Sites/Villages	£1.50
Bridges/Viaducts	£3
Castles	£1.50
Cathedrals	£1
Chapels	£3
Churches	£2
Crystal Palace	£3
Follies	£5
Greetings/Town Names	£1.50
Holiday areas	£1
Hotels	£6
Interiors	£1
Lake District scenery	£1
Landscapes	£1
Manor Houses	£3
Monuments/Memorials	£3
Multi-view	£3
Municipal Buildings	£3
Parks	£3
Seaside/Common views	.50
Special Events	£20
Stately Homes	£1.50
Much photographed buildings	£1

Every dealer will have his own idea of the value of any card backed up by a specialised knowledge of his own area, so at best, the prices above should only be taken as a broad general average, capable of movement up or down as determined by the particular card.

TOPOGRAPHICAL

Mansfield, R/P £20

Guiseley Post Office R/P £20

Burnham-On-Crouch R/P £15

Chessington, Bones Gate R/P £15

Smethwick, Cape Hill R/P £15

Burford, High Street. R/P £15

R/P Shopfront £30

TOPOGRAPHICAL

Trottiscliffe, Post Office. R/P £25

Cranbrook , R/P £18

Easton, Church Street R/P £15

West Kirby R/P £7.50

Colwyn Bay R/P. £18

Thurlestone, Post Office R/P £20

Armly, Branch Road R/P £12

Shenfield Village R/P £20

TOPOGRAPHICAL

Blackpool R/P £15

Witham,   R/P £15

Dartford, East Hill. £15

Branscombe R/P £15

Horning village R/P £18

Sutton Valence R/P £12

Altrincham   R/P £12

Rusthall, High Street R/P £20

Office Workers R/P £10

Bus conductors tea break R/P £35

Spectacular shopfront £25

Airship arriving in Croydon R/P £30

Thornton Heath laundry cart £40

Motor Garage R/P £25

Baines Dairy shopfront R/P £25

SOCIAL HISTORY

This is Topographical by another name and the same comments apply. You can almost name your own price for the better RP studies and the scarce cards of local history interest. At the same time there are a great many interesting cards in this classification which are very reasonably priced.

It is pointed out that for all relevant entries e.g. Fairs . Post Offices . Public Houses . Street Markets . Windmills etc. the stated price is a broad average figure for a card, either RP or Printed, fully identified and showing a 'Close-up at a named location', with Real Photographic cards being the most desirable. Unlocated cards and middle or far-distance views would be priced accordingly.

Please see WHAT THE PRICES MEAN on P.30 ***

AGRICULTURE

Agricultural Shows	£12
Carting	£12
Crofters	£6
Dalesmen	£5
Farm Machinery/Tractors etc	£15
Farms	£8
Farmworkers	£6
Flower Picking	£6
Fruit Picking	£6
Herdsmen	£5
Trees	£1.50

Harvesting

Reaping	£5
Threshing machines/Located	£35
/Unlocated	£20
Hay Carts/RP studies	£8
General Harvesting scenes	£3

Hop Picking

Demonstrations in Kent	£75
Real Photographic scenes/Located	£20
/Unlocated	£10

There are many superb RP studies of Hop Picking. Everything depends upon location.

Cooper's Series/Maidstone/RP	£12
The "Kent" Series/Invicta	
Pub: G.A. Cooper/A.N. Hambrook	£8
Young & Cooper/Bw	£8
/Coloured	£4

There are certain Y&C coloured cards which are very common.

Filmer's Home Hop Picking Series	£8
T.A. Flemons/Tonbridge	£8
"Solochrome" Series/E.A. Sweetman	£6
"Solograph" Series/E.A. Sweetman	£6

For Hampshire/Worcestershire etc. follow the price guide above.

Foreign Hop Picking	£5

Lavender Industry

Fields/Growing	£8
Picking	£10
Carting	£35

Ploughing

Oxen in Sussex/RP	£25
/Printed	£8
Plough Horses	£3
Ploughing/General scenes	£2

Sheep

Lambing	£6
Shearing	£12
Sheep Dips	£12
Sheepdog Trials	£12
Shepherds	£6
/South Downs/RP studies	£10

CANALS

Aqueducts/Bridges/Locks	£8
Barges/Close-up	£40
Canal construction/Workers	£40
Disasters	£40
Events/Gatherings, etc.	£40
Military Canals	£3
Tunnels	£8

Hop Picking. R/P £10

Regents Canal, R/P £20

Narrow Canals

Spectacular Real Photographic	£50
Real Photographic	£10/£15
Coloured/Sepia/BW	£6
Common views/Hythe, Llangollen etc.	£2

Ship Canals

Caledonian/Crinan/Exeter etc.	£2
Manchester Ship Canal	£5

River Navigations

Traffic/Close-up	£15
General views	£6

As with other Subjects, a particularly good card or an unusual view on a seldom photographed Canal, would fetch a price well in excess of these general figures.

Coal Mining rescue team R/P £20

COAL MINING

Coal Miners

Groups/Portraits	£20/£30

Collieries

Surface/Close-up	£20/£30
/Middle Distance	£10
Somerset Coalfield	£20
Underground	£10
Models	£6
Pit Girls	£10
Open-cast Mining	£30

Art Type	£2
Coal Picking	£60

Certain views of Collieries in South Wales, published by M.J.R.B. have been remaindered and are therefore worth considerably less than the prices given above.

Series

Kinsley Evictions 1905	£50

For full details on this series please refer to PPV 2003

M. Brookes/Pontypridd	£10
Cannock Chase	£10
Clay Cross Co./Set 25	£10
Timothy's Series/South Wales	£10
Other series	£10

A number of Collieries produced series of cards depicting work both at the surface and underground.

Disasters

Hamstead Colliery	£15
Senghenydd Colliery	£30
Other Named Events	£25
In Memoriam Cards	£25
In Memoriam Gothard	£20/£75
Rescue Teams	£20

CRIME & PUNISHMENT

Judges/Barristers	£5
Prisons	£5
Prisoners at Work	£5
Warders at Dartmoor	£1.50
Prisoners at Portland	£1.50

CYCLING

Close-up RP studies	£6
Tandems	£10
Tricycles	£15
Military	£4
Greetings/Romantic	£3
Comic Sketches	£3

Advert Cards

Poster Type	£40
Others	£15

See also SPORT

DISASTERS

Coast Erosion/Landslips	£12
/Black Rock/Brighton	£3
Explosions	£20
Floods	£20
Frozen Seas	£6
In Memoriam Cards	£20
Lightning Damage	£18
Snow Damage	£15
Storm Damage	£18

Subsidence	£20
Wrecked Buildings/Piers	£15
War Damage/WW1 Air Raids	
/Ramsgate	£12
/Scarborough	£8
Other locations	£15

Earthquakes
Essex 1884	£8
Other locations/GB	£20
Messina	£1.50
San Francisco	£5
Other locations/Foreign	£3

Events
Faversham 1916/Funeral scenes	£15
Lincoln Typhoid Outbreak 1905	£60
Louth Floods 1920	£18
Lynmouth Floods 1952	£8
Newport Dock 1909	£50
Northwich Subsidence	£12
Norwich Floods	£12
Southend Pier	£10
Vanguard Motor Accident/	
Handcross 1906	£10
Weston Super Mare Storm 1903	£12
Worthing Pier	£10

DOMESTIC LIFE
Corkscrews	£8
Knitting	£4
Weddings/Brides/Groups	£2
/Wedding Cakes	£2

Country Houses
Buildings	£3
Domestic Servants	£5
Gardens	£2
Kitchens	£5

Photography
Cameras/Equipment	£8
Greetings/Romantic	£4
Comic Sketches	£6
Stereoscopic cards	£4

These are cards with two adjacent pictures, best viewed through a Stereo viewer for full effect.
There are many different series and subjects.

Telephones
Correspondence cards	£8
Telephone in photograph	£4
Telephone Exchanges/Operators	£10
Greetings/Romantic	£3
Comic Sketches	£2

FAIRS
Amusement Parks	£5
Southend Kursaal	I£5
Wall of Death/Action photos	£15

/Arenas	£8
Fetes	£12
Seaside Fairs/Water Chutes	£5

Feats/Wagers
Walking Round the World	£10
/George M. Schilling	£5
/Man in the Iron Mask	£5
Niagara Falls Barrel	£5
Other Stunts	£10

Markets
| Animal Markets | £15 |
| Street Markets | £15 |

See note on pricing at beginning of section.

London Markets
Club Row	£8
Farringdon Road	£5
Petticoat Lane	£5
Billingsgate Market	£8
Smithfield Market	£8
Woolwich	£5

Hull Fair, Bioscope £20

Travelling Fairs
Barnet Horse Fair	£20
Cosham Fair	£25
Hampstead Heath/A&G Taylor	£60
/Star Series	£5
Hull Fair	£20
Mitcham Fair	£20
Nottingham Goose Fair	£10
Oxford Fair	£15
Other named locations	£25
Fairground Equipment	£20
RP studies/Published c.1950	£5

See note on pricing at beginning of section.
There are in circulation many privately produced, postcard-size plain back photographs of Fairground equipment. Most of these have been printed in quantity from an existing negative and consequently have only a nominal value.

FIRE BRIGADE

Firemen	£12
Fire fighting/Identified	£12
/Unidentified	£6
Fire Stations	£18
Tuck Oilettes	£8

Fire Engines

Hand Drawn	£35
Horse Drawn	£35
Motor	£35

Fires

Bon Marche/Brixton	£5
Lewes	£6
Selby Abbey	£3
Other GB Fires	£12
Art Sketches	£3

Fire at Harrow R/P £12

FISHING INDUSTRY
Deep Sea Fishing

Fish sales on quayside	£15
Fish Markets	£3
General quayside scenes	£3
Herring Girls	
/Gutting/Packing Herring	£6
/Spectacular RP studies	£15
Fishermen	£3
Mending Nets	£3
Fishwives at Newhaven etc.	£1
French scenes/Concarneau etc.	£3
Other French scenes	£2
Foreign scenes	£1.50

It is pointed out that in the 'Fish Markets' classification there are a number of very common cards, worth about £1.50 each, which are always turning up.
Unfortunately it is not possible to list these individually without showing illustrations, but you have been warned.

Trawlers/Drifters

RP Trawler studies	£12
General studies	£6
/c.1960 RP studies	£1.50
On board Trawler	£12
Trawler fleet at sea	£3

Tuck Oilette Series

2317 Toilers of the Sea	£4
2761 Toilers of the Sea	£4
2817 Toilers of the Sea	£4
6690 Toilers of the Deep	£4

Local Industry

Keddle Net Fishing/Rye	£25
Prawn Fishermen/Bognor	£15
Coracle Fishermen	£5
Cockle Gatherers	£10
Cockle Vendors	£15

GIPSIES
Camps

GB locations	£35
/Unlocated	£12
Alien Immigrants/Pub. Hartmann	£6
Macedonian Gipsies at Epping	£10

On the Road

GB locations	£35
/Unlocated	£12

HUNTING
Tuck Oilette Series

2732 Fox and Stag Hunting	£4
2758 Hunting	£4
3596 Hunting in the Shires	£4
9801 In the Hunting Field	£4

Miscellaneous

Photographic groups/Named Hunts	£6
/Un-named Hunts	£3
Other photographic studies	£3
The Owl Series	£1.50
Comic Sketches	£2
Art Studies	£3

INDUSTRIAL

Delabole Slate Quarry	£5
Gas Works	£15
Greenwich Telescope	£2
Power Houses	£6
Printing Works	£6
/Evening News	£8
Royal Mint/Two sets of 12 cards	
Price per set	£1.50
Saltworks	£25
Science Museum Series	£3
Steelworks	£12

Cotton Mills

Interior/Machines	£8

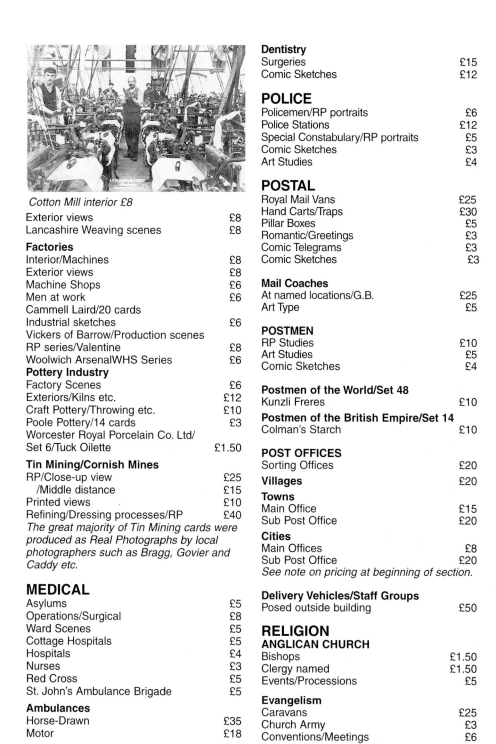

Cotton Mill interior £8

Exterior views	£8
Lancashire Weaving scenes	£8

Factories

Interior/Machines	£8
Exterior views	£8
Machine Shops	£6
Men at work	£6
Cammell Laird/20 cards	
Industrial sketches	£6
Vickers of Barrow/Production scenes	
RP series/Valentine	£8
Woolwich Arsenal/WHS Series	£6

Pottery Industry

Factory Scenes	£6
Exteriors/Kilns etc.	£12
Craft Pottery/Throwing etc.	£10
Poole Pottery/14 cards	£3
Worcester Royal Porcelain Co. Ltd/	
Set 6/Tuck Oilette	£1.50

Tin Mining/Cornish Mines

RP/Close-up view	£25
/Middle distance	£15
Printed views	£10
Refining/Dressing processes/RP	£40

The great majority of Tin Mining cards were produced as Real Photographs by local photographers such as Bragg, Govier and Caddy etc.

MEDICAL

Asylums	£5
Operations/Surgical	£8
Ward Scenes	£5
Cottage Hospitals	£5
Hospitals	£4
Nurses	£3
Red Cross	£5
St. John's Ambulance Brigade	£5

Ambulances

Horse-Drawn	£35
Motor	£18

Dentistry

Surgeries	£15
Comic Sketches	£12

POLICE

Policemen/RP portraits	£6
Police Stations	£12
Special Constabulary/RP portraits	£5
Comic Sketches	£3
Art Studies	£4

POSTAL

Royal Mail Vans	£25
Hand Carts/Traps	£30
Pillar Boxes	£5
Romantic/Greetings	£3
Comic Telegrams	£3
Comic Sketches	£3

Mail Coaches

At named locations/G.B.	£25
Art Type	£5

POSTMEN

RP Studies	£10
Art Studies	£5
Comic Sketches	£4

Postmen of the World/Set 48

Kunzli Freres	£10

Postmen of the British Empire/Set 14

Colman's Starch	£10

POST OFFICES

Sorting Offices	£20

Villages £20

Towns

Main Office	£15
Sub Post Office	£20

Cities

Main Offices	£8
Sub Post Office	£20

See note on pricing at beginning of section.

Delivery Vehicles/Staff Groups

Posed outside building	£50

RELIGION
ANGLICAN CHURCH

Bishops	£1.50
Clergy named	£1.50
Events/Processions	£5

Evangelism

Caravans	£25
Church Army	£3
Conventions/Meetings	£6

Gipsy Smith	£3
Personalities	£3
Wesleyan Churches	£3

Oberammergau

Actors/Portraits	£1
Production scenes/Views	£1

ROMAN CATHOLICISM

Cardinals/Bishops	£1.50
Priests named	£1.50
Events/Processions etc.	£2
Lourdes scenes	£1

Popes

Coronation Souvenir Cards	£5
Jubilee Cards	£5
Mourning Cards/Leo XIII	£5
Funeral Processions	£3
Portraits	£2

MISCELLANEOUS

Angels/Saints etc.	£4
Lord's Prayer	£1.50
Mission Societies	£2
Missionaries	£3
/In the Pot	£3
Monks/Local Industry	£2

For Churches and Religious buildings see
TOPOGRAPHICAL

RETAIL TRADE
Delivery Vehicles

Hand Carts	£35
Horse-drawn Carts	£40

Horse drawn cart R/P £40

Milk Floats	£50
Motor Vehicles	£30

See also MOTOR TRANSPORT

Public Houses
Delivery Vehicles/Staff Groups

posed outside building	£50
Close-up view	£15
Pub in street scene	£8

See note on pricing at beginning of section.
A pub in a street scene would be priced as a
Topographical card. It must also be borne in
mind that there are many very common pubs
to be found on postcards. For example:
The Star/Alfriston
Cat and Fiddle/New Forest
Jerusalem Inn/Nottingham and many others
too numerous to list. These are worth much
less than the quoted prices and only through
experience will you learn which ones they are.

Breweries

Guinness Brewery Scenes	£8
6x4 size	£6
Local Breweries	£30

Close Up R/P £25

Shop Fronts
Delivery Vehicles/Staff Groups

posed outside building	£50
Special Displays/Meat Hanging etc.	£40
Grocer/Tobacconist/Newsagent etc.	
Spectacular Close-up RP/Located	£25
/Unlocated	£12
Other displays/Located	£10
/Unlocated	£4
Picture Postcard Displays	£50
Arcades	£10
Rationing queues	£40
Station Bookstalls/W.H.S. etc.	£20

See note on pricing at beginning of section.
There are far more unlocated Shop Fronts
than those which can clearly be assigned to
a particular town or village.

RURAL LIFE

Allendale Wolf	£5
Barrel Organs/Men	£60

Blacksmiths	£18	Morris Dancers	£15
Bootmakers	£25	Well Dressing	£6
Brusher Mills	£5	Witches	£5
Children's Games	£5		
Chimney Sweeps	£25	**Funerals**	
Cliff Climbers	£8	Celebrities	£18
Coopers	£18	Special Events/Processions	£12
Cornish Pasties	£2	Other Funerals	£6
Deer Stalking	£3	**Lacemaking**	
Flower Shows	£6	GB locations/Named Lacemakers	£25
Hermits	£12	Industrial/Factory scenes	£6
Hunting/Shooting	£3	Belgium	£8
Milkmaids	£3	France	£6
Odd Characters	£12	Other Foreign	£6
Open Air Gatherings	£5	**Performing Bears**	
Ox Roasts/Pig Roasts	£25	GB locations	£75
Pea Picking	£5	/Unlocated	£30
Peat Digging	£6	Foreign	£10
Seaweed Gathering/Wracking	£3	**Refuse Collection**	
Spinning/Weaving	£4	Dustcarts	£40
Irish Spinning Wheels	£1.50		
Street Furniture/Troughs	£6		
Street Parades/Processions	£15		

SCHOOLS

Universities/Colleges	£2
Public Schools/Eton etc.	£2
Grammar/Secondary	£6
Village Schools	£8
Classroom groups/Identified	£8
/Unidentified	£1.50

Price is governed by the subject and location.

Tobacco Auctions/USA	£6
Trug Making	£40
Village Crafts	£3
Village Folk	£2
Village Life	£3

There are a number of Tuck Oilette series on this theme, which would carry the price of the respective Artist.

Water Carts	£30
Watercress Growing	£20
Wheelwrights	£30
Workers in the fields	£5

Charcoal Burning

Actual work in progress/RP	£25
Huts/Forest clearings etc.	£5

Folklore

Banbury Cross	£1.50
County Humour/Dialect	£1.50
Customs & Traditions	£1.50
Dunmow Flitch	£8
Ducking Stools/Stocks	£1.50
Epitaphs	£1.50
Ghosts	£1.50
Gretna Green	£1
Lady Godiva	£5

There are many cards of different personalities playing this part.

Legends	£1.50
Maypole Celebrations/Located	£15
/Unlocated	£5

SEASIDE

Donkeys	£3
Bathing Machines	£5

On the promenade R/P £8

Pierrot/Beach Shows	£5
Piers	£3
Punch & Judy	£12
Sand Models	£3
Seaside Amusements	£5

Beach Scenes

Animated RP	£10
General scenes	£1.50

HOLIDAY CAMPS

Butlins

Pre-1960	£4/£8
1961 onwards	£2

Butlins produced cards with inset pix of their respective Holiday Camps.

Pontins/Warners etc.

Pre 1960	£3
1961 onwards	£1.50

Local Camps/Holiday Villages

Pre 1960	£3
1961 onwards	£1.50
Caravan Parks	£3

There exist many modern 6x4 size cards of Holiday Camps which would be worth less than the prices quoted above.

Pontin's, South Devon R/P £3

Mill, Steam R/P £12

WATERMILLS

Scarce types	£12
Middle range	£4
Common types	£2
Fires/Disasters	£25
Art types	£1
Foreign	£1.50

WINDMILLS

Scarce types	£20
Middle range	£12
Common types	£3
Fires/Disasters	£30
Art types	£1
Foreign	£2

See note on pricing at beginning of section. With both Watermills and Windmills it is difficult to be more specific, without listing and illustrating every card. In both cases there are some very common cards which are always turning up. With Watermills, those at Laxey, Groudle Glen and Guy's Cliff are familiar to all collectors,while in Windmills, Salvington, Rottingdean and Wimbledon are virtually unsaleable. Beyond these, there is a broad band of middle range cards, which although relatively common, are usually saleable if priced realistically. At the top of the range are cards which are seldom found, and where only a few copies may exist.

Also with Windmills there are many post-1945 cards which would carry half the prices.quoted above.

Only knowledge and experience can be your guide.

WELFARE ORGANISATIONS

Workhouses	£10
N.S.P.C.C.	£12
Y.M.C.A./Y.W.C.A.	£3
John Grooms's Crippleage	£1.50
Lord Mayor Treloar Home	£1.50
Newcastle-upon-Tyne Street Life/ Pub. Thompson & Lee	£15
Waifs and Strays	£3
Childrens' Homes	£5
Orphanages	£5

Charities/Fund Raising

Flag Days	£15
Fund Raising Animals	£12
T.B. Fund Raising	£8

See also MILITARY/WW1

Dr. Barnardo

Portraits	£3
Funeral Procession at Barkingside	£20
Homes	£3
Children at Work	£3
Children in group photos	£3
'Our Young Migrants in Canada'	£12

This was a scheme now discredited where Barnardos sent children to the Colonies. Believed to be two sets of 6 cards.

Salvation Army

Bands	£6
Gen. Booth/Visits G.B.	£18
Gen. Booth/Memorial Card	£8
Gen. Booth/Portraits	£3/£12
Miscellaneous interest	£3

Boy Scout R/P £5

YOUTH ORGANISATIONS
SCOUTING
Baden Powell

Tuck Empire Series	£25
Early Vignettes/Coloured	£25
/b.w.	£12
Relief of Mafeking	£30
Portraits	£12
Visits	£20

Portraits/Groups

Tuck R. & Sons/Payne H	£25
Other Series	£10
Camps/Located	£10
/Unlocated	£5
Scouts/Troops Identified	£10
/Unidentified	£2
Comic Sketches	£10

National Series
Published by Millar & Lang in sets of 6 cards.

Prices are for individual cards.

Series 749	£10
Series 760	£10
Series 845	£10
Series 858	£10
Series 919	£10
Series 1000	£10
Series 1002	£10
Series 1044	£10
Series 1572	£10
Price per set of those listed above	£75
Other Millar & Lang issues	£8

Personalities

Jack Cornwell V.C.	£10

Miscellaneous

H.Q. Official Cards	£15
Jamborees	£15

A special postmark on these cards adds to their value.

Tuck R. & Sons/Our Boy Scouts/ Oilette Series 9950/Animal Heads W.H. Ellam	£100
Price per set	£750
Scouts of the World/Set 111 USA 1968/Price for complete set	£75

GIRL GUIDES
Leaders

Lady Baden Powell	£10
Princess Mary	£5
Princess Elizabeth	£5
Other Leaders	£5

Portraits/Groups

Official Cards	£5
Identified	£5
Unidentified	£1.50

MISCELLANEOUS

Boys Brigade	£10
Church Lads Brigade	£6
Other Organisations	£3

Scout Troop, Sunbury R/P £10

LONDON LIFE
and other Social History Series

Many Edwardian postcard firms published series of cards reflecting the Life and Labour of those times, while other companies produced long series covering Events and Disasters. These cards today are highly prized, and in many cases form a unique historical record of social conditions. The value of the Picture Postcard as a contemporary reference can be clearly seen in many of the examples listed below.

Market Report

As always, restricted by a limited number of buyers, Not a lot of demand at the fairs but these cards will always sell at auction, generally to people trying to complete the set. Because of this, valuations given here are more of a guide than an attempt at accurate pricing.

ARISTOPHOT

391 Flower Girls	£10
392 Omnibus	£25
395 Policeman	£10
398 Omnibuses in a row	£15
401 Feeding Pigeons	£15
413 Street Vendors	£12
414 Hansom Cab	£20
415 Sandwich Types	£10
417 Boot Cleaner	£12
418 Fine Ripe Cherries	£10
419 London Beer	£20

BEAGLES J. & CO.

001 The Costermonger	£12
002 The Policeman	£12
003 The Shoe Black	£12
004 The German Band	£12
005 The Parcel Post	£12
006 The Flower Sellers	£10
006 The Horse Omnibus	£18
007 A Newsvendor	£12
008 The Flower Sellers	£10
008 The Street Organ	£15
010 The Knife Grinder	£15
011 Drinking Fountain & Cattle Trough	£10
013 The Pavement Artist	£12
014 The Paper Boy	£12
015 The Telegraph Messenger	£12
018 The Milkman	£18
018 The Flower Sellers	£10
019 The Baker	£15
020 The Postman	£15
022 The Chelsea Pensioner	£10
411 Dust Cart	£18
646K A London Policeman	£12
647N Policeman holding up the traffic	£12
648E City of London Ambulance	£18

W. HAGELBERG
Series 3490

Thames Embankment	£8
Coffee & Cocoa Stall	£8
Middlesex Street/Old Petticoat Lane	£8

JOHN WALKER

22607 Street Music	£25
22671 Petticoat Lane	£15
22672 Petticoat Lane	£15

LL/LOUIS LEVY
London Types

301 Beefeater at the Tower of London	£8
302 Pavement Artist	£8
303 The Fireman	£12
325 Policeman	£8

G. SMITH
Types of London Life

01 Pavement Artist	£8
04 Flower Seller at Piccadilly Circus	£12
05 Newsboy	£12
05a A Newsboy	£12
06 Shoe Black at Trafalgar Square	£12
07	
08 The Fireman	£12
09 A Bus Driver	£15
10 Police Ambulance	£15
11 Policeman holding up Traffic at the Bank	£12
12 Postman	£12
13 Messenger Boy	£12
14 Street Sweeper	£15
15 Fruit Seller	£15
16 Hot Chestnut Man	£15
17 The Lord Mayor's Coachman	£12
18 Punch & Judy Show at National Portrait Gallery	£15
19 A Horse Bus	£15
20 A Messenger Boy	£12
21	
22 Sentry at Buckingham Palace	£8

Research by Philip Richards who informs me that although this is the main series of Gordon Smith "Types of London Life", there are certain titles known in another un-numbered series, as well as other cards in the style within the publisher's general range.

PHOTOCROM CO.
Celesque Series/Coloured
London Types

Covent Garden Porter	£6
Shoe Black	£10
Flower Seller	£6
The Smithfield Market Porter	£6
The Bus Conductor	£10
The Pavement Artist	£6
The Recruiting Sergeant	£6
The Street Hawker	£10
The Newsboy	£6
The Life Guard	£6
The Orderly Boy	£10
The Postman	£10
The Chelsea Pensioner	£6
The Lighterman	£10

CHARLES SKILTON

Set of 12 cards c.1940	£18

TUCK R. & SONS

A10 A Policeman	£12
A11 The Recruiting Sergeant	£12
A12 A Fruit Hawker	£18
A13 Flower Vendors	£12
A14 A Messenger Boy	£12
A15 A Shoeblack	£18
A16 A Pavement Newsvendor	£12
A17 A Sandwichman & Newsvendor	£18
A18 A Cabman on the Rank	£18
A19 A Policeman controlling Traffic	£12
A20 A Pavement Hawker	£18
A21 A Pavement Artist	£12

WYNDHAM SERIES

6335 Hawking Butcher	£30
7579 Fish Stall	£30
7587 Mending Door Mats	£30
7588 Penny Scales	£30
7589 Salt & General Merchant	£30
7590 Sweep snow away	£30
7591 The Potman	£30
7592 Shrimps	£30
7593 Mixed Quartette	£30
7594 Caravan Carpenter	£30
7595 Hot Potatoes	£30
7596 Fruit Merchant	£30
7597 Pussy's Butcher	£30
7598 Sweeps	£30
7599 Muffins	£30
7600 Toy Vendor	£30
7601 Old Clo	£30
7602 Dustman	£30
7603 Shoeblack	£30
7604 Shoeblack	£30
7605 Street Musician	£30
7606 Whelks	£30
7607 Laces	£30

STAR SERIES
Set of 36 cards

01 Good Old Hampstead. The Cockney's Paradise
02 Milk Fresh from Tin Cow at St. James' Park.
03 The Nurse's Paradise, Hyde Park.
04 Feeding the Ducks in a London Park
05 Feeding the Pigeons in a London Park
06 The Fountains. Trafalgar Square.
07 Sweep O.
08 O.H.M.S.
09 The Little Bird will tell your Fortune for one Penny
10 Shoeblack and Cabby.
11 Fireman and Escape.
12 On Guard. Buckingham Palace.
13 Recruiting Sergeant and a Policeman. "On Point Duty".
14 Aliens.
15 Harmony.
16 A free Drink for Man's Best Friend.
17 Fine Fruit and Fresh Flowers. Farringdon Market, Farringdon Street.
18 Covent Garden.
19 All a Blowing and a Growing.
20 A Hot Day. Give us a Taster Jack.
21 Kerbstone Merchants. "Wonderful Pennorths". Ludgate Hill.
22 Paper Kiosk outside the "Prudential" Holborn. A well-known Landmark.
23 Regent Circus. "Fresh from Market".
24 The Busy Bargees. River Thames.
25 Off to a Fire.
26 Changing the guard. Horseguards.
27 Fatigue Duty. Buckingham Palace Road.
28 Motor Bus.
29 Electric Tram and "2d" Tube Station.
30 A Free Drink in a London Park.
31 London Bridge
32 Piccadilly Circus
33 Rotten Row. Hyde Park.
34 Mansion House and Cheapside.
35 G.P.O. and St. Martin's le Grand.
36 Holborn Viaduct and City Temple.

Price Range: £3/£6. (The printing technique of this series leaves much to be desired).

A & G TAYLOR
Orthochrome Series/Coloured

243 Taking Lessons from the Artist	£6
245 Cat's Meat!	£10
246 The Ice Cream Merchant	£10
247 The Crossing Sweeper	£10
248 Brother Professionals	£6
250 On His Majesty's Service	£10
251 "Here you are, Sir! Shine Sir?"	£10
254 London Postman making collection	£10

ROTARY PHOTOGRAPHIC CO.
London Life/Series 10513

01 Fireman	£25
02 Postman	£25
03 Street Orderly Boy	£25
04 Taxi-Cab Driver	£25
05 Newspaper Boy	£25
06 Pavement Artist	£20
07 Hot Chestnut Seller	£35
08 Lifeguardsman Sentry	£20
09 Toy Seller	£25
10 "Votes for Women"	£60
11 District Messenger	£25
12 Flower Seller	£25
13 Omnibus Driver	£35
14 Hansom "Cabby"	£35
15 Bootblack	£30
16 Hawker	£25
17 City Police Constable	£25
18 Flower Sellers	£20
19 Fortune Teller	£25
20 The Brewers Man	£35
21 District Messenger Boy	£25
22 Big Bens Telescopeman	£25
23 Post Office Telegraph Boy	£30
24 LCC Tramcar Conductor	£35
25 Reuter Telegraph Co.'s Messenger	£20
26 The Milkman	£35
27 The Baked Potato Man	£35
28 A Woman Pavement Artist	£25
29 City Police Motor Ambulance	£30
30 "Votes for Women"	£55
31 Billingsgate Porter	£25
32 Smithfield Market Porter	£35
33 Covent Garden Porters	£35
34 Chelsea Pensioner	£25
35 Firemen at Work	£20
36 Street Fruit Hawker	£35
37 Street Orderly Man	£35
38 Boy Scouts	£35
39 Chimney Sweep	£25
40 Sandwich Board Man	£35
41 Automatic Road Sweeper	£35
42 Royal Exchange Constable	£25
43 Newspaper Boys with latest news	£30
44 Ice Cream	£35
45 An Apple Woman	£25
46 Recruiting Sergeants	£20
47 Coster in his Donkey Cart at Covent Garden Market	£35
48 Flower Sellers at Oxford Circus	£35
49 Underground Tube Train Conductor	£45
50 Boulters Lock on Ascot Sunday	£35
51 A Scene at Henley during Regatta Week	£35
52 A Racecourse Scene at Epsom	£35
53 The King is Coming	£35
54 Opera enthusiasts. Queue outside Covent Garden Opera House	£35
55 A Night Watchman	£35
56 A Coffee Stall Supper, "Al Fresco"	£35
57 A Whelk Stall	£35
58 A Motor Bus. One of London's Red Generals	£45
59 Postman collecting the Midnight Post	£35
60 Fireman at work at a midnight Fire	£30
61 An Underground Railway Lift Man	£35
62 GPO Royal Mail Motor	£35
63 Knives and Scissors Grinder	£35
64 A Baker's Man	£35
65 A Flower Seller	£35
66 A Coal Man	£40
67 A Butcher	£35
68 A Hospital Nurse	£45
69 Early Morning in Rotten Row, Hyde Park	£25
70 Football. Chelsea V Aston villa at Stamford Bridge	£50
71 Arrest of a Militant Suffragette	£75
72 Rushing to a Fire at Night	£30
73 Steam Roller at work	£35
74 The Dustman	£35
75 A helpful member of our Dumb Friends League	£35
76 A Boy Scout's Band	£45
77 "Four Wheeler" Cab	£45
78 A City Window Cleaner	£35
79 Turkish Baths Advertiser	£35
80 A Labour Demonstration	£45
81 A Crossing Sweeper	£35
82 In Smithfield Meat Market	£35
83 Lifeguard at Whitehall	£35
85 "The policeman's lot is not a happy one"	£25
87 Feeding pigeons outside St. Paul's Cathedral	£20
88 In Billingsgate Market	£35
89 The Opening of the London Season	£35
90 Queen Alexandra Buying Roses	£20
91 A Coaching Meet in Hyde Park	£20
95 Fire Brigade drilling before Chief Officers	£45
96 Firemen wearing the smoke helmet	£45
98 Motor Fire Engine and Escape	£45
99 Fire Brigade drill at Headquarters	£45

There are also Tinted Cards known with a 10514 Series Number. More information is needed here.

LONDON LIFE/ART SERIES

Kyd	£10
Rotophot Cries of London	£3
Sauber	£5
Tuck R. & Sons Oilette Series 9015	£6

ROTARY LONDON LIFE

OUR DUMB FRIENDS' LEAGUE TRACE HORSE HELP GIVEN

10513-75   LONDON LIFE.   A HELPFUL MEMBER

10513 66   LONDON LIFE.   A COAL MAN.   ROTARY PHOTO, E.C.

10513-50   LONDON LIFE.   BOULTER'S LOCK ON ASCOT SUNDAY.   ROTARY PHOTO, E.C.

ROTARY LONDON LIFE

10513-10   LONDON LIFE.   "VOTES FOR

10513-47   LONDON LIFE.   COSTER IN HIS DONKEY CART AT COVENT GARDEN MARKET.   ROTARY PHOTO. E.C.

10513-80   LONDON LIFE.   A LABOUR DEMONSTRATION.   ROTARY PHOTO, E.C.

LYNMOUTH FLOODS

Francis Frith & Co., Reigate
LYH 30 "Watersmeet Valley", ptd., horiz.   £3
?Ditto. but RP
?LYH 31
?LYH 32
LYH 33 "Glen Lyn", ptd., horiz.   £3
?Ditto, but RP
LYH 34 "The Main Street", ptd.horiz.   £3
Ditto, but RP   £2
LYH35 "East Lyn",ptd.,horiz.   £2
?Ditto, but RP
?LYH 36 "Lynton Hill Corner", ptd., horiz
Ditto, but RP   £12
?LYN 37-41
?lyn 42 "View from the Quay", ptd., horiz
Ditto, but RP   £8
?LYH 43
?LYH 44 "Harbour and Quay from Lynton Hill",
ptd.,horiz.
Ditto, but RP   £6
LYH 139 "Old Lynmouth/New Lynmouth",
R.P., vert.

Harvey Barton & Son, Bristol

41850 (Lyndale Hotel and temporary footbridge), R.P., horiz.   £15
1   Ditto, but without border   £15
41851 (Lyndale Hotel entrance), R.P., horiz £8
2   Ditto, but without border
£8   41852 (Houses at the bottom of
Lynton Hill), R.P. Horiz.   £15
3   Ditto, but without border
£15   41853 (West Lyn Hotel and Lyn
Valley Hotel), R.P., horiz.   £15
4   Ditto, but without border   £15

unnumbered multi-view of above 4 views with
central pre-flood view in oval,R.P. horiz.   £6

41854 "August 15th 1952/ Lynmouth/ August
16th 1952", R.P., vert.
Then and now comparison of West Lyn Hotel
and Lyn Valley Hotel,   £12

46268 "Lynmouth 1952/ Lynmouth 1953" R.P.,
vert.,then and now comparison of harbour   £6

46269 "Lynmouth 1952/ Lynmouth 1953" R.P.,
vert.,   then and now comparison looking
seawards   £6

Photochrom Co. Ltd., Tunbridge Wells

"The Electric Power Station and Flood", R.P.,
horiz   £8
"The Cottage Tea Gardens and Café, River
Side", R.P., horiz.   £10
"Lynn Valley Hotel", R.P., vert   £15
"Site of Shelley's Cottage", R.P., horiz.   £18

E.A.Sweetman & Son, Tunbridge Wells

C10412   "Old Lynmouth / New Lynmouth"
R.P., vert.,   then and now comparison looking
inland   £6
C10413 ?
C10414 "Old Lynmouth / New Lynmouth" R.P.,
vert., then and now comparison looking seawards   £6

Anonymous

"Lynmouth Floods August 15th 1952", R.P.,
horiz., 5 different views, with letters N or M in
the stamp box   £10/15

Blackmore Series

"Lynmouth Disaster   Aug 15th-16 1952", R.P.,
horiz., with footbridge in foreground and
Lyndale Hotel entrance on left   £15
Ditto, same title, R.P. horiz., looking seawards,
with debris in foreground and bulldozer middle
distance   £15

**For details on Warner Gothard of Barnsley,
The Liverpool Strike cards of 1911,
The Senghenydd Pit Disaster 1913 and
The Kinsley Evictions 1905
Please refer to Picture Postcard Values 2003**

OVERSEAS TOPOGRAPHICAL

Please read the following explanation before consulting prices:

1. Every country listed in this section could support its own catalogue. Many of them produced literally millions of postcards, and although I have now begun to sub-classify many countries, a process which will be continued in future editions of this Catalogue, it must be clearly understood that at best, all one can really do in the pages which follow, is to put the reader in touch with the broad general price area for any particular card.

2. The degree of classification of any one country is a reflection of the demand for that country. France catalogues in much greater depth than Luxembourg for example, because the demand is there. Readers may like to think about this, when choosing a country to collect? With many countries there exist definite market indications which allow me to list Town and City Street Scenes, while other `non-collected' countries can at present only be covered either with a general `Street Scene' heading, or, in many cases, with just a single price for the whole country!

3. To achieve a logical presentation, I have in all cases used the term `Street Scenes', but where applicable, e.g in small islands, this is taken to mean all population centres, hut settlements, native villages, dirt-track roads etc. I don't need to be told that there are few `Streets' in Tibet or Nepal - I have deliberately chosen to use this term throughout the listings to achieve a correct balance.

4. Railway Stations are in all cases taken to be Town or Village stations. It is suggested that main City stations or termini be treated as `General Views', unless of course you are faced with a quite spectacular card. With all Foreign cards you will find a great many which are virtually worthless. These include Beach Scenes • Cathedrals • Churches • Countryside • Gardens • Historic Buildings • Lake Scenes • Landscapes • Mountains • Parks • Religious Buildings • River Scenes • Ruins • Stately Homes • Waterfalls • WW1 Shell Damage • Volcanoes etc.

5. As far as possible within the confines of a logical presentation, I have listed countries under the name by which they were known at the turn of the century. Where applicable, I have also given the modern name of the country in brackets, followed by the date this name was adopted. (This is not necessarily the date of independence).

Prices...

... are given for both **Unused** and **Used** cards. With **Unused,** prices may be taken as a broad, general average for the classification to which they refer. However, in all classifications there will be some very common cards which are worth much less than the stated figure, whilst on the other hand there will be cards which are worth more. With **Used** cards, prices are for Postcards which are of non philatelic origin, bearing the correct postal rate for the period and distance involved, and with a clear cancel on the address side only. **The price given represents a basic value for any correctly used Postcard of that country.**

It is pointed out that some postally used cards from certain countries or Islands are particularly rare, and may fetch a price considerably in excess of that quoted. In these cases, and where these conditions also apply to unused cards, a + sign has been entered.

The + sign has also been used where a realistic market value has not yet been established. This does not necessarily mean that the Postcard in used form is particularly rare, although certainly worth the price quoted. At best, all one can do within the limitations of a Catalogue of this kind, is to offer the reader a general indication of value for the cards in which he is interested.

Market Report
Another good year for overseas cards, in which they have reflected the general pattern of post-card collecting, where the better images and cards from smaller and more elusive countries have sold well, while the vast bulk of common Europe, and major British Colonies can be picked up by the box-full.

	Unused	Used
ADEN		
South Yemen 1967		£8
Street Scenes	£4	
General Views	£2	
AFGHANISTAN		£8+
Afghan War	£4	
Ethnic	£3	
Street Scenes	£4	
General Views	£2	
ALBANIA		£3+
Ethnic	£3	
Street Scenes	£4	
General Views	£1.50	
ALGERIA		£3+
Street Scenes	£2	
General Views	£1	
ANDAMAN ISLANDS		
General Views	£5	
ANDORRA		£5+
Street Scenes	£6	
General Views	£1	
ANGOLA		£5
Street Scenes	£6	
General Views	£2	
ANGUILLA		£15+
Street Scenes	£12	
General Views	£8	
ANTIGUA		£8+
Street Scenes	£10	
General Views	£2	
ARGENTINA		£3+
Ethnic	£3	
Railways	£6	
Street Scenes/Town	£4	
/City	£2	
/Rural	£4	£3
General Views	£1	
ASCENSION		£25+
Royal Visit	£25	£80+
General Views	£15	
AUSTRALIA		£3
Aborigines	£4	
Animals	.50	
Bush Life	£3	

	Unused	Used
Dairy Industry	£3	
Farming	£3	
Industrial	£8	
Mining	£6	
Railway Stations	£12+	
Sheep Farming	£1.50	
Street Markets	£5	
Timber Industry	£4	
Trades/Workers	£4	
USA Fleet Visit	£18	
Street Scenes/Town	£6	
/City	£2	
/Rural	£8	
General Views	.75	
AUSTRIA		£2
Costume	£1.50	
Industrial	£3	
Railway Stations	£8	
Street Markets	£6	
Trades/Workers	£6	
Street Scenes/Town	£3	
/City	.75	
/Rural	£5	
General Views	.75	
AZORES		£3
Street Scenes	£6	
General Views	£3	
BAHAMAS		£5
Hurricane 1933	£10	
Ethnic	£3	
Street Scenes/Town	£8	
/Rural	£10	
USA coloured views	£2	
General Views	£2	

Bahamas, Nassau Hotel R/P £6

	Unused	Used
BAHRAIN		£20+
Street Scenes	£8	
General Views	£4	
BARBADOS		£6
Railway	£12	
Ethnic	£3	
Street Scenes	£5	
General Views	£1.50	
BASUTOLAND		
Lesotho 1966		£15+
Ethnic	£2	
Street Scenes/Town	£8	
/Rural	£12+	
General Views	£3	
BECHUANALAND		
Botswana 1966		£15+
Ethnic	£5	
Street Scenes	£10+	
General Views	£3	
BELGIAN CONGO		
Zaire 1971		£4
Street Scenes	£6	
General Views	£1.50	
BELGIUM		.50
Costume	£1	
Dog Carts	£3	
Industrial	£6+	
Railway Stations	£8+	
Street Markets	£4	
Synagogues	£25	
Trades/Workers	£3	
WW1 Shell Damage	£1	
Street Scenes/Towns	£4	
/City	.50	
General Views	.50	
BERMUDA		£6+
Ethnic	£3	
Street Scenes/Town	£6	
General Views	£2	

	Unused	Used
BHUTAN		£15+
Ethnic	£4	
Street Scenes	£10+	
General Views	£3	
BOLIVIA		£6+
Ethnic	£2	
Railways	£6	
Street Scenes/Town	£5	
/Rural	£6	
General Views	£2	
BORNEO		£8
Street Scenes/Town	£12+	
/Rural	£15+	
Dutch	£6	
BOSNIA & HERZEGOVINA		
Yugoslavia 1929		£2
Street Scenes	£4	
General Views	£2	
BRAZIL		£3
Ethnic	£3	
Railways	£6+	
Street Scenes/Town	£5+	
Street Scenes/City	£2	
General Views	.7	

2 Portage Camaria Falls Cuyuni River, British Guiana.

British Guiana, railway workers Pr. £5

	Unused	Used
BRITISH GUIANA		
Guyana 1966		£8
Ethnic	£5	
Sugar Industry	£4	
Street Scenes/Town	£4	
/Rural	£8+	
General Views	£2	
BRITISH HONDURAS		
Belize 1973		£10+
Timber Industry	£8	
Street Scenes/Town	£10+	
/Rural	£15+	
General Views	£3	

Bermuda, Golf Course R/P £6

	Unused	Used
BRITISH NEW GUINEA		
Papua New Guinea 1975		£15+
Ethnic	£10+	
Street Scenes	£20	
General Views	£8+	
BRITISH SOMALILAND		
Somalia 1960		£8
Street Scenes	£15	
General Views	£6	
BRITISH VIRGIN ISLANDS		£12
Street Scenes	£15	
General Views	£6	
BRUNEI		£8
Street Scenes	£12	
General Views	£8	
BULGARIA		£1
Ethnic	£3	
Street Scenes	£4	
General Views	£1	
BURMA		£8
Ethnic	£5	
Street Scenes	£4	
General Views	£2	
CAICOS ISLANDS		£15
Street Scenes	£15+	
General Views	£12	
CAMBODIA		£10+
Kampuchea 1979		
Temples	£1	
Street Scenes	£8+	
General Views	£2	
CAMEROON		£10
Street Scenes	£8	
General Views	£2	
CANADA		£2
Farming	£1	
Indians	£4	
Industrial	£5	
Lake Steamers	£3	
Mining	£3	
Railway/CPR Views	£4	
Railway Stations	£8	
Street Markets	£3	
Trades/Workers	£3	
Street Scenes/Town	£4	
/City	£2	
/Rural	£8+	
General Views	.50	
CANAL ZONE		£3
Ethnic	£3	
Panama Canal	£3	
Street Scenes	£8	
General Views	£1.50	

	Unused	Used
CANARY ISLANDS		£3
Ethnic	£2	
Street Scenes	£3	
General Views	£1	

Canary Islands, Tenerife R/P £5

	Unused	Used
CAPE VERDE ISLANDS		£3
General Views	£5	
CAROLINE ISLANDS		
Pelew Islands, Ethnic		£5
CAYMAN ISLANDS		£10+
General Views	£10	

Cayman Islands, Georgetown R/P £6

	Unused	Used
CEYLON		
Sri Lanka 1972		£1
Ethnic	£2	
Tea Plantations	£3	
Street Scenes/Town	£5	
/City	£3	
General Views	£1	
CHAD		£6
Street Scenes	£8+	
General Views	£1	
CHATHAM ISLAND		£10+
General Views	£8	
CHILE		£3+
Ethnic	£2	
Railways	£10+	
Street Scenes/Town	£4+	
/City	£2	
General Views	£1	

	Unused	Used
CHINA		£6
Ethnic	£3	
Street Scenes/City	£4	
/Rural	£10+	
General Views	£2	
CHRISTMAS ISLAND		£20+
Atomic Tests	£6	
General Views	£18	
COCOS ISLANDS		£25+
General Views	£18	
COLOMBIA		£4
Ethnic	£3	
Railways	£10+	
Street Scenes	£5	
General Views	£2	
COMORO ISLANDS		£8+
General Views	£3	
COOK ISLANDS		£10+
Street Scenes	£10	
General Views	£8	
CORFU		£2
Street Scenes	£5	
General Views	£1	
COSTA RICA		£6+
Ethnic	£3	
Street Scenes	£8	
General Views	£2	
CRETE		£2
Ethnic	£5	
Street Scenes	£6	
General Views	£2	
CUBA		£2
Street Scenes	£4	

Cuba, Havana R/P £4

	Unused	Used
General Views	£1	
CURACAO		
Netherlands Antilles		£6+
Street Scenes	£8	
General Views	£1	
CYPRUS		£5
Ethnic	£6	

	Unused	Used
Street Scenes	£8	
General Views	£2	
CZECHOSLOVAKIA		£3
Street Scenes	£3	
General Views	.75	
DAHOMEY		
Benin 1975		£6
Street Scenes	£8	
General Views	£3	
DANISH WEST INDIES		
Virgin Islands/USA 1917		£15+
Ethnic	£5	
Street Scenes	£5	
General Views	£3	
DANZIG		
Poland 1945		£5
Street Scenes	£6	
General Views	£1.50	
DENMARK		£2
Costume	£1	
Street Scenes/Town	£5	
/City	£1	
General Views	.75	
DOMINICA		£3
General Views	£2	
DOMINICAN REPUBLIC		£2
General Views	£2	
DUTCH GUIANA		
Suriname 1975		£5

Dutch Guiana Pr. £3

	Unused	Used
General Views	£3	
DUTCH NEW GUINEA		
Street Scenes	£7	
General Views	£3	
EASTER ISLAND		
General Views	£5	
ECUADOR		£4
Ethnic	£4	
Railways	£10+	
Street Scenes/Town	£6	
/City	£3	
General Views	£2	
EGYPT		£1
Ethnic	£2	

Fiume, R/P 46 images on one card £6

	Unused	Used
Street Scenes/Town	£5	
/City	£1.50	
General Views	£1	
FIUME		
Yugoslavia 1947		£5
Street Scenes	£6	
General Views	£1.50	
FORMOSA		
Taiwan		£12+
Street Scenes	£10+	
General Views	£3	
FRENCH GUIANA		£4
General Views	£3	
FRENCH GUINEA		
Guinea 1958		£4
General Views	£4	
FRENCH INDIAN SETTLEMENTS		
India 1950/54		£2
General Views	£2	
FRENCH OCEANA		£10+
Street Scenes	£8+	
General Views	£4	
FRENCH SOMALILAND		
Djibouti 1977		£5

	Unused	Used
Street Scenes	£2	
General Views	£1	
ELLICE ISLANDS		
Tuvalu 1978		£10+
Street Scenes	£15	
General Views	£8	
EL SALVADOR		£4
Ethnic	£3	
Railway	£10+	
Street Scenes	£5	
General Views	£2	
ERITREA		
Ethiopia 1952		£1.50
Ethnic	£4	
Street Scenes	£8	
General Views	£1.50	
ESTONIA		
Russia 1940		£6
Ethnic	£3	
Street Scenes	£8	
General Views	£1.50	
ETHIOPIA		£5+
Ethnic	£3	
Street Scenes	£6	
General Views	£2	
FALKLAND ISLANDS		£20+
Events	£25+	
Penguins & Birds	£6	
Sheep Farming	£12+	
Whaling	£15+	
Street Scenes	£20+	
General Views	£10+	
FANNING ISLAND		£15+
General Views	£8+	
FAROE ISLANDS		£10+
General Views	£6+	
FIJI		£5
Ethnic	£6	
StreetScenes	£10+	
General Views	£3	
FINLAND		£4
Costume	£1.50	

Djibouti, R/P   £6

Street Scenes	£8	
General Views	£1.50	
FRENCH SOUDAN		
Mali 1960		£3
Street Scenes	£5	
General Views	£1.50	
FRANCE		.50
Animal Markets	£6	
Canals	£1.50	
Costume	.50	
Dog Carts	£25+	
Farming	£1	
Fetes	£3	
Fishing Industry	£3	
Fish Markets	£5	
Industrial	£5	
Mining	£5	
Railway Stations	£4	
Street Markets	£4	
Synagogues	£25	
Trades/Workers	£6	
Watermills	£2	

France is arguably the leading postcard collecting country in the world, and its cards have been catalogued to a fine degree by Neudin and Fildier, whose annual publications are strongly recommended to those readers who wish to go more deeply into the subject.

	Unused	Used
GABON		£4
Street Scenes	£10	
General Views	£2	
GAMBIA		£8+
Street Scenes	£8	
General Views	£3	
GERMAN EAST AFRICA		£10+
Burundi 1962/Rwanda 1962/Tanzania 1961		
Ethnic	£5	
Occupation 1914/18	£6	
Street Scenes	£8	
General Views	£3	
GERMAN NEW GUINEA		
Papua New Guinea 1975		£15+
Ethnic	£8	
Street Scenes	£10	
General Views	£4	
GERMAN SOUTH WEST AFRICA		
Namibia		£8+
Ethnic	£8	
Street Scenes	£10	
General Views	£3	

Germany Pr.£3

	Unused	Used
GERMANY		£1.50
Animal Markets	£5	
Costume	£1.50	
Farming	£1.50	
Industrial	£5	
Mining	£4	
Railway Stations	£8	
Rhine Steamers	£3	

	Unused	Used
Street Markets	£5	
Synagogues	£25	
Trades/Workers	£5	
Street Scenes/Town	£3	
/City	£1	
General Views	.75	
GIBRALTAR		£1
Street Scenes	£3	
General Views	.50	

Gibraltar, The Jew's Market Pr.   £3

	Unused	Used
GILBERT ISLANDS		
Kiribati 1979		£12+
Street Scenes	£12	
General Views	£8	
GOLD COAST		
Ghana 1957		£6
Ethnic	£6	
Railway	£10	
Street Scenes	£8	
General Views	£2	
GREECE		£1
Ethnic	£3	
Postal Stationery	£5	
Street Scenes	£4	
General Views	£1	
GREENLAND		£10+
Ethnic	£6	
Street Scenes	£10	
General Views	£4	
GRENADA		£3+
Street Scenes	£5	
General Views	£1.50	
GUADELOUPE		£3
Street Scenes	£8	
General Views	£1.50	
GUAM		£10+
Street Scenes	£8	
General Views	£6	

	Unused	Used
GUATEMALA		£3
Street Scenes	£6	
General Views	£2	
HAITI		£3
Street Scenes	£6	
General Views	£1.50	
HAWAII		£5
Ethnic	£4	
Street Scenes colour	£3	
Street Scenes photo	£10	
General Views	£1.50	
HELIGOLAND		£6
Street scenes	£15	
General Views	£6	
HONDURAS		£4
Ethnic	£4	
Railway	£10	
Street Scenes	£8	
General Views	£2	
HONG KONG		£8+
Ethnic	£4	
Peak Railway	£6	
Street Scenes Photo	£10	
Street Scenes colour	£6	
General Views	£2	
HUNGARY		£2
Ethnic	£3	
Street Scenes	£4	
General Views	£1	
ICELAND		£10+
Ethnic	£5	
Street Scenes	£8	
General Views	£2	

Iceland, Col. Pr.   £2

INDIA		£2
British Rule/Barracks etc.	£3	
Ethnic	£2	

	Unused	Used
Gold Mining/Court Size	£15	
Street Scenes	£3	
General Views	£1.50	
IRAQ		£5
British Occupation	£3	
Street Scenes	£8	
General Views	£1.50	
ITALY		£2
Costume	£1	
Customs & Traditions	£3	
Industrial	£5	
Railway Stations	£8	
River Steamers	£3	
Street Markets	£6	
Trades/Workers	£3	
Street Scenes/Town	£3	
/City	.50	
IVORY COAST		£8
Street Scenes	£10	
General Views	£2	
JAMAICA		£3
Ethnic	£3	
Railway	£10	
Sugar Industry	£3	
Street Scenes	£5	
General Views	£1	

Jamica, Linen c.1940's   £3

JAPAN		£2
Costume	£1	
Ethnic	£2	
Tea Houses		£2
Yokohama Earthquake		£3
Street Scenes/City		£3
/Rural		£5+
General Views		.75
JAVA		
Street Scenes		
General Views		£3
KENYA		
Ethnic	£6	
Street Scenes	£6	
General Views	£1.50	

	Unused	Used
KERMADEC ISLAND		£20+
General Views	£5	
KOREA		£5+
Street Scenes	£5	
General Views	£2	

Korea, Fuzan Pr. £5

	Unused	Used
KUWAIT		£15+
Street Scenes	£8	
General Views	£4	
LABUAN		£15+
Street Scenes	£12+	
General Views	£8	
LAOS		£10
Street Scenes	£10	
General Views	£3	
LATVIA		
Russia 1940		£4
Ethnic	£5	
Street Scenes	£4	
General Views	£1.50	
LEBANON		£5
Ethnic	£3	
Street Scenes	£4	
General Views	£1.50	
LIBERIA		£10+
Street Scenes	£8	
General Views	£2	
LIBYA		£1
General Views	£2	
LIECHTENSTEIN		£3
Street Scenes	£6	
General Views	£2	
LITHUANIA		
Russia 1940		£5
Ethnic	£4	
Street Scenes	£5	
General Views	£2	
LORD HOWE ISLAND		£20+
General Views	£12	

	Unused	Used
LUXEMBOURG		.50
Street Scenes	£2	
General Views	.50	
MACAO		
Street Scenes		£12
General Views	£5	
MADAGASCAR		£3
Street Scenes	£6	
General Views	£1	

Madagascar   Pr. £3

	Unused	Used
MADEIRA		£3
Street Scenes	£3	
General Views	£1	
MAFIA ISLAND		£25+
General Views	£6	
MALAYA		
Malaysia 1963		£5
Ethnic	£4	
Railways	£10	
Rubber Industry	£3	
Street Scenes	£6	
General Views	£1.50	
MALDIVE ISLANDS		£10+
General Views	£8	
MALTA		.50
Ethnic	£2	
Street Scenes/RP	£5	
/Coloured	.50	
General Views	.50	
MARTINIQUE		£1
Volcano 1902	£3	
Street Scenes	£8	
General Views	£1	
MAURITANIA		£3
Street Scenes	£8	
General Views	£2	
MAURITIUS		£4
Railways	£12	
Street Scenes	£8	
General Views	£2	

	Unused	Used
MEXICO		£2
Ethnic	£3	
Railways	£10	
Street Scenes	£4	
General Views	£1	
MIDDLE CONGO		
Congo 1960		£6
Street Scenes	£8	
General Views	£2	
MOLUCCA ISLANDS		
General Views	£5	
MONACO		.50
Street Scenes	£1	
General Views	.50	
MONGOLIA		£8+
General Views	£6	
MONTENEGRO		
Yugoslavia 1929		£5
Street Scenes	£8	
General Views	£1.50	
MONTSERRAT		£12
General Views	£8	

Montserrat Pr. £5

	Unused	Used
MOROCCO		£2
Street Scenes	£3	
General Views	£1	
MOZAMBIQUE		£4
Street Scenes	£5	
General Views	£1	
MUSCAT & OMAN		
Oman 1970		£30+
Street Scenes	£8	
General Views	£6	
NAURU		£25+
General Views	£10	
NEPAL		£6+
Street Scenes	£6	
General Views	£2	

	Unused	Used
NETHERLANDS		.50
Canals	£1	
Costume	.75	
Customs & Traditions	£1	
Industrial	£3	
Railway Stations	£5	
Street Markets	£5	
Trades/Workers	£5	
Windmills	£1.50	
Street Scenes/Village	£5	
/Town	£2	
/City	.50	
General Views	.75	

Nevis Col. Pr. £8

	Unused	Used
NEVIS		£10+
General Views	£8	
NEW CALEDONIA		£10+
Street Scenes	£8	
General Views	£3	
NEWFOUNDLAND		£4
Fishing Industry	£3	
Railway Stations	£10	
Street Scenes	£8	
General Views	£2	
NEW HEBRIDES		£15+
Vanuata 1980		
Street Scenes	£10+	
General Views	£5	
NEW ZEALAND		
Dairy Industry		£3
Farming		£1.50
Industrial		£5
Maoris		£3
Railway Stations		£10+
Sheep Farming		£1
Street Markets		£5
Trades/Workers		£5
Street Scenes/Town		£6
/City		£3
General Views		.75
NICARAGUA		
Ethnic		£6
Railways		£12+

199

	Unused	Used
Street Scenes	£8+	
General Views	£3	
NICOBAR ISLAND		£10+
General Views	£5	
NIGER		£3
Ethnic	£8	
Street Scenes	£6	
General Views	£1.50	
NIGERIA		£1
Ethnic	£3	
Railways	£8	
Street Scenes	£5	
General Views	£3	
NIUE		£10+
General Views	£8	
NORFOLK ISLAND		£20+
General Views	£18	
Street Scenes	£20	
NORTH BORNEO		
Sabah 1964		£15+
Ethnic	£6	
Street Scenes	£12+	
General Views	£4	
NORTHERN RHODESIA		
Zambia 1964		£6
Ethnic	£4	
Railways	£10+	
Street Scenes	£8	
General Views	£1.50	
NORWAY		£1
Costume	£1	
Street Scenes/Town	£5	
/City	£3	
General Views	.75	
NYASALAND		
Malawi 1964		£4
Ethnic	£4	
Street Scenes	£6	
General Views	£3	
OCEAN ISLAND		£15+
General Views	£8	
OUBANGUI-CHARI		
Central African Republic 1960		£5
General Views	£3	
PALESTINE		
Israel 1948		£1
British Occupation	£4	
Ethnic	£3	
Religious Sites	.50	
Street Scenes	£6	
General Views	.75	

Palestine, R/P £4

	Unused	Used
PANAMA		£4
Ethnic	£3	
Railways	£10+	
Street Scenes	£5	
General Views	£1.50	
PAPUA SE NEW GUINEA		
Street Scenes		£10
General Views		£6
PARAGUAY		£3
Ethnic	£4	
Railways	£12+	
Street Scenes	£8	
General Views	£2	
PEMBA ISLAND		
Ethnic	£6	
General Views	£6	
PERIM ISLAND		
General Views	£5	
PERSIA		
Iran 1935		£4+
Street Scenes	£5	
General Views	£2	

Peru, Mollendo, R/P £8

	Unused	Used
PERU		£5
Ethnic	£5	
Railways	£10+	
Street Scenes	£6+	
General Views	£2	

	Unused	Used
PHILIPPINES	£3	
Street Scenes	£8	
General Views	£1.50	

Philippines, Manila R/P £8

PHOENIX ISLAND		£10+
General Views	£5	
PITCAIRN ISLAND		£25+
Ethnic	£20	
General Views	£15	
POLAND		£2
Ethnic	£3	
Street Scenes	£3	
General Views	£1	
PORTUGAL		£2
Costume	£1.50	
Industrial	£3	
Railway Stations	£8	
Street Markets	£5	
Trades/Workers	£4	
Street Scenes/Town	£4	
/City	£1	
General Views	.50	
PORTUGUESE GUINEA		
Guinea-Bissau 1974		£5
Street Scenes	£8	
General Views	£1.50	
PORTUGUESE INDIA		
India 1961		£1.50
General Views	£1.50	
PORTUGUESE TIMOR		
East Timor		£5
Street Scenes	£8	
General Views	£2	
PUERTO RICO		£4
Street Scenes	£8	
General Views	£2	
REUNION		£3
Ethnic	£6	
Street Scenes	£5	
General Views	£3	

	Unused	Used
RUMANIA		£1
Ethnic	£3	
Street Scenes	£4	
General Views	£1	
RUSSIA		£3
Costume	£1.50	
Ethnic	£4	
Industrial	£6	
Railway Stations	£8	
Street Markets	£4	
Trades/Workers	£6	
Street Scenes/Town	£5	
/City	£1.50	
General Views	£1	

Russia, Vladivostok R/P £5

ST. CROIX		£5+
Street Scenes	£6	
General Views	£4	
ST. HELENA		£12+
Boer War	£20	
Street Scenes	£10	
General Views	£3	
ST. KITTS		£5+
Street Scenes	£10	
General Views	£3	
ST. LUCIA		£8+
Street Scenes	£8	
General Views	£2	
ST. MARTIN		£8+
Street Scenes	£8	
General Views	£3	
ST. PIERRE & MIQUELON		£10+
Street Scenes	£8	
General Views	£2	
ST. THOMAS & PRINCE ISLAND		£6+
Street Scenes	£6	
General Views	£2	
ST. VINCENT		£8+
Street Scenes	£8	
General Views	£3	

	Unused	Used
SAMOA		£12+
Ethnic	£6	
Street Scenes	£10	
General Views	£5	
SAMOS		£10+
Street Scenes	£5	
General Views	£5	
SAN MARINO		£2
Street Scenes	£4	
General Views	£2	
SARAWAK		£10+
Ethnic	£8	
Street Scenes	£10	
General Views	£6	
SARDINIA		£1.50
Street Scenes	£5	
General Views	£1	
SAUDI ARABIA		£12+
Street Scenes	£6	
General Views	£4	
SENEGAL		£3
Street Scenes	£8	
General Views	£1	
SERBIA		
Yugoslavia 1929		£5
Ethnic	£4	
Street Scenes	£8	
General Views	£1.50	
SEYCHELLES		£12+
Street Scenes	£10+	
General Views	£5	

	Unused	Used
SIERRA LEONE		£5
Ethnic	£3	
Railways	£8+	
Street Scenes	£6	
General Views	£1	
SIKKIM		
India 1975		£10+
General Views	£4	
SINGAPORE		£3
Ethnic	£6	
Railway Stations	£12	
Street Scenes	£8	
General Views	£2	
SOLOMON ISLANDS		£15+
Street Scenes	£10+	
General Views	£6	
SOMALILAND		
Somalia 1960		£10+
Street Scenes	£8	
General Views	£3	
SOUTH AFRICA		.50
Ethnic	£3	
Industrial	£3	
Mining	£3	
Railways	£8	
Railway Stations	£10	
Trekking	£1.50	
Street Scenes/Town	£5	
/City	£1	
General Views	.50	
SOUTHERN RHODESIA		
Zimbabwe 1980		£5
Street Scenes	£8	
General Views	£1.50	

Samoa, Pr. £5

Spain, Majorca R/P £3

	Unused	Used
SIAM		
Thailand		£8+
Street Scenes	£10+	
General Views	£3	

	Unused	Used
SPAIN		£2
Bullfighting	£2	
Costume	£1	
Industrial	£3	
Railway Stations	£6	
Street Markets	£4	

	Unused	Used
Trades/Workers	£3	
Street Scenes/Towns	£3	
/City	£2	
General Views	.50	
SPANISH GUINEA		
Equatorial Guinea 1968		£4
Street Scenes	£8	
General Views	£2	
SUDAN		£4
Ethnic	£4	
Street Scenes	£8	
General Views	£1	
SUMATRA		£3
Street Scenes	£6	
General Views	£1	
SWAZILAND		£10+
Ethnic	£4	
Street Scenes	£8	
General Views	£4	
SWEDEN		£2
Costume	£1	
Street Scenes/Town	£5	
/City	£1.50	
General Views	.75	
SWITZERLAND		£2
Costume	£1	
Customs & Traditions	£1	
Industrial	£3	
Lake Steamers	£1.50	
Mountain Railways	£3	
Railway Stations	£8	
Trades/Workers	£5	
Street Scenes/Town	£3	
/City	£1	
General Views	.50	
SYRIA		£3
Street Scenes	£4	
General Views	£1.50	
TANGANYIKA		
Tanzania 1961		£6
Ethnic	£5	
Street Scenes	£8	
General Views	£1.50	
TASMANIA		£4
Street Scenes	£6	
General Views	£1	
THURSDAY ISLAND		£10+
General Views	£8	

	Unused	Used
TIBET		£15+
Ethnic	£6	
Street Scenes	£6	
General Views	£3	
TIMOR		£5+
Street Scenes	£5	
General Views	£2	
TOBAGO		£4+
Street Scenes	£6	
General Views	£3	
TOGO		£6
Ethnic	£6	
Street Scenes	£5	
General Views	£4	
TONGA		£10+
Ethnic	£10	
General Views	£8	
TRANSJORDAN		
Jordan 1946		£4
Street Scenes	£6	
General Views	£1.50	

Trinidad, San Fernando Pr. £5

	Unused	Used
TRINIDAD		£1.50
Ethnic	£3	
Oil Industry	£3	
Street Scenes	£5	
General Views	£1.50	
TRISTAN DA CUNHA		£100+
General Views	£80+	
TUNIS		£4+
Street Scenes	£3	
General Views	£1	
TURKEY		£4+
Ethnic	£2	
Street Scenes	£3	
General Views	£1	
TURKS ISLANDS		£12+
Street Scenes	£12	

Farmers Market, Los Angeles R/P £4

Vietnam, Saigon Pr. £8

	Unused	Used
General Views	£12	
TUVA		
Russia 1944		£10+
Street Scenes	£8	
General Views	£4	
UGANDA		£5+
Ethnic	£4	
Street Scenes	£6	
General Views	£2	
UPPER VOLTA		
Burkina 1984		£5+
Street Scenes	£8	
General Views	£1.50	
URUGUAY		£3
Ethnic	£4	
Railways	£10	
Street Scenes/Town	£5	
/City	£3	
General Views	£1.50	
U.S.A.		£2
Cattle	.50	
Indians	£6	
Industrial	£4	
Mining	£8	
Railway Stations	£6	
Steamboats	£4	
Street Scenes/Town	£4	
/City	£1	
General Views	.50	
VENEZUELA		£4
Ethnic	£5	
Railways	£10	
Street Scenes	£5	
General Views	£1.50	

	Unused	Used
VIETNAM		£3
Ethnic	£6	
Street Scenes	£8	
General Views	£3	
WAKE ISLAND		
General Views	£6	
YEMEN		£5+
Street Scenes	£6	
General Views	£4	

Yugoslavia, Brioni Island R/P. £6

	Unused	Used
YUGOSLAVIA		£2
Ethnic	£3	
Street Scenes	£6	
General Views	£1.50	
ZANZIBAR		£8
Ethnic	£8	
Street Scenes	£6	
General Views	£1.50	

STAMPS ON POSTCARDS

In response to many enquiries we receive about the value of Stamps found on Postcards, it must be pointed out that the picture postcard invariably carried the minimum postage rate, and these low-denomination Stamps are virtually worthless. Realistically, the only value in a used card would be if it has been stamped and posted from an 'unusual' country, or small island, or if it bears a cancellation of some interest.

INLAND POSTAGE RATES

1 October 1870 - 3 June 1918 - ¹/₂d
3 June 1918 - 13 June 1921 - 1d
13 June 1921 - 24 May 1922 - 1¹/₂d
24 May 1922 - 1 May 1940 - 1d

FIRST DAY OF ISSUE

QUEEN VICTORIA

¹/₂d Blue Green	17 April 1900	£500

KING EDWARD VII

¹/₂d Blue Green	1 January 1902	£40
1d Red	1 January 1902	£40
¹/₂d Yellow Green	26 November 1904	£35

KING GEORGE V

¹/₂d Green (three-quarter profile, hair dark)	22 June 1911	£30
1d Red (three-quarter profile, Lion unshaded)	22 June 1911	£40
¹/₂d Green (three-quarter profile, Hair light)	1 January 1912	£40
1d Red (three-quarter profile, Lion shaded)	1 January 1912	£45
*British Empire Exhibition 1924. (1d Red)	23 April 1924	£15
*British Empire Exhibition 1925. (1d Red)	9 May 1925	£30
U.P.U Congress 1929 (¹/₂d or 1d)	10 May 1929	£12
¹/₂d Green	19 November 1934	£5
1d Red	24 September 1934	£5
Silver Jubilee 1935. (¹/₂d or 1d)	7 May 1935	£6

* Postcards bearing Wembley Park 1924 or 1925 handstamp or slogan cancel on exhibition cards would justify a premium.

KING EDWARD VIII

¹/₂d Green	1 September 1936	£6
1d Red	14 September 1936	£12

KING GEORGE VI

¹/₂d Green	10 May 1937	£1
1d Red	10 May 1937	£1

POSTMARKS ON POSTCARDS

This is a vast and complex field, and part of the much wider area of Philately. There are thousands of different postal markings and stamps to be found on the backs of picture postcards, and indeed there is a similar number of specialised philatelic books devoted to all aspects of this subject.

In a postcard Catalogue of this kind, it is only possible to give a very rough indication of price for postmarks likely to be found on picture postcards. Readers requiring more specialised information or catalogues are referred to any good stamp dealer, or to one of the many books available on the subject.

IMPORTANT. Prices quoted are for complete, clear postmarks in every instance. Partial or indistinct strikes, generally have very little value.

CIRCULAR DATE STAMP

English type - 50p   Scottish type - 75p upwards
The most common of all postmarks

SINGLE RING

50p upwards   Small 'thimble' circular ring
                               £1 upwards

DUPLEX

£1 upwards
Certain obscure or limited types may be worth up to £10 each

SQUARED CIRCLES

Three different types £1 each
For lesser used types - £2 upwards to £40

MACHINE CANCELLATIONS

There are many varieties and different types
As examples shown £1 each

MACHINE CANCELLATIONS £1-£3

Two different examples of the E (Crown) R Type. Used in London (£5) Liverpool (£20)

CACHETS

50p

Handstamps applied other than by the Official PO. Other common types are 'Summit of Snowdon', "Beachy Head'

METER MARKS

50p

Normally meant for business use

POSTAGE DUES

From £1 upwards

Surcharge marks for under-paid mail, many varieties

(i)

(ii)

(iii)

EXAMINATION MARKS

Post Office Examiner's marks applied to wrongly sorted mail. Usually stamped in black but type (iii) sometimes found in violet. 75p - £2 each

N.B. There is a larger type as (iii) which was used for checking the bulk posting of circulars, etc. Price 50p each

RUBBER DATE-STAMPS

often in blue or violet, used by smaller offices
£3 - £10 if superb coloured

ISLANDS

Circular Date Stamps
Examples shown, Gorey £3, Sandwick Shetland £5. Others such as Lundy Island £40,
St. Kilda £25. Chief offices of Jersey, Guernsey and I.O.M are common

---

SLOGANS

50p upwards
Mostly common, but there are exceptions amongst many hundreds of different types

209

SKELETONS

A temporary hand-stamp used for a limited period. Of varying sizes usually 27 - 39 mm in diameter. Price subject to wide fluctuation £3-£10 upwards

EXHIBITIONS

Edinburgh 1908   Crystal Palace Code 3
£6   (below date) £20
A complex field where price depends upon the particular exhibition and date
£1. - £50

TRAVELLING POST OFFICES	SORTING CARRIAGES & TENDERS
£5	£5
Another type of railway postmark	Railway postmarks - where many types
Many different £1.50 - £30	and varieties exist

RECEIVED FROM H.M.SHIP. NO CHARGE TO BE RAISED

RECEIVED FROM H M SHIP	**DUMB CANCELS**
£1.50	£1.50
Naval security markings	Naval security markings

ARMY CAMPS
Many different varieties £2 - £20

ARMY & FIELD POST OFFICES

P.B.2	Field Post Office G
1919 Archangel	France 1915
£25	£1 upwards

A popular specialist field - with wide price fluctuations

ROYAL HOUSEHOLDS

There are several different date-stamped as
example above.
All are scarce £12 upwards

SEA POST MARKS

£1.50 upwards
A common Maritime strike

PAQUEBOTS

£2   £5

Typical examples of a very wide and complex field in maritime postal history

STEAMERS

£12 upwards
Used for mail carried by Paddle
Steamers. Other varieties could be
worth more.

RAILWAY SUB-OFFICES

75p+
R.S.O. postmarks. Certain types
are worth more

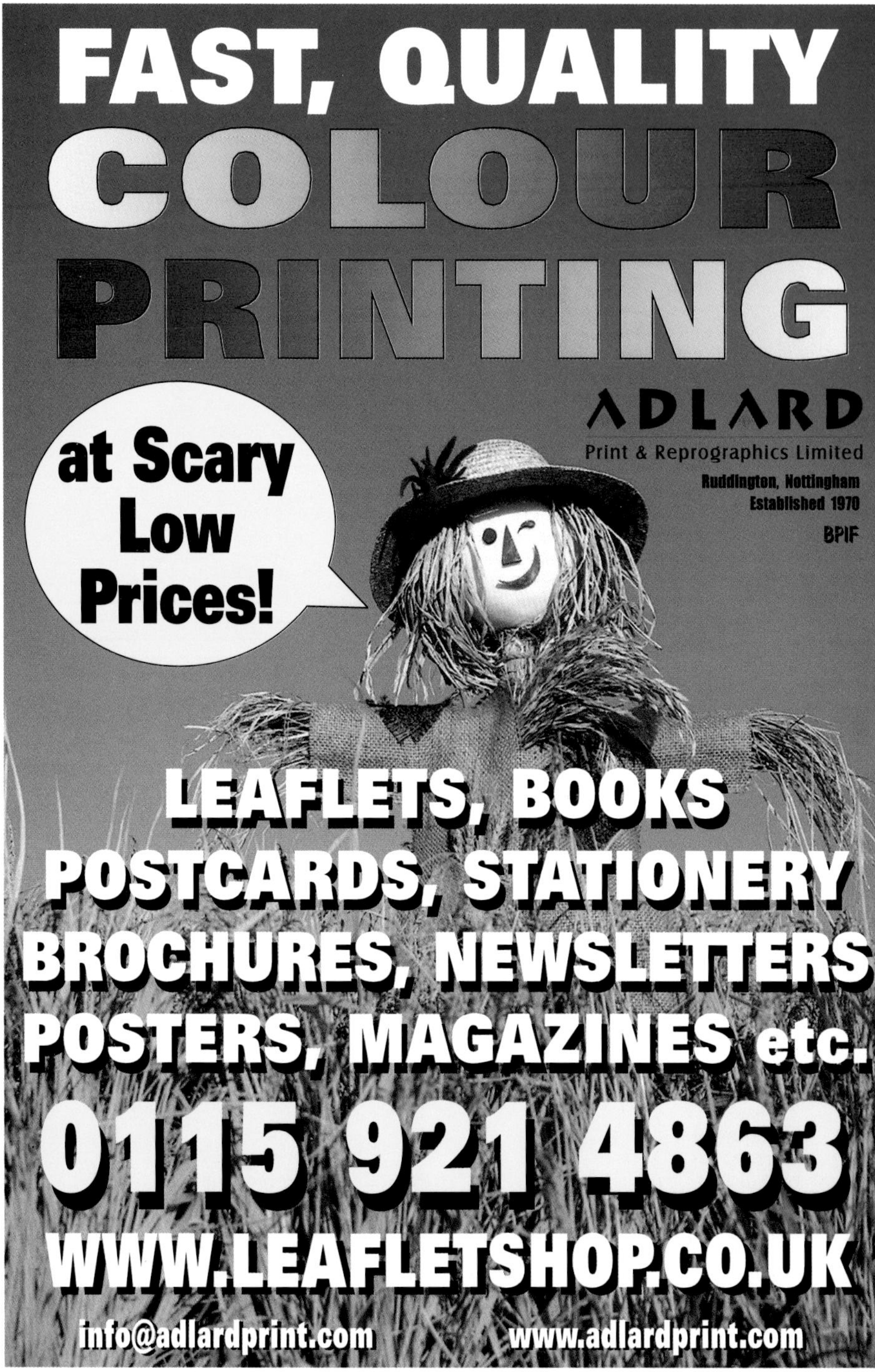
FAST, QUALITY
COLOUR
PRINTING
ADLARD
Print & Reprographics Limited
Ruddington, Nottingham
Established 1970
BPIF
at Scary Low Prices!
LEAFLETS, BOOKS
POSTCARDS, STATIONERY
BROCHURES, NEWSLETTERS
POSTERS, MAGAZINES etc.
0115 921 4863
WWW.LEAFLETSHOP.CO.UK
info@adlardprint.com
www.adlardprint.com

CHRISTMAS POSTMARKS
For delivery on Christmas Day
1903 - 1909

 Bury

(i)
£50 - £300

(ii)
£50 - £300

(iii)
£50

initials   *City & Towns known to have used such cancellers*

ADJ	Altrincham (i) (ii)		Newton Le Willows (ii)
	Ashton Under Lyne (ii)		Norwich (ii)
	Birkenhead (ii)		Oldham (ii)
BL	Bolton (i)		Ormskirk (ii)
BD	Bradford (i)		Prescot (ii)
BC	Bury (i)	PR	Preston (i)
CE	Carlisle (i)		Reading (ii)
	Douglas, I.O.M (ii)	RO	Rochdale (i)
DR	Dover (i)		Runcorn (ii)
	Dukinfield (ii)		St. Helens (ii)
ECC	Eccles (ii)	SCR	Sale (i)
GW	Glasgow (i)	SP	Southport (i)
	Glossop (ii)		Stalybridge (ii)
HU	Hull (i) (ii)	SP	Stockport (i) (ii)
	Hyde (ii)	WF	Wakefield (i)
KU	Knutsford (i) (ii)	SL	Walsall (i)
LE	Leicester (i) (ii)	WA	Warrington (i) (ii)
	Leigh (ii)	WIP	Widnes (i) (ii)
	Liverpool (ii)	WI	Wigan (i) (ii)
MC	Macclesfield (i)		
MR	Manchester (i) (ii) (iii)		

INDEX TO ADVERTISERS

INDEX